Complexity, Organizations and Change

Compl...
commu...
living v...
society as a whole.

Complexity, Organizations and Change, available in paperback for the first time, describes and considers ideas and insights from complexity science and their use in organizations, especially in bringing about major organizational change. It is about transforming the way people think about organizations, about their design, the way they operate and, most importantly, the people who co-create them.

This book explains the history and development of complexity science in an accessible way for the non-scientific reader, describing key concepts and their use in theory and practice. These concepts are fleshed out with real-life examples from organizations in the UK, Europe and the USA. These include an in-depth case study of an organization which used complexity principles as part of a strategic change intervention. From this, useful models for introducing a complexity-based change process are derived.

Complexity, Organizations and Change will appeal to academics, researchers and advanced students who are interested in complexity science and what it means for strategy, organization and management theory and organizational change.

Elizabeth McMillan is currently a Research Fellow at the Open University where she co-founded the Complexity Science Research Centre. She is also a co-founder and a Director of the UK Complexity Society and a Fellow of the Chartered Institute of Personnel and Development, with many years experience as a senior manager.

Routledge Studies on Complexity in Management

1 Complexity, Organizations and Change
Elizabeth McMillan

Complexity, Organizations and Change

An essential introduction

Elizabeth McMillan

London and New York

First published 2004
by Routledge
2 Park Square, Milton Park, Abingdon, Oxon OX14 4RN

Simultaneously published in the USA and Canada
by Routledge
270 Madison Ave, New York, NY 10016

This edition published in paperback 2006

Routledge is an imprint of the Taylor & Francis Group

Transferred to Digital Printing 2006

British Library Cataloguing in Publication Data
A catalogue record for this book is available from the British Library

Library of Congress Cataloging in Publication Data

ISBN 0-415-31447-X (hbk)
ISBN 0-415-39502-X (pbk)

To my late Mother and to Simon – a son for all seasons.

Contents

Illustrations

Figures

Tables

Preface

For most of my working life I have been a personnel professional. I have worked in a number of different organizations and experienced a variety of organizational cultures, management styles, and human behaviours. As I collected my professional qualifications and became more and more immersed in the ways of management so I found I was travelling on two parallel journeys. I was digesting, sometimes uncomfortably, huge amounts of data about how to do things rationally, logically, efficiently and effectively. Yet at the same time I was aware that the reality of my everyday experiences did not always match the theory I was absorbing. As a young manager I had plenty of theory and very little practice with which to hone my critical skills. However, as I became more experienced and learnt from others around me so I became increasingly more and more uncomfortable with many aspects of modern management and organization theory. Then in 1993 three events happened which were to significantly change the direction of my life and lead in 2002 to the writing of this book.

I was unexpectedly introduced to chaos theory in the novel, *Jurassic Park*, by Michael Crichton, who refers to chaos to explain the turbulent events that unfold in the dinosaur park. A few months later I was introduced to the work of Ralph Stacey and recommended to read James Gleick's book, *Chaos*. At about the same time I became involved in a strategic change intervention at the organization where I worked, the Open University. This gave me an opportunity to try out some of the ideas that were surfacing in my mind and to introduce influences from chaos, and later complexity, into a major strategic change programme.

The programme which originally had been planned for a few months, ran for four years, and as it drew to its close I was given a secondment to study full time for my doctorate and to use the programme to provide the raw data for my case study research.

Thus my life took a totally unpredictable turn and almost 10 years later I find myself working as a research fellow in the Technology Faculty and writing this book. It's a far cry from working in the hurly burly of a busy personnel department, wrestling with budgets, strategic plans, internal politics, crises of one sort or another, and all the many demanding minutiae that make up a manager's life – but what proof that we live in an unpredictable world!

Acknowledgements

There are many people who I should acknowledge for the assistance and encouragement they have given me in preparing and writing this book. I particularly should thank Dave Wield, Helena Dolny, Roger Spear, Ysanne Carlisle, Marlene Gordon and Cathy McNulty. I should also mention Sue Oreszczyn who first suggested the idea of a book, and all my family and friends who have given me so much love and support.

1 Introduction

In my view, there is today a considerable amount of outdated and unhelpful thinking about the world of organizations. Too many current approaches to organizational change are drawn from a world view that is no longer consonant with the early twenty-first century. Traditional notions of organizations and how to manage them may have suited more stable times, but they do not offer effective solutions to organizations coping with the fast-flowing uncertainties of the modern world. Monolithic bureaucracies with their vast economies of scale seemed appropriate to the industrialized world of the early twentieth century, but they struggled to survive with the transformations brought about by modern technologies and globalization trends. Toby Tetenbaum (1998) lists six major characteristics which, for her, encapsulate these changes.

1 New technologies which have transformed communications, electronics, consumer markets and speeded up industries.
2 Globalization, which has resulted in a world that is evermore connected and interdependent as information, money and goods move around the planet.
3 Globalization and new technologies, which together have sharpened competition and precipitated the rise and fall of market leaders.
4 Change, which is now happening faster than ever before in our known history.
5 Speed – an 'incredible increase in technological speed is matched in business (product life cycles are measured in months not years) and in people's lives (most of us feel we are running as fast as we can merely to stay in place)' (Tetenbaum 1998: 23).
6 Complexity and paradox which are increasing as a result of all these changes and are making more and more difficult demands on managers used to seeking certainties and 'either/or' type solutions in order to bring about the ideals of stability and order.

Thus, in recent decades, the landscape in which organizations exist has changed almost beyond recognition, however, I do not believe that mainstream organization theory and practice have kept pace with these developments. Traditional management literature still considers the world from a linear cause and effect perspective and advocates controlling and planning processes as the way to help an organization survive and succeed. These notions are based on ideas and approaches derived from a classical, traditional, scientific world view that was developed some 300 years ago. It is a view rooted in the science and philosophy of the seventeenth century entwined with an emerging scientific methodology. It is a view and a way of looking at the world that is so woven into the fabric of western thought and everyday life as to be indiscernible. It is the air that we breathe. This book argues that though the natural order still unfolds as it always did, the world we have created and where we live our everyday lives has significantly changed, but our thinking has yet to make the same kind of shift. Modern science has combined research and imaginations and made them fact, for example, in the shape of laser applications, multimedia communications, robotics, interplanetary vehicles, nanotechnology and a range of biotechnologies. I believe that it's time that mainstream management and organization theory and practice caught up.

The prevalent literature on organizations and management has been challenged in recent years by a number of writers. People like Gareth Morgan and Charles Handy have broken with tradition and offer insightful and innovative ways of reconsidering life in organizations. Morgan in his book *Images of Organization* uses metaphor to explore our notions of organizations in an exciting and transforming way. Handy in *The Age of Unreason* and *The Empty Raincoat* offers new and challenging visions of the future of life and work. The development of ideas on learning and the learning organization, by people like Peter Senge, Margaret Dale, Mike Pedler, John Burgoyne and Tom Boydell, offers a demonstrably useful set of ideas for today's organizations. Ricardo Semler, the Brazilian manager, describes in his book *Maverick* how he broke the established rules and approaches to management to forge a dynamic and egalitarian workplace. Thus the contemporary literature on managing organizations is being injected with some powerful and fresh ways of thinking.

Recently another set of management literature reminiscent of the more radical ideas on change has been emerging – the literature based on the new sciences. This has been informed by ideas from chaos theory, complexity science and research at the Santa Fe Institute in the USA and in European institutions. These ideas have been taken up by people who have a major interest in organizations and organizational change, people like Ralph Stacey, Margaret Wheatley, Ikujiro Nonaka, and Richard Pascale. I would argue that truly radical thinking on organizations is needed if we are to better understand the world in which we live and work and that drawing on these scientific understandings can help us to achieve this.

The emergence of complexity science as the last century drew to a close had profound implications for the scientific community and a world view based on Newtonian–Cartesian thinking. Complexity now challenges the predominant scientific tradition which many consider to be highly successful, and it is making a radical and significant contribution to new scientific thinking and understanding. It challenges long held notions of predictability and the importance of small events or minor differences. This has major implications for our notions of change, how it occurs, the types and degrees of change and thus for strategic planning and associated activities. Complexity science challenges the ubiquitous use of over-simplified, linear approaches to events and happenings that has led to the development of unreal thinking and unrealistic models of the world. Further, it restores the importance of emotion and intuition to their rightful place alongside rationality and logic and it takes a holistic perspective on a world that has both consciously and unconsciously become over reductionist and compartmentalized.

Paradigm shifts are, of course, very difficult to achieve as established paradigms tend to be strongly supported by those who have built their reputations or advanced their careers by embracing such a perspective. Further, they are usually deeply rooted in people's thinking and in the way they unconsciously interpret the world around them. They are often accepted unquestioningly and are only seriously questioned by very few original thinkers. However, ideas and insights derived from complexity science have now spread across the western world and are being explored and applied in many non-scientific domains such as education, politics, philosophy, management, economics and social studies. A considerable number of writers, thinkers and pragmatists now consider that a new paradigm is coming into being – the complexity paradigm. It is a view which I support and which I shall explore further in this book.

But how can understanding of the complexity paradigm significantly and pro-foundly affect the way people think and act in society at large, and most specifically in organizations? Does it offer helpful new ways of interpreting and understanding the world of organizations? This book seeks to explain and describe how viewing the world from a complexity paradigm perspective can shed fresh light on a range of organizational problems and issues, and suggest innovative and ground-breaking ways of reshaping the organizational world so that it is more in tune with the times. It does so by seeking to build on the existing management literature base which draws on complexity science. Also it reviews some existing mainstream theories and practice and looks at complexity influenced activities in a number of organizations. It offers an in-depth case study of a traditional, complex and complicated organization that used complexity ideas to challenge and change the predominant culture, as a real life example of complexity ideas at work. Observa-tions, models and some new knowledge derived from this detailed case study are offered in the belief that they may help organizations to cope more effectively with the waves of uncertainty and change that already are the hallmark of the twenty-first century.

In writing this book I have considered a sweep of ideas and insights based on an approach to the literature on complexity that is wide-ranging and eclectic, including writers from many backgrounds and disciplines. The case study I present investigates in considerable detail a change process in one organization, but overall I have attempted to provide an integrative and holistic approach. One that combines the fine detail that comes with close investigation with a focus that takes a more distant and all embracing perspective. Organizations play a very large role in both our working and non working lives and thus a key role in the overall dynamics of society and I have sought to acknowledge this in the approach I have taken in this book.

The new sciences encourage us to look not just for formal structures and content but for patterns, flows and processes. Thus in writing this book I have sought to add to the existing literature on complexity and management by focusing on the people dimension, that is the behaviours, emotions and learning patterns and processes that flow through an organization and give it its life and characteristics.

I have spoken broadly of complexity science and the complexity paradigm and they will be explored in more detail in other chapters of this book, but what is my overall view of this brave new science and why and how do I intend to discuss its many aspects? For the reader who is largely unfamiliar with complexity science territory it perhaps needs to be stated first of all that complexity science involves a broad spectrum of disciplines: biology, physics, mathematics, chemistry and meteorology. I also would include chaos theory and evolutionary biology as features of complexity science. Thus understanding the many facets of complexity science would appear to offer a serious challenge to those with limited scientific education. So why does this book offer a broad overview of the history and development of complexity science and describe at some length complexity theories and ideas? The answer is that, in my view, anyone interested in complexity science and its applications in management and organizations should understand the origins of the ideas they may be working with. Only by understanding the basic concepts on which applications and theories are derived will the intelligent reader be able to form their own sound judgements. Having the knowledge and understanding to critique ideas derived from complexity is, in my opinion, essential if one is not to be misinformed, mislead or even cheated by expensive consultants bearing gifts.

A major aim of this book is to build a bridge between the world of science and the world of organizations and management, and to contribute to the ongoing debate about complexity science and its applications. Thus I describe the new sciences in order to investigate their relevance outside the scientific arena. It is not my aim in this book to assume the role of the expert scientific researcher nor to critique any scientific theories. (Indeed, I do not consider myself qualified to do so.) The ideas and theories put forward are drawn from the mainstream of the new sciences, and overall, are well accepted within that realm. Thus the main tenets of complexity science are covered but the list is meant to be informative and illuminating rather than exhaustive. Inevitably some names may be missing.

As complexity science is multidisciplinary, to cover all the main theories and ideas presents a significant challenge. In order to address this I have chosen to refer to the work of a number of well-known scientists in different disciplines and also to scientific writers who are recognized for their work on interpreting the work of others researching in the field. For example, James Gleick's (1993) book on chaos describes the history and development of chaos and discusses the work of major contributors such as Lorenz, Feigenbaum and Mandelbrot. This is now considered by many to be the best introduction to the origins and essence of chaos.

As scientific knowledge increased over the last decades, so more and more sub-disciplines emerged with a focus on their own highly specialized domain. Biology, for example, is one traditional discipline that now has many new branches or specialisms and each specialism tends to have its own particular way of framing and describing the world. So, if one is considering a particular life event or a scientific phenomenon, which interpretation is the right one? The answer is, of course, that there is no right interpretation and this is a very important message for anyone coming to understand the complexity paradigm. I shall illustrate this by describing a story that Steven Rose tells in his book *Lifelines*.

Five biologists are sitting by a pool enjoying a picnic when a frog that was sitting close by makes a sudden leap into the water. This prompts a discussion between the biologists on why the frog jumped. One of them, a physiologist, states that the creature jumped because the muscles in the frog's leg are responding to signals from the brain, which is itself responding to a message from the frog's retina when the snake was spotted. Rose describes this as a 'simple "within level" causal chain' whereby one event follows another 'all within a few thousandths of a second' Rose (1998: 10). But this explanation is challenged by another of the biologists, an ethnologist. The physiologist has explained how the frog jumped but not the reason why. The animal behaviourist explains that the creature jumped in order to avoid being eaten by the snake. It was a goal-directed action and can only be understood within its environmental and social contexts. Thus the ethnologist views the notion of cause quite differently from the physiologist.

The third biologist is a developmentalist and finds the other two explanations inadequate. From a developmental point of view the only reason why the frog can jump is because during its development from fertilized egg to adult frog its brain, nerves and muscles were wired up in such a way that such a sequence of activity was highly probable in the circumstances. As Rose (1998: 12) observes: 'the onto-genetic approach introduces a historical element into the account: the individual history of the frog becomes the key to understanding its present behaviour'.

The fourth biologist, an evolutionist, however, is not satisfied by any of the explanations to date. The evolutionary explanation is that the frog jumped because 'during its evolutionary history it was adaptive for its ancestors to do so at the sight of a snake; those ancestors that failed to do so were eaten, and hence their progeny failed to be selected' (Rose 1998: 12).

Finally, the fifth biologist, a molecular biologist, speaks up and claims that they have all missed the point.

> The frog jumps *because* of the biochemical properties of its muscles. The muscles are composed largely of two interdigitated filamentous proteins, called actin and myosin, and they contract because the protein filaments slide past one another. This behaviour of the actin and myosin is dependent on the amino acid composition of the two proteins, and hence on chemical properties, and hence on physical properties.
>
> (Rose 1998: 13)

So here we have five different, yet valid explanations, from five different sub-disciplines of biology. So who do we believe? As Rose points out, we have to consider all of the explanations and possibly others too. There is no one simple answer and it is an approach which I have sought in writing this book. The one right answer or explanation is a way of thinking that belongs to the old scientific paradigm, yet one encounters it everywhere, even in writings on complexity science. It should also be borne in mind that simple causal methods of explanation tend to paint linear pictures. Rose reminds us that notions of 'cause' have been troublesome since the days of Aristotle, so it may be more advisable to think in terms of clear temporal sequences. Again I shall endeavour to avoid the pitfalls of cause and effect approaches, but I have to acknowledge that it is embedded well into my thinking as part of my traditional educational experiences. That is not to say that it is without value, but it tends to oversimplify the complexities of our world, and can encourage inappropriate, and sometimes over simplistic interpretations of complex issues.

Scientists have their own 'languages', for example, the language of the physicist is not always understandable by the chemist and vice versa. Further, as the above story illustrates there are specialist terms used by sub-disciplines within mainstream disciplines. Thus, as scientific research builds up ever more massive knowledge databases, so the many languages of science increase their vocabularies and sub-languages emerge along with new sub-disciplines. I have sought in this book to write in a way that is accessible to the non-scientific reader and to avoid a vocabulary that is highly scientific wherever possible. I have thought for some time that complexity science needs to develop an accessible language that is rooted in verifiable science, but is not itself exclusively scientific and dependent upon an esoteric scientific vocabulary to explain itself.

The new sciences challenge many aspects of the existing paradigm and in so doing indirectly offer a challenge to the way organizations are structured and behave. If complexity provides us with explanations about how the world works then, I would argue, these explanations should be of value in considering how organizations work and how to change them. I was able to test this hypothesis in a real life laboratory and the ideas and insights I present in this book draw heavily on empirical data from my research and a range of practical experiences.

This book aims to embrace many aspects of how organizations might be transformed by using ideas drawn from complexity science. Therefore it seeks to consider a spectrum of implications, whether they have been strategic, operational or employee based. But there is a special emphasis on considering the role that the people in an organization play in transforming that organization. The term 'people' refers to everyone who works in an organization regardless of role or status. I would contend that they, rather than high level, strategic planning processes and formal change interventions, especially top-down ones, are the real key to understanding organizational change. Thus this book argues that it is human dynamics which bring about real 'second order' change and renewal. That is change that is not surface but deep down, where thinking and behaviours become significantly different.

So far this chapter has sought to introduce the main underpinning themes of the book and the approaches I have taken in writing it. In the final section of this introduction I outline the contents on a chapter-by-chapter basis.

A complete chapter in this book, Chapter 2, is dedicated to the history and development of those ideas and theories, and those chiefly credited with their development, which have collectively become known as complexity science. Thus a significant part of this chapter includes the basic tenets of chaos theory and draws heavily on the writing of Gleick (1993). The following are included in this section: the butterfly effect (or sensitive dependence on initial conditions) and the work of Edward Lorenz; Benoit Mandelbrot and the development of fractal geometry; strange attractors; notions of order and disorder; the edge of chaos; concepts of universality; patterning and flow. The chapter then moves on to the emergence of complexity science with reference to the writings of Fritjof Capra; the work of Ilya Prigogine on dissipative structures and self-organization; John Holland on complex adaptive systems and emergence; and Stuart Kauffman and others on biology and fresh interpretations of evolution. This chapter also includes a brief discussion on the use of the terms 'chaos' in the ordinary vernacular.

In order to explore the importance of the ideas and theories arising from the new science it was important to consider the background against which they arose. Thus Chapter 3 describes the origins and development of the classical, scientific tradition founded by Galileo, Newton, Descartes and others. This established a mechanistic, linear view of the world which took a reductionist, cause and effect approach to science. Human beings were seen as machine-like and the intellect was highly valued and the senses disregarded. In spite of challenges from the Romantics in the early nineteenth century and from quantum physics and relativity theory in the twentieth century this world view continued to exert a very powerful influence on all aspects of life. Many early technologists and the founders of industrial society in the Western world looked to science to provide ideas and models as to how to establish their new industries. This chapter includes a review of mainstream organization theory and practice including: organizations as machines; bureaucracy; classical management theory; scientific management; the behavioural influences; and developments in the 1970s and 1980s. The end of the twentieth century saw organizations trying to cope with rapid change and uncertainty and experimenting with a host of ideas including downsizing and business process re-engineering, and the emergence of learning organization concepts. This chapter considers how much ideas derived from the classical, scientific view still exist in today's organizations and refers to Handy (1990, 1993), Morgan (1986) and others to offer considerable evidence to support the view that the influence is still a powerful one. Also included is a discussion of the significance of language and metaphor because of the insights they offer us into organizational life.

Many organizations and their managers assume that change can be managed and controlled in an orderly fashion until the new desired state is arrived at. This is a mechanistic, linear approach to change which assumes that equilibrium can be achieved and maintained in a rapidly changing world and is typified by the use of deliberate strategies as described by Mintzberg and Waters (1989). Chapter 4 looks at how the way organizations think about change affects their ability to handle it. It includes a brief survey of how perceptions of change and the nature of change have changed over time, from the ancient world of Heraclitus to the modern world of David Bohm (1980) and complexity science. In so doing it aims to reinforce emerging understandings on the reality of change, especially in organizations.

This chapter considers and critiques some of the mainstream theories and approaches to change that are widely taught and practised. It also refers to important writers on strategic management like Mintzberg and Waters (1989) and Quinn (1989) who have contributed to major developments in current thinking on strategic management. In spite of this, however, there is much evidence to suggest that traditional thinking on change management and the old mindset still prevail.

In order to understand and describe the changes explored in the case study in Chapter 6, I have referred also in Chapter 4 to writers such as Morgan (1986), Stacey (1992, 1996a) and Nonaka (1988) and their interpretations of the different kinds of change. The work of Carlisle and McMillan (2002) is also included in order to make a comparison between a Newtonian–Cartesian approach to strategic change and a complexity paradigm-based approach to strategic thinking and action. The importance of learning and the many forms it may take powerfully underpins the writings of these definitions of change and this led to considering the work of Dale (1994) and Senge (1992, 1994) on learning organizations.

Morgan (1986) contends that writing on the management of change falls into two main categories. One is a descriptive approach which attempts to identify and list manifestations of change as discrete events. The second approach attempts to describe change via abstract concepts such as amounts of uncertainty or turbulence. Morgan considers that these approaches succeed in describing and classifying the nature of change but fail to explain its underlying dynamic. In describing the changes that took place at the Open University between 1993 and 1996 I have attempted to blend the two approaches Morgan describes and explain them via understandings of change drawn from complexity. Thus I describe both apparent and unapparent changes. In other words, the discrete, observable events and waves of change or turbulence, but also those less observable events and flows which are part of the human response and often emerge only over time. Thus some explanations regarding the basic dynamics of change in organizations are put forward.

Having considered some ideas on managing change in organizations in Chapter 4, Chapter 5 moves on to consider how complexity science may be used to reinterpret the world of organizations and management. It describes how different features such as the butterfly effect, fractals, the edge of chaos, self-organizing principles, and understanding of complex adaptive systems may be used in renewing organizations, and provides examples from a number of organizations in Europe and the USA. It explores new approaches to strategic change and describes how some organizations are creating a new kind of order that does not use controlling approaches. In other words, how they are breaking out of old ways of thinking as they come to better understand the complexity approach. It describes how self-organizing principles derived from complexity can encourage the emergence of real creativity and innovation. Further, it describes some of the new perspectives and understandings that may emerge when organizations are viewed in a non-linear way.

This chapter also reviews and discusses the work of a number of key writers on organizations who draw on the new sciences for their ideas and insights. It covers some of their ideas and approaches and how they believe they may be used to achieve organizational transformation and renewal. Nonaka (1988), for example, was one of the first to explore how ideas from chaos could be used in organizations through his observations of transformation in Japanese companies. He draws heavily on the work of Prigogine and his work on dissipative structures. Wheatley (1994) and Pascale *et al.* (2000) write on their research and experiences in the USA. Stacey (1992, 1993, 1996a; *et al.* 2000) draws on extensive reading and his own research in a range of organizations, and provides the most extensive and comprehensive insights on the uses of the complexity in organizations. I use Stacey and others to review some of the important literature on organizational transformation derived from complexity science.

Chapter 6 provides a brief history of the Open University. It describes some of its main features, including how it was set up, its structure, purpose and culture and to do so draws on a range of internal publications. Further, it describes the financial, environmental and strategic planning situation in early 1993 in order to establish the context out of which the strategic change programme, named 'New Directions' emerged. It is this programme which provides the case study presented in this book and which is the subject of this chapter. This chapter provides an outline of the story of the programme on a chronological basis, and describes the different events as they unfolded. Thus it sets the stage for the case study, offers information on the real life activity and provides some of the factual evidence.

The New Directions Programme originally started out as a series of consultative workshops on the university's new strategic action plan. These were led by the Pro Vice Chancellor, Strategy. They were planned to take place over a few months but most unexpectedly developed into a complex and far-reaching change process which extended over four years. This process was underpinned and energized by emergent self-organizing principles. A range of complex, interactions developed between different individuals and different staff groups as the programme unrolled. An unpredicted response dynamic emerged within the organization and rich learning experiences took place. But how effective had it been as an organizational change process and how had understandings of complexity science influenced the programme and events? The programme had created two teams of volunteers who were particularly successful in organizing and delivering on their projects. What was the essential nature of these teams and did they have any connections with ideas from complexity? Why had the team members volunteered to participate in such a specific way in the change process? These and other key questions I sought to answer via an analysis of the case study data and my conclusions are presented in this book.

The Open University was set up in the late 1960s and early 1970s and broke the mould in higher education with its delivery of distance learning and open access policies. It was an innovative organization which experimented with radical ideas for course design and delivery, and in so doing developed the course team approach to teaching and experiential learning. However, as the university grew so it became more formalized and bureaucratic and a number of contradictions emerged. It set out to be a democratic institution that sought to involve the staff in its governance, yet the procedures it set up to do this excluded many of them, particularly the more junior grades. Thus, by the 1990s, the formal structures and bureaucratic procedures dominated a compartmentalized organization within which informal groups, course teams and innovative individuals sought to work creatively across it.

The university is a many faceted institution with a large administrative function, and a multiplicity of cultures and management styles. In some areas of the university there is a large measure of democracy and staff empowerment with managers that are keen to innovate and change. However, there are many areas with Taylorist approaches to management, where the senior staff have a strong attachment to the status quo and resist all attempts at real change. Thus the university is a richly complex and complicated organization and so is a very good organization on which to base a case study on organizational change.

Chapter 7 considers the evidence derived from the case study on the New Directions Programme to illustrate and suggest how approaches and ideas derived from complexity science are relevant and useful in organizational change processes. It is possible by studying the New Directions initiative to identify and explain the role that ideas emerging from complexity contributed to the change process. This suggests how approaches to organizational change derived from complexity can be operationalized and practically useful.

Of all the writers on complexity in organizations, I have used Ralph Stacey most when interpreting some of the ways in which complexity could be used. His work provided especially valuable signposts and yardsticks against which to consider my own research data. Stacey's (1996a) nine-point complexity theory of organization provided a useful theoretical framework within which to examine and consider the case study data in the light of complexity principles. Nonaka's (1988) research was also used as a source of comparison. Stacey's work on self-organizing systems and especially self-organizing teams was also used as a theoretical framework within which to consider the data on teams and team working.

Finally, Chapter 7 offers a model of participative strategic change which is based on the findings of the case study and which supports a democratic approach to strategy formation and delivery.

All change interventions can provoke hostile responses and a change process based on innovative approaches and complexity is no exception, and needs not only operational support but also high level political support. In my view, without support from those who are powerful at the top of the organization the process will be short-lived. Further, continued powerful support and the right environment are needed if the process is not to slow down and fade away. In Chapter 8 I suggest that using ideas from complexity should be especially successful in organizations which are prepared to provide the right climate and environment to support such a process. Such organizations will to be prepared to cut across any existing hierarchical boundaries, to allow all staff to challenge and debate strategic priorities and to experiment with new ideas, and will be ready to genuinely listen and respond to the outcomes. They will also be prepared to set up empowered teams of volunteers to tackle change projects on their own terms.

Human systems have a real capacity for self-organization and this chapter demonstrates how given the right environment a spontaneous, self-organizing dynamic can emerge within an organization. One that will stimulate and energize a range of changes. One that can influence policy making and strategic planning by filtering into the senior management processes. Further, it discusses the importance of team working and democracy. It tells how by setting up self-organizing teams specific change projects can be accomplished or issues addressed. These are all observable changes. Most significantly the emergence of self-organization within human groups creates opportunities for learning both theoretical and experiential. Learning may be simple or first level, such as an acquisition of new skills, or it may be complex or adaptive learning, such that mindsets are moved and people see the world afresh. These changes within an individual contribute significantly to the flow of change within an organization although they may only be observable over time. If sufficient learning takes place within a self-organizing system then it becomes a complex adaptive system.

Chapter 8 is also all about future choices and focuses on the need to consider possibilities for the future. It suggests that one way to introduce a complexity approach to organizational change is to use a 'twelve principles' model. This provides guidance on how to create the right environment and climate for such an intervention, behavioural aspects and practical suggestions. It also incorporates a 'transition strategy' model which is derived from the case study research. This offers a theoretical bridge between traditional approaches to strategic change and an approach based on complexity science. Drawn from a real-life example, it provides a useful tool for thinking about strategic change in the working world.

This chapter contends that an understanding of the nature of organizational structure and its underpinning design principles are key to organizational trans-formation. Further, it proposes that the use of design principles derived from complexity science should lead to the development of new structural forms that are flexible, responsive and resilient. It compares the 'classical' model of organiza-tion design with a complexity-based model and in proposing a radical rethink offers the 'fractal web' as a possible model for such an organization structure. This is a speculative model of organization structure and design based on complexity principles.

This chapter and the book conclude with some final reflections on the emergence of the complexity paradigm and the implications it offers for organizational change.

In conclusion the aims of this book are as follows:

- To enable those unfamiliar with the complexity paradigm to understand how it developed and its important features without the need for a scientific education or background.

- To further develop this understanding by describing the relationship between organizations and classical science from an historical perspective.
- To explore theories, attitudes and ideas on change and organizational change, in particular, in order to widen perspectives and set the context for the modern organization.
- To consider the possibilities the complexity paradigm offers when considering changing and reshaping organizations.
- To share with the reader examples of the ways in which a wide variety of organizations have used ideas and insights from the complexity paradigm to move their organizations forward or to create a new kind of organization.
- To provide a major real-life example of complexity ideas in practice in a well-known complex and complicated organization.
- To provide new theoretical and practical insights into the use of complexity principles in bringing about organizational changes.
- To encourage the reader who is new to the complexity paradigm to want to learn more and to offer the 'experienced' reader some new theory and some new real-life insights based on original research.

2 Introducing complexity

No one doubts that it was plain, honest reductionist science that allowed us to
unlock so many of the secrets of the Universe. ... But clear, strong, and powerful
though it may be, it is not enough by itself to explain the facts of life.

(Lovelock 1989: 214)

This chapter is designed to offer those new or unfamiliar with complexity science
('complexity', 'complex adaptive systems' or 'complex systems', as it is sometimes
known), an understanding of the basic tenets of chaos (the forerunner of complexity), and complexity science. The histories and the descriptions and definitions
offered are not exhaustive, nor are they meant to be, and their purpose is not a
scientific one. They are provided on the basis that an all round understanding of
the scientific background is necessary if one is to explore, with any degree of
confidence, the insights and ideas they may offer in organizational and management
contexts. Further, I hope that this chapter will enable readers to question the validity
of any proposals by writers on organizational theory and practice when they draw
on complexity science in support of their ideas.

Chaos

Chaos theory or chaos science is defined in a number of ways and one very succinct
and interesting definition offered by Gleick (1993: 3) is that 'WHERE CHAOS
BEGINS, classical science stops'. This definition reminds us that many early chaos
researchers were intrigued and challenged by areas that the laws of classical science
failed to provide answers for and they were often particularly attracted to some of
the more difficult questions. Classical science suggested a mechanistic view of the
world and this encouraged scientists to search for fixed theories using linear methods
and simple cause and effect approaches. Mathematicians and physicists tended to
focus their researches on systems perceived to be linear in that they exhibited
predictable patterns and cause and effect arrangements. This encouraged the
development of linear equations and other linear methods of exploration and
explanation. Non-linear systems were considered too unpredictable and too
dynamical to be effectively researched. To seek understanding of these ubiquitous

systems involved calculations that were too demanding, too time consuming and too complicated, that is until the advent of computers. The use of computer technology made it possible to use non-linear equations and to begin significant researches into non-linear systems. Thus computer technology and scientific curiosity led to the emergence of the principles of chaos science. Over time this had a profound effect on an essentially linear view of the world and in so doing challenged many long-held assumptions.

Chaos or chaos science is a science that seeks to explain phenomena that have always existed, but its focus upon them is new and it has a multidisciplinary approach that breaks with a western scientific tradition that had become increasingly reductionist. It is new, too, because most of its significant explanations and theories were first mooted in the last thirty five or so years, whereas traditional, classical science has been pre-eminent for over 300 years.

The use of the term chaos theory often misleads people. *The Concise Oxford Dictionary* (1976: 166) defines chaos as a noun meaning 'formless primordial matter; utter confusion'. In Brewer's *The Dictionary of Phrase and Fable* (1978: 237) the reference to chaos reads:

> Chaos (kaos). Confusion: that confused mass of elemental substances supposed to have existed before God reduced creation into order. The poet Hesiod is the first extant writer that speaks of it.
> 'Light, uncollected, through the chaos urged
> Its infant way, nor order yet had drawn
> His lovely train from out the dubious gloom.' (Thomson: Autumn, 732–4)

In everyday life people tend to think of chaos as some kind of madness when systems break down, when life seems to be getting out of control and the natural order of things disintegrates. Chaos in the biblical sense has strong associations with darkness and disorder. However, the development of chaos theory or chaos science gave the everyday term 'chaos' a new scientific meaning. In the scientific sense chaos is not about darkness, breakdown, confusion and disorder. The scientific use of the term describes processes that appear to be random or chaotic, but in fact are not. Paradoxically, this apparent 'chaos' is not an aberration in the planned scheme of things, but reflects deeper more complex patterns and swirls of order than had previously been expected and understood. They are processes that have their own kind of internal order and their own kind of process principles.

The British mathematician Ian Stewart (1997) describes chaos theory as an exciting new area of mathematics concerned with non-linear dynamics. But chaos science embraces a wide range of disciplines: physics, biology, meteorology and chemistry, as well as mathematics. It is holistic in nature and approach and concerned with universal systems and processes. Chaos researchers search for explanations and patterns that connect rather than divide, that link together and create new approaches, and that encourage new ways of viewing the world, ways that help us to better understand the nature of our complex universe.

Chaos science is about understanding and explaining the apparent disorder that exists in the universe. Further, it has challenged the prevalent view of how the world works and discovered new laws and even new kinds of laws. It is considered by many to be a subset of complexity science for it was the discovery of chaos theory which stimulated further explorations into the behaviour of complex systems and dynamics which are the essence of complexity.

Chaos – a brief history

But when did chaos science first come into being? It has its origins in the late 1960s and the 1970s when a number of scientists from a wide range of disciplines became uneasy and sometimes dissatisfied with existing scientific explanations. These often ignored minor aspects in order to uphold an important theory or law. Galileo, it is known, had to disregard the non-linear effects of friction and air resistance in order to achieve his results. Chaos researchers were fascinated by the unpredictable nature of the universe and sought to understand and explain things radically differently. By the 1980s, chaos had become a fast growing movement that had created its own range of special techniques using computers and specialized graphics.

Table 2.1 shows the major concepts of chaos science and some of the key researchers associated with them.

A major landmark in the emergence of the new science was the proposition of the 'butterfly effect' or 'sensitive dependence on initial conditions'. This phrase was coined by Edward Lorenz, a meteorologist at the Massachusetts Institute of Technology. Working in the 1960s, he discovered that small variables in weather conditions could have a major impact on developing weather patterns. Lorenz's discovery posed a significant challenge to prevalent theories of predictability and disturbed the scientific community. It is one of the main tenets of chaos.

In the 1960s and 1970s the study of the behaviour of pendulums by a number of physicists led to further discoveries.

> Those studying chaotic dynamics discovered that the disorderly behavior of simple systems acted as a *creative* process. It generated complexity: richly organized patterns, sometimes stable and sometimes unstable, sometimes finite sometimes infinite, but always with the fascination of living things.
>
> (Gleick 1993: 43)

The American, Stephen Smale, at the University of California at Berkeley, went back to Henri Poincaré, the great French mathematician, building on his work on qualitative dynamical systems, such that by the 1970s Smale's work had become more widely recognized as opening up a whole new branch of mathematics.

The Australian-born, Robert May, whose work on fish populations demonstrated that whatever changes take place, there emerges an underlying pattern of order as population changes repeat themselves over different yearly cycles. There is order

Table 2.1 Developments in chaos science

Time period	Theory/ concept	Key researcher	Discipline	Country of birth/ experience
1854–1912	Topology (strange attractors)	Henri Poincaré	Mathematics	France
1970s	Sensitive dependence on initial conditions	Edward Lorenz	Meteorology	USA
	Strange attractors	David Ruelle	Mathematics and Physics	Belgium and France
		Floris Takens	Mathematics	Holland
		Edward Lorenz	Meteorology	USA
1980s	Chaotic properties of dynamical systems	Stephen Smale	Mathematics	USA
	Notions of order and disorder	James Yorke	Mathematics	USA
	Order within chaos	Robert May	Biology and physics	Australia and UK
	Fractals	Benoit Mandelbrot	Mathematics	France and USA
	Universality	Mitchell Feigenbaum	Physics	USA
	Flow	Albert Libchaber	Physics	France

within apparent chaos. May argued that the standard scientific education misled scientists about the overwhelming non-linearity of the world. His work showed how a logistic equation could be responsive to small differences in starting values and reaffirmed the importance of 'sensitive dependence on initial conditions' discovered by Lorenz.

Benoit Mandelbrot, a Polish-born mathematician who moved to France as a boy, is credited with devising a new form of geometry – fractal geometry. Fractals are everywhere around us in nature but until Mandelbrot devised his new geometry there was no qualitative means of measuring the natural world. His work was to significantly influence the new generation of mathematicians who were working on chaos theory.

Mitchell Feigenbaum, a US physicist who spent a great deal of his time walking, flying among the clouds and pondering over the nature of light and colour, developed the concept of 'universality'. He showed that universality was both a qualitative phenomenon and a quantitative one that applied not only to patterns, but also to numbers.

In the 1960s and 1970s most scientists thought very differently to today when they sought to interpret the world around them. Now an alternative set of ideas exists, a new way of viewing the world, that has arisen out of the serious, painstaking, and often inspired, research of the early chaos pioneers. Chaos encouraged holistic thinking in science and it brought together a whole range of disciplines that were heading down their own exclusive paths. Furthermore, as Gleick (1993) points out, the discoveries of the chaos scientists were not only new but were often new ways of understanding old ideas. Others like Einstein, Poincaré and Maxwell had seen many of the aspects of chaos but these had then been forgotten.

It was the development of computers and computer technology which enabled scientists to solve complex dynamical equations and to unravel some of the mysteries of chaos which had been observed by an earlier generation. Thus enabled by developments in computer technology a new set of concepts arose.

Chaos – main themes and theories

The butterfly effect – sensitive dependence on initial conditions

Edward Lorenz is credited with the discovery of the phenomenon of 'sensitive dependence on initial conditions' although the French mathematician, Poincaré coined a similar expression when he too pointed out the existence of such phenomena in an essay in 1903. In the 1960s, Lorenz, was working using a simple computer program that simulated weather patterns. One day he took a shortcut and instead of keying in the usual sequence that started the weather cycle, he chose instead to start it up using only half the sequence. He returned to his program after a coffee break assuming that the change was inconsequential and that a small numerical difference was like a small puff of wind, it would have no major impact on the overall, large scale patterns of the weather. However, as the program progressed the weather patterns that emerged started to become increasingly different from the previous ones, until all further resemblance disappeared. Small changes over a period of time had produced significant differences. The small perturbations in the behaviour of the weather were what made the weather systems so changeable, unpredictable and complex. From then on Lorenz believed that long-range weather forecasting was impossible. His discovery later became known as the 'butterfly effect' as a result of his paper: 'Predictability: does the flap of a butterfly's wings in Brazil set off a tornado in Texas?' given at the annual meeting of the American Association for the Advancement of Science in December 1979.

The butterfly effect demonstrates that all systems are exceptionally sensitive to their initial or starting conditions and that small variations over a period of time can lead to major changes in a non-linear system. Poincaré's research in this field had been forgotten and until Lorenz's work everyone had believed that small differences averaged out and were of no real significance. The butterfly effect showed that small things mattered, further, it demonstrated the near impossibility of predicting with any real degree of accuracy, the long-term outcomes of a series of events.

But, as the US biologist Stuart Kauffman (1996) points out, it is important to realize that because a system is not predictable in the long term, it does not mean that it is impossible to understand or even to explain its behaviours. Also that it should be possible to build theories that offer explanations for the generic properties of the system without necessarily knowing the small details.

Paradoxically, complex dynamical systems, like the weather systems, studied by Lorenz are not, as a whole, unstable although they exhibit unstable behaviours. The system may appear to be behaving erratically and unpredictably at first glance, but observation over a longer time period or on a wider panorama or visual scale will show patterns emerging that echo each other and weave around to form an unexpectedly stable tapestry of behaviours. It may well be a bizarre tapestry of strange and unusual shapes, but there will be an overall pattern that emerges and unites it as an orderly whole. This theme occurs again and again as one explores different aspects of chaos theory and it resonates with notions such as strange attractors, and concepts of patterning and universality which are discussed later.

The butterfly effect challenges traditional ideas of cause and effect and concepts of predictability. As a result many long-held scientific notions have had to be reviewed and, of course, it has major implications for notions of long-term planning and the wisdom of commitment to long-term strategies. For the UK science writer, John Gribbin:

> The classic example of chaos at work is in the weather. If you could measure the positions and motions of all the atoms in the air at once, you could predict the weather perfectly. But computer simulations show that tiny differences in starting conditions build up over about a week to give wildly different forecasts. So weather predicting will never be any good for forecasts more than a few days ahead, no matter how big (in terms of memory) and fast computers get to be in the future. The only computer that can simulate the weather is the weather; and the only computer that can simulate the Universe is the Universe.
>
> (John Gribbin 1999: 9)

This is a serious point to bear in mind when reading accounts of computer simulations and the validity of the possible predictions (e.g. economic and business forecasts) they can offer you if they are dealing with many different factors with in built differences, however small or subtle.

Strange attractors

Edward Lorenz is also renowned for what is known as the 'Lorenz attractor', sometimes known as the 'butterfly attractor'. This is an example of a 'strange attractor' (a term coined by David Ruelle and Floris Takens). A strange attractor is a way of describing and visualizing in geometric form the behaviour of a dynamical system over a period of time. It concerns a 'basin' of attraction within which a range of similar but non-repeating behaviours take place, behaviours which seem to be magnetically drawn or pulled together within the 'basin'. These 'basins' and the patterns formed by the different trajectories or paths the system takes within the 'basin' are represented by using computer-generated graphics. The Lorenz attractor was called the 'butterfly attractor' because when the different trajectories of the system were mapped by Lorenz the image that unfolded on the computer screen formed a figure of eight, not unlike that of a butterfly's wings.

David Ruelle, a Belgian-born mathematical physicist, created the term 'strange attractor' in order to describe and explain the patterns of behaviour of turbulence in fluids.

> Like so many of those who began studying chaos, David Ruelle suspected that the visible patterns in turbulent flow – self-entangled stream lines, spiral vortices, whorls that rise before the eye and vanish again – must reflect patterns explained by laws not yet discovered.
>
> (Gleick 1993: 138)

Working with the Dutch mathematician, Floris Takens, Ruelle began to develop the notion of the strange attractor and in 1971 they published their findings. It was to be some years, however, before their work was fully recognized.

A strange attractor has two distinct features. Firstly, it shows great sensitivity to initial conditions. Secondly, it has fractal properties. The nature of fractals is discussed in the next section. Because of its sensitivity to initial or starting conditions it means that it is impossible to accurately predict the precise behaviours of the system involved and thus, for example, to accurately plot in advance each trajectory on a computer screen. A strange attractor has been likened to dropping a small ball or a marble into a large bowl or basin. The ball will roll around up and down the walls of the bowl repeating this upwards and downwards movement until all its energy is spent and it finally comes to rest. The trajectories taken by the ball when plotted by a computer and produced on a computer screen would show the repeating patterns of behaviour made by the ball. Patterns of movement up and down and around the bowl are all very similar in shape although each one is uniquely different and follows its own individual pathway. The trajectories may touch or cross each other but they are always different. The ball is sensitive to initial conditions, in that should you repeat the same exercise again, then the trajectories taken by the ball although similar in pattern would be different. They are different because the ball responds to slight changes in the shape of the bowl, to small specks of dust or tiny smears of moisture and all these things affect the rolling of the ball. Everyone drops the ball in a slightly different way. And everyone knows what kind of behaviour to expect of a small ball dropped into a large basin. The behaviour witnessed is the phenomenon of the strange attractor.

Although a dynamical system may appear to be chaotic and unpredictable it does have a shape and never moves outside the bounds of its strange attractor. The British weather, for example, behaves like a strange attractor. It is an extremely dynamical system and can vary considerably from week to week and from day to day and is renowned for its unpredictability. But it always behaves like the British weather. There are no periods of monsoon or desert-like weather conditions. Its unpredictability is part of its strange attractor behaviour and so it always behaves within certain bounds.

Although the potential for chaos resides within every system, chaos when it emerges never moves outside the bounds of its strange attractor. No point or pattern of points is ever repeated, and one might think that this shows a totally messy system with no order. But the chaotic behaviour exhibited is not random and unrestrained, it is has its own kind of patterning and its own form of determinism. In other words, it has its own kind of internal order. The strange attractor may weave a range of complex, exotic patterns, each one different, yet the whole is creating and exhibiting a new kind of order. It is order within apparent chaos.

The discovery of the strange attractor enabled scientists to consider how dynamical systems behave in more ways than had previously been considered possible.

Fractals

The term 'fractal' was coined by Benoit Mandelbrot to describe a new type of geometry, one that concerned irregular shapes that repeated themselves up and down the scales of length. Conventional, Euclidian geometry is a geometry that describes and measures the many attributes of the man-made world – a world of buildings, roads, squares, rooms and so on. It describes essentially simple shapes, such as straight lines and smooth circles. It cannot measure the irregular, uneven and sometimes fuzzy features of the natural world. Mandelbrot's new geometry is a universal geometry that can capture the amazing diversity of shapes in the living world. It is able to describe all the many different and complicated aspects of nature ranging from hard rocky landscapes, coastlines, and mountain tops to nebulous clouds and living things such as plants, corals, vegetables, trees and nervous and cardiovascular systems. Fractal shapes are everywhere in nature.

The property whereby fractal objects repeat themselves on different size scales is known as self similarity. Coveney and Highfield (1995: 172) refer to self similarity as this 'property of endlessly manifesting a motif within a motif within a motif'. Thus, they suggest, if one looks at the shape of the edge of a clover leaf one will discover that the edge itself contains still smaller clover type shapes. They humorously highlight this by quoting the satirist Jonathan Swift's observation written in 1733:

> So, naturalists observe, a flea
> Hath smaller fleas that on him prey
> And these have smaller fleas to bite 'em
> And so proceed *ad infinitum.*

Fractal principles give us valuable insights into how nature creates our world using a few simple guidelines. An excellent and oft-quoted example of this is the way a fern is built up from a few basic rules. It starts with a basic shape and builds up into what we recognize as a fern by constantly repeating this pattern on a series of different size scales. The same principles apply to many types of trees which are designed using branching patterns. These patterns form the underlying design of their leaves, their twigs, their branches and their trunks. Another example of a fractal structure is the blood circulatory system in the body. It has an extensive web of intertwining veins and arteries all branching out in fractal patterns.

If we use fractal geometry, however, then we see things differently – on different scales. Gleick (1993) cites the example of a hurricane which in one way is a violent storm and a particular atmospheric event. However, seen in fractal terms it is part of a vast continuum that extends from gusts of air on a city street to the enormous cyclonic systems that race across the planet. Further, the use of fractals encourages us to break away from the traditional, quantitative, reductionist approach to measurement. Fractal geometry is a geometry of the whole and one that is all about qualitative rather than quantitative measurement and appreciation.

Scientists from a range of disciplines are now using fractals to describe the appearance and properties of a wide range of objects, materials, processes and behaviours. These include polymers, metals, the human heart, plant properties and wild life activity. Some organizations are using fractal principles in order to operate more effectively. They are attempting to stand back from studying separate aspects and are focusing on overall shapes, themes and patterns. Business analysts too use fractals to study the patterns in behaviour of the stock market. Even the world of art has been explored using observations based on fractal patterning approaches. An analysis of the paintings of the US artist Jackson Pollock shows that his patterns are essentially fractal, in that 'they display the finger-print of nature' (Taylor *et al.* 1999: 25).

> Pollock's contribution to the evolution of art is secure. He described nature directly. Rather than mimicking it, he adopted the language of nature – fractals – to build his own patterns. In doing so he was, in many ways, ahead of his contemporaries in art and science.'
>
> (Taylor *et al.* 1999: 28)

Order within chaos

Explorations of chaos involve research into the apparently random behaviour of dynamical systems. A significant aspect of this research is the notion of order within chaos. This puts forward the idea that within the most seemingly disorderly of systems there are elements of order and thus a kind of unexpected stability. This notion emerged from the work of a number of researchers and Robert May when he was working as a biologist. May was interested in understanding the behaviour of wildlife populations and their boom and bust cycles.

May developed a computer program designed to simulate the different changes in fish population sizes. He investigated hundreds of different values, setting feedback loops in motion and watching to see where and whether the numbers would settle to a fixed point. It was as if he were able to study his own fish pond. Like Lorenz he created a bifurcation diagram which plotted the behaviour of the system at different parameters. It showed clearly that when the parameters are low the fish population becomes extinct. As the parameters rise so does the equilibrium of the population. Then as it rises further the equilibrium splits into two and the population starts to alternate between two different levels. The bifurcations become faster and faster then the system turns chaotic and the population visits infinitely many different values. One would think that in the chaotic period the changes were completely random but in fact, in the middle of this chaos, stable cycles return. For example, the pattern of changing population may repeat itself on a three- or a seven-year cycle. These appeared on the computer graph like windows of order within the chaotic sector. Also when portions of these parts of the graph are magnified they turn out to resemble the whole diagram – a fractal pattern.

Thus pockets of order exist within the most chaotic and disorderly of living systems. Coveney and Highfield (1995) tell how a simple linear system in a bifurcation cascade (also known as period doubling) moves into chaos. The further the system moves from equilibrium, the more chaos one would expect to see. However, on close inspection one sees that there are islands or windows of regularity between areas of chaos. Lovelock (1989) refers to the ecologist C.S. Holling, who observes that the stability of all large-scale ecosystems depends on the existence of such internal chaotic stabilities. The existence of order within chaos is to be found everywhere in the natural world.

The edge of chaos

Complex living systems appear to have the ability to balance order and chaos and this place of balance is known as 'the edge of chaos'. The edge of chaos is a place, or rather a zone, where the parts of a system never quite lock into place, and yet never quite break up either. Kauffman (1996) uses water as an analogy to describe the edge of chaos. Water exists as solid ice, liquid water and as gaseous steam. Kauffman's hypothesis is that if any living system becomes too embedded or too deeply involved in the frozen, highly-ordered area (ice), then it becomes too rigid to undertake the complex activities necessary to sustain and develop life. On the other hand, if the system becomes too embedded in the gaseous chaotic zone (steam) then it would suffer from a complete lack of order and again would be unable to carry out all the activities necessary to survive. Thus the best place for a living system to exist is in the fluid area (water) which lies between the two other areas. This is the space between order and chaos and it offers the best possibilities for the successful development of complex activities. This is the edge of chaos. In this position a complex living system is best placed to take advantage of dipping into and even blending, if needed, attributes from either of the other two zones without experiencing the disadvantages.

Biological life forms appears to exist in a balance between regularity and disorder. This provides them with sufficient stimulation and freedom to experiment and adapt but also with sufficient frameworks and structure to ensure they avoid complete disorderly disintegration. Observations and computer simulations of ant colonies provide some evidence for this balance between order and chaos and the existence of the edge of chaos. Ants as individuals behave in a chaotic fashion. They rush about, have a rest, then rush about again, thus moving from an active pattern to a stable or inactive one. But their individual behaviours reflect the overall pattern of the colony which as a whole has an orderly rhythmic pattern to it. Further, experimental studies have showed that the pattern of their behaviour is affected by population density.

> Evidently ants have a sense of density in the colony, since they regulate it at a fairly constant value. As ants come and go from the nest, changing the density, rhythmic activity patterns appear and disappear, replaced by disordered activity. This suggests that the colonies are regulating their densities so that they live at the edge of chaos.
>
> (Goodwin 1997a: 176)

The science writer, Mitchell Waldrop, describes the edge of chaos as the place:

> were [sic] the components of a system never quite lock into place, and yet never quite dissolve into turbulence either. The edge of chaos is where life has enough stability to sustain itself and enough creativity to deserve the name of life. The edge of chaos is where new ideas and innovative genotypes are forever nibbling away at the edges of the status quo, and where even the most entrenched old guard will eventually be overthrown. ... The edge of chaos is the constantly shifting battle zone between stagnation and anarchy, the one place where a complex system can be spontaneous, adaptive, and alive.
>
> (Waldrop 1994: 12)

Universality, patterns and rhythms

The concept of universality is a feature of chaos theory and is applicable to many living systems. In 1975 Mitchell Feigenbaum, a US physicist, discovered that very different systems would behave in a similar way when moving from an orderly state into a chaotic one, in other words, that they behaved in a universal fashion.

Mathematician Ian Stewart (1997) explains how Feigenbaum discovered that a particular number, approximately 4.669, is associated with period doubling cascades. If, for example, a tap was dripping then a small turn of the tap to increase the flow leads to a change in the sounds and the rhythm of the falling drops. The sound would move, say, from a two-drop rhythmic pattern to a four-drop pattern. Another small turn of the tap would then increase the pattern to an eight-drop one and so on with each small turn of the tap. The length of the pattern keeps on doubling until it reaches a point, known as the Feigenbaum point, at which the pattern sequence disappears. There is no discernible patterning and the system has entered chaos. What is interesting is that it takes smaller and smaller increases in the water flow to introduce greater and greater changes.

> Feigenbaum's number δ tells us how the period of the drips relates to the flow rate of the water. To be precise, the extra amount by which you need to turn on the tap decreases by a factor of 4.669 at each doubling of the period.
>
> (Stewart 1997: 141)

Further:

> The Feigenbaum number δ is a quantitative signature for any period-doubling cascade, no matter how it is produced or how it is realized experimentally. That very same number shows up in experiments on liquid helium, water, electronic circuits, pendulums, magnets, and vibrating train wheels. It is a new universal pattern in nature, one that we can only see through the eyes of chaos; a *quantitative* pattern, a number, emerges from a qualitative phenomenon. One of nature's numbers.
>
> (Stewart 1997: 142)

The natural world is full of rhythms and rhythmic cycles and universal patterning. There are the rhythmic cycles of the human body, rhythmic responses by plants and animals to the moods (seasons) of our planet, tidal ebbs and flows and the complex rhythmic patterns used by animals as they move. Stewart points out that there are several kinds of patterning: numerical patterns, patterns of form and patterns of movement as well as fractal patterning. Numerical patterns include the lunar cycle of twenty-eight days; animals that have two or four legs; insects with six legs and spiders with eight. Stewart also writes of the strange patterns created by flower petals whereby nearly all flowers have a number of petals which conforms to a number taken from the sequence 3, 5, 8, 13, 21, 34, 55, 89. He cites the example of the lily which has three petals, the buttercup with five, delphiniums with eight, marigolds with thirteen, asters with twenty-one and daisies which may have thirty-four, fifty-five or even eighty-nine petals. The fascinating thing about this pattern is that the numerical sequence is created by adding the previous two numbers together. For example, three plus five equals eight, and five plus eight equals thirteen and so forth.

Patterns of form include the wave patterns that are universally found in the sea and in the atmosphere as well as in the world's deserts. There are the stripes and spots that abound throughout the animal kingdom. Patterns of movement are to be found in the way animals, fish, birds, insects, snakes, and even bacteria move and change position.

Fractal patterns are found everywhere in nature as they repeat themselves over and over on different size scales from the repeating patterns of mountain ranges and rugged coastlines to the fine details on a coral fan living in a warm sea.

Complexity

Complexity is a science that is both very new and very wide ranging so that is difficult to define it, or even to know where to map its boundaries. It is inter-disciplinary with a growing range of interdisciplinary applications. It is its many aspects and applications that make a neat, concise yet apposite, definition difficult.

Some writers refer to the study of complex systems rather than complexity or complexity science. How one describes a complex system is considered by Allen (2001) to be straightforward.

> It is any system that has within itself a capacity to respond to its environment in more than one way. This essentially means that it is not a mechanical system with a single trajectory, but has some internal possibilities of choice or response that it can bring into play.'

(Allen 2001: 150)

Further, he states that almost any situation is a complex system and therefore people, groups, families, organizations and cities are all complex systems.

I would enrich Allen's description by adding some other significant attributes. Thus one useful working definition might be: that complexity science is concerned with the study of the dynamics of complex adaptive systems which are non-linear, have self-organizing attributes and emergent properties. Complex adaptive systems, self-organization and emergence are described in subsequent sections in this chapter.

The use of the term complexity to describe this new science in part derives from the nature of the systems which are studied. These dynamical systems are made up of many interacting parts which create patterns that become increasingly more and more complex. However, although these patterns are incredibly complex and complicated there is an underlying simplicity to them. Complexity scientists work to understand these systems better and to uncover and explain the principles that underpin them.

Complexity science is holistic in nature. It seeks to understand why the whole universe is greater than the sum of its parts and in so doing to discover the natural order that prevails throughout our universe. Furthermore, the holistic nature of complexity gives a new perspective and fresh insights into difficult concepts, such as the nature of life, of consciousness and intelligence, that traditional science has struggled to understand (Coveney and Highfield 1995).

Complexity is considered by many scientists to have enormously wide-ranging applications with considerable potential for understanding the nature of the universe and its multitude of complex systems. It has been found to have applications in a wide variety of complex systems that may be biological, ecological, physical, social or economic.

How does one define the relationship between chaos and complexity? Whenever one reads of one then references to the other abound. Chaos was first recognized in the 1960s and 1970s and complexity emerged a little later. Thus chaos theory was first on the scientific scene, but complexity is inextricably interwoven with chaos concepts. It is clear that in many ways they have a symbiotic relationship.

Notions of order and disorder, predictability and unpredictability, regularity and chaos are features of complex systems. Yet these terms belong to the language of chaos science. The distinguished science writer, Roger Lewin (1993) ponders on the difference between chaos and complexity and suggests that chaos is always very random with very little order, whereas complexity is about structure and order. However, as the previous section on chaos will have shown, order unexpectedly exists within chaos and chaotic systems. Thus, in chaos, we have a very paradoxical science. Furthermore, it is not possible to study some aspects of complexity without understanding references to chaos theory and the next sections of this chapter will further demonstrate this.

Like chaos science, complexity is viewed by many as a scientific revolution that is creating new ways of explaining and describing the world. These are far removed from traditional, linear, reductionist approaches. Complexity research is trying to answer all the questions that do not easily fit into conventional categories and to do so in new and often untried ways. Further, I would argue that complexity is changing not only the way we think about the universe but also the assumptions that underpin conventional science.

The new science of complexity is twenty-five or so years old, yet many are describing its theories as highly significant not only for the scientific community but for the world at large. It is also seen as having great import for the future. Many writers and researchers claim that a new paradigm is emerging: the complexity paradigm.

Complexity science – a brief history

Complexity emerged and developed as a major area of scientific study from the work of a number of scientists during the 1970s and early 1980s. It was to receive further recognition and a considerable boost with the establishment of the Santa Fe Institute in New Mexico. Santa Fe brought together a wide range of researchers from different disciplines, including economics and computer science, and created a broadly based scientific community which sought to explain and apply concepts from this new science.

Table 2.2 shows the major features of complexity science and some of the key researchers associated with them.

One of the first scientists to research and develop theories that led to the foundation of complexity as a new science was a Russian-born, physical chemist, Ilya Prigogine. Prigogine developed the theory of 'dissipative structures' which was the first description of what is also called, 'self-organizing systems'. Self-organization and self-organizing systems are a key concept in complexity science. Prigogine was fascinated by the way that living organisms are able to survive in highly unstable, or far from equilibrium, conditions. In order to understand this better he decided to study a non-living situation called the Bénard instability, which

Table 2.2 Developments in complexity science

Time period	Theory/ concept	Key researcher	Discipline	Country of birth/ experience
1960s–1970s	Dissipative structures (Self-organization)	Ilya Prigogine	Chemistry	Russia and Belgium
	Self-organization/ Self-organizing systems	Herman Haken	Physics	Germany
	Self-organization, evolution and	Stuart Kauffman	Biology	USA
	complexity	Brian Goodwin	Biology	Canada and UK
	Patterns and patterning	Ian Stewart	Mathematics	UK
	Self-organization/ Autopoiesis	Humberto Maturana	Biology	Chile
		Francisco Varela	Biology	Chile
1980s	Edge of chaos	Chris Langton	Anthropology and computing	USA
1990s	Complex adaptive systems	John Holland	Mathematics	USA
		Murray Gell-Mann	Physics	USA
	Emergence	Chris Langton	Anthropology and computing	USA

is a phenomenon of heat convection (Capra 1996). This is now considered a classical case of a self-organizing phenomenon. Capra (1996: 89) gives a description of Prigogine's analysis of the Bénard cell and his work on another self-organizing phenomenon, the Belousov–Zhabotinskii reaction.

Prigogine was awarded the Nobel Prize in 1978 for his work on showing how systems existing in highly unstable conditions can induce changes in themselves that can lead to new patterns of order and stability emerging. His work was considered of such ground-breaking importance, that the Nobel committee in awarding recognition for his research, stated that he had fundamentally transformed and revised the science of thermodynamics. Prigogine's research offered a new view of things. Instead of a world where systems ran down and were subject to an ongoing deterioration, he showed that systems were essentially non-linear, dynamic and able to transform themselves into new states of being. Thus the concept of dissipative structures offered an alternative view to that implied by Newton's second law of thermodynamics. It suggested that Newton's law may still apply, but only in situations where a system is in equilibrium, that is to say, in a very stable and unchanging state.

Dissipative structures or self-organizing systems are the basic structures of all living systems, including human beings, and understanding of this concept is now being used in technology, economics, sociology, biology, medicine and many other aspects of life including politics and business.

Hermann Haken, a German physicist, is another world-renowned scientist associated with complexity science. Haken studied lasers and found that the transition from normal light to laser light involved a self-organizing process typical of systems operating far from equilibrium. In 1970 he published his non-linear laser theory. This makes it clear that although the laser needs external actions on it to keep it in its disordered state, the co-ordination of the light emissions are carried out by the laser itself, and thus it is a self-organizing system (Capra 1996).

In the 1980s the Austrian physicist, Eric Jantsch, argued strongly that living systems had self-organizing tendencies. Jantsch not only further developed ideas on self-organization, building on Prigogine's work, but also considered some aspects of autopoiesis and evolution thus linking together developments in modern biology with developments in physics, chemistry and systems thinking. His holistic approach is very reflective of the essence of complexity as an interdisciplinary science concerned with wholeness and connection.

Biologists have also played an important role in the development of complexity science. Two key figures are the US biologist Stuart Kauffman and the UK-based biologist Brian Goodwin. Both have contributed through their research and their writing to our understanding of self-organizing systems, notions of the edge of chaos, and evolution and complexity.

In the 1980s, the US computer scientist, John Holland's use of computer modelling led to the serious study of complex, adaptive systems at the Santa Fe Institute. Complex adaptive systems with their self-organizing attributes and emergent properties are the central concept which underpins complexity science. Today there is recognition that in the natural world these systems include immune systems, brains, ant colonies, ecologies and even human cultural, political and social systems.

Another important concept is the notion of emergence or emergent properties. Holland played an important role in the development of this concept during the 1970s and 1980s, as did Chris Langton, a former student of Holland's.

Since the end of the last century there has been a steady and increasing stream of discovery and data which has spread concepts and ideas from complexity across Europe and the USA. This has swelled understanding of complexity science, refining and expanding on existing research such that it is now a well recognized, if not entirely uncontentious, scientific domain. It is not a discipline, which is essentially a compartment within the house of science, but rather, for its supporters, a new house which has remodelled and built upon the foundations of classical science creating an entirely original edifice.

Complexity – main themes and theories

Self-organizing systems

Complexity science is concerned with systems that have the capacity to spontane-ously self-organize themselves into even greater states of complexity. The concept of self-organization first appeared in the 1940s and 1950s when cybernetic scientists started to explore neural networks. Heinz von Foerster, a physicist and cyberneticist, was a major contributor to the development of a theoretical understanding of self-organization and by the late 1950s he had developed a model of self-organization in living systems. This model was built upon and refined by other researchers including Ilya Prigogine, Hermann Haken, Manfried Eigen, James Lovelock and Lynn Margulis (Capra 1996). However, Prigogine's work on dissi-pative structures is recognized as central to the development of understanding of self-organizing systems.

> According to Prigogine's theory, dissipative structures not only maintain themselves in a stable state far from equilibrium, but may even evolve. When the flow of matter and energy increases, they may go through new instabilities and transform themselves into new structures of increased complexity.
>
> Prigogine's detailed analysis ... showed that, while dissipative structures receive their energy from outside, the instabilities and jumps to new forms of organization are the result of fluctuations amplified by positive feedback loops. Thus amplifying 'runaway' feedback, which had always been regarded as destructive in cybernetics, appears as a source of new order and complexity in the theory of dissipative structures.
>
> (Capra 1996: 89)

The feedback loops within the system produce rich patterns, thus we are reminded of the importance of patterns, and the principle of patterning found in chaos science.

Wheatley (1994) points out that self-organizing systems are sometimes known as self-renewing systems because they dissipate their energy in order to renew themselves. This ability to create new structures and new ways of behaving marks a significant difference between the early concept of self-organizing systems first devised by the cyberneticists.

Thus self-organizing systems need energy to ensure that self-organization or renewal takes place and in order to do this they need to be open to their environ-ments. By being open they can exchange matter and energy and so stay alive and far from equilibrium.

Spontaneity is an important feature of self-organizing systems as they interact and reshape themselves. The ability to spontaneously self-organize, for example, enables fish to shoal to protect themselves from predators, birds to flock for foraging or protection, and social ants and termites to organize themselves so that their nests or mounds are built and their young fed. People, too, unconsciously self-organize themselves and create small communities, towns, markets and economies to help meet their material needs. People, insects and animals, like birds in flight, respond and adapt to the actions of those nearby so that they unconsciously organize themselves.

Self-organizing systems are to be found everywhere in the natural world. A hurricane, for example, is a self-organizing system which derives its energy from the sun, this in turn drives the wind and takes rain from the oceans. A living cell is a self-organizing system which takes its energy from food and excretes energy as heat and waste. Self-organization is the principle which underlies the emergence of the wide variety of complex systems and complex forms that exist whether physical, biological, ecological, social or economic.

A good real-life example of human self-organization at work is provided by the fuel protest in the UK in the autumn of 2000. This shows how people can effectively self-organize themselves, even in a world that tends to follow more traditional command and control principles. In early September a group of farmers meeting in Wales spontaneously decided it was time to take action over the high price of diesel fuel. With agriculture in depression and many farmers struggling to survive, the high tax on diesel, essential for farm vehicles, was considered a tax too far. They left the meeting and picketed a local oil refinery in protest. British hauliers, who also felt that they were being disadvantaged in comparison with other Europeans, joined in. Using mobile phones and word of mouth the protest spread rapidly and within a week 75 per cent of fuel deliveries had been halted, as refineries and fuel depots across the country were effectively blockaded. The army was placed on standby, operations on the NHS were cancelled, petrol stations ran out of fuel, and the prime minister, Tony Blair, was faced with a major challenge to his authority. All this because a group of angry farmers and hauliers spontaneously decided to take action about a key issue and were able to rapidly and effectively communicate and organize themselves using modern communications technology.

Complex adaptive systems

As stated earlier, complexity science is very much concerned with the study of self-organizing systems and complex adaptive systems. Complex adaptive systems are self-organizing, but they differ from some self-organizing systems in that they *learn* to adapt to changes in circumstances. For example, a laser beam is a self-organizing system, it has changed as a result of changing circumstances, but learning is not part of, nor a by-product of, its adaption process.

Complex adaptive systems are adaptive, because they do not respond passively to events, but they actively seek benefits from any situation. For example, the human brain is always organizing and reorganizing its billions of neural connections in order to learn from its experience, and economies constantly respond to changes in trading and lifestyles. Thus complex adaptive systems are to be found everywhere in the natural world, for example, in cells, the brain, developing embryos, insect colonies and in the human world where they include cultural, social, economic and political systems.

Waldrop (1994) describes a conversation with John Holland about the nature of complex adaptive systems. Holland considers that these systems wherever they are found share certain crucial properties. First of all, they are:

> network of many 'agents' acting in parallel. In a brain the agents are nerve cells. ... In an economy, the agents might be individuals or households ... each agent finds itself in an environment produced by its interactions with other agents in the system. It is constantly acting and reacting to what the other agents are doing.
>
> (Waldrop 1994: 145)

Thus there is no central controlling feature to complex adaptive systems. Control is dispersed within the system. Competition and collaboration between the different agents in the system leads to the emergence of coherent behaviours.

Second, Holland defines a complex adaptive system as a system with many levels of organization, with agents at one level acting as the building blocks for agents at a higher level. Thus, for example, an individual worker will collect with others to form a group, a group of workers will make up a department, and a group of departments will form a division.

Another property of complex, adaptive systems, and one which Holland considered very important, is that they are constantly reconsidering and reorganizing themselves as they gain experience. Holland continues:

> Succeeding generations of organisms will modify and rearrange their tissues throughout the process of evolution. The brain will continually strengthen or weaken myriad connections between its neurons as an individual learns from his or her encounters with the world. ... At some deep fundamental level, ... all these processes of learning, evolution, and adaption are the same. And one of the fundamental mechanisms of adaption in any given system is this revision and re combination of building blocks.
>
> (Waldrop 1994: 146)

Learning is key to understanding how a complex adaptive system differs from a system that is a self-organizing system. This is explained by Murray Gell-Mann in Lewin (1993) when he describes how a turbulent liquid flow is a complex system in that it is full of rippling eddies of different sizes, and therefore is a system with information it. But it is not a system that devises a general scheme of things from this, nor a system that uses the information in such a way as to predict or to better interpret its environment.

According to Gell-Mann, complex adaptive systems are pattern seekers which interact with their environment, learn from their experiences, and then adapt, non-living complex systems do not.

Another property of living, complex adaptive systems, according to Holland, is that they anticipate the future.

> From bacteria on up, every living creature has an implicit prediction encoded in its genes ... every complex adaptive system makes predictions based on its various internal models of the world – its implicit or explicit assumptions about the way things are out there. Furthermore, these models are much more than passive blueprints. They are active ... And like any other building blocks they can be tested, refined, and rearranged as the system gains experience.
>
> (Waldrop 1994: 146)

Thus an adaptive system is able to take advantage and learn from what the world around it is able to tell it.

Goodwin (1997b) in his valedictory lecture at the Open University, suggested that complex adaptive systems have evolved so that they are attracted to the edge of chaos. They have done so because it is here that such systems can exist at maximum dynamical activity which is necessary for their survival.

Finally, complex adaptive systems are always changing, always transforming themselves, which is why, according to Holland, standard mathematics found them so difficult to analyze.

Emergence

The concept of emergence is a main theme that flows through studies of complexity. It is a phenomenon of the process of evolving, of adapting and transforming spontaneously and intuitively to changing circumstances and finding new ways of being. And in doing this, something else, something complex, unexpected and enriching takes shape. Emergence in seen in the properties of ecosystems, food chains, embryo development, human societies, insect swarms, and especially in complex adaptive systems.

The renowned entomologist Edward O. Wilson, at Harvard, considers that emergence is the core feature of complexity and contends that it is shared by insects and humans alike. Social ants, like human beings, have discovered that by working together rather than operating individually they are better equipped to rear the next generation and to survive in the world. For both species obtaining food, defending territories, and building and repairing homes are all better achieved by working collectively. Individual ants may not have great intelligence, but by working together they create an intelligence as a group that is greater than the sum of the individual parts, or ants. The cells in the human brain work together to provide a powerful collective intelligence and the emergence of consciousness. People create amazing city structures that are different in density, design and atmosphere to individual homes. By working collectively something greater emerges, a new entity which transforms the lives of everyone concerned.

Waldrop (1994) describes a computer simulation which attempted to show the essential nature of flocking behaviour in birds, herding in sheep and the schooling behaviour of fishes. The simulation created an environment full of obstacles and programmed each 'boid' or birdlike agent to follow three simple rules of behaviour. These were: try to maintain a minimum distance from other objects, including other boids; try to fly/move at the same speed as other boids in the vicinity; try to move towards the perceived centre of the mass of boids. Interestingly, there is no rule that says form a flock. The rules, referred only to what an individual boid could see and do. Every time the simulation was run flocks were formed. However, the boids were scattered they still formed up into flocks that were able to navigate around hazards in a fluid and natural way. This is truly emergent behaviour.

Chris Langton (Waldrop 1994) of the Santa Fe Institute describes how a global order emerges from the interactions in a local, dynamical system and in so doing a whole new set of properties emerge. Thus from a set of interactions at a local level new global level properties can emerge. This global level system then feeds back and interacts with the local interactions, so creating a circular feedback process.

Evolution and complexity

Lewin (1993) explores complexity in the context of the ebb and flow of life on earth and comments that Darwin saw the process of natural selection as essentially a gradual process that produced small changes incrementally over long time periods. However, in the 1960s and 1970s Harry Whittington discovered that the Cambrian period had seen a massive explosion in evolutionary innovation, which was later followed by a massive extinction. Other scientists too found evidence of massive changes in the number and variety of species. Also during the 1970s Niles Eldridge and Stephen Gould put forward the notion of 'punctuated equilibrium'. Their researches of the fossil record showed that the evolution of different species takes place in steps separated by long periods of apparent stability. This approach has led to the punctuated equilibrium view of strategy.

Thus it is only comparatively recently that other views of the way life on earth developed has arisen. The reality is that change is not gradual, it is often dramatic and overwhelming, and the landscape may be completely transformed as to be unrecognizable. The accepted view that evolution was a slow, incremental, step by step, 'let's select the best option' approach is not the only way nature has created the amazing diversity of life forms on planet earth. This has major implications for the way we think about change and transformation in organizations.

New interpretations of natural selection have arisen from complexity. Brian Goodwin in conversation with Roger Lewin (Lewin 1993) points out that natural selection did not cause organisms, nor did genes. In his view, organisms caused themselves. In other words, they are the emergent properties of self-organizing and developmental processes. They emerge over time from a biological attractor which is part of a complex dynamical living system, such as a whirlpool in the sea.

With reference to May and Novak, Coveney and Highfield (1995) point out that co-operation and self-organization was as essential for evolution as natural selection. They contend that the former create more complex structures and forms whereas the latter chooses which of these will survive.

Kauffman (1996) argues that all organisms and organizations are structures that have evolved. He writes:

> We are all, cells and CEOs, rather blindly climbing deforming fitness land-scapes. If so, then the problems confronted by an organization – cellular, organismic, business, governmental, or otherwise – living in niches created by other organizations, is pre-eminently how to evolve on its deforming land-scape, to track the moving peaks.
>
> (Kauffman 1996: 247)

Fitness or adaptive landscapes are used by biologists to consider different species and their survival history or their future chances. High peaks on this landscape represent optimum places to be, lower peaks less so and the valleys are places where a species can become trapped or stuck. This landscape, however, is constantly changing as each participant species moves and evolves across it. Kauffman observes that whatever the individual peaks and troughs, expansions or extinctions, the system itself appears to evolve into a balanced state, the edge of chaos. Thus the landscape itself is constantly changing as each species moves and evolves across it. How a species survives depends very much on how it explores and moves across this landscape. If it is too timid it could get caught in the foothills or if it is too bold it may get trapped on a peak. Successful species strike a balance somewhere between the two and flow along the ridges towards new regions of fitness.

Lewin (1993) refers to the importance of connectedness in evolution. Connectedness is a vital part of any living system, if living systems are to be disturbed into creating huge numbers of new life forms and also precipitating massive extinctions.

Connectedness is a theme that links with concepts of patterning and concepts of organization. It implies more than spatial relationships. One senses a mysterious, unifying rhythm at work between all the entities within a system and again this resonates with aspects of chaos theory.

Conclusion

This chapter has explored the development of the new sciences of chaos and complexity and some of their main features in order to devise a framework within which to explore the world of organizations and organizational life.

This new science is not satisfied with the elegant constructs of the logical, rational world of classical science which is discussed in the next chapter. It is more concerned with understanding the complexities, paradoxes and difficulties encountered in the real world. This is the world of dynamic complex systems that behave spontaneously and unpredictably. This is the world of human systems too, and therefore organizations are as much a part of this system as storm clouds or ant colonies. As the renowned economist Brian Arthur (quoted in Waldrop 1994) states:

We are part of nature ourselves. We're in the middle of it … we are all part of this interlocking network. If we, as humans, try to take action in our favor without knowing how the overall system will adapt – like chopping down the rain forest – we set in motion a train of events that will likely come back and form a different pattern for us to adjust to, like a global climate change.

(Waldrop 1994: 333)

Brian Goodwin (1997a), in writing that organisms have to be understood as dynamical systems and cannot be reduced to the properties of their genes, wonders whether complexity science research is leading to the development of a new science of qualities. This is currently the subject of considerable debate.

The recognition of species as natural kinds, the generic forms of living nature that arise by creative emergence from a dynamic process located at the edge of chaos, carries with it implications about our relationships with the species that make up the intricate web of mutual dependence which makes our life on this planet possible.

(Goodwin 1997a: 215)

The next chapter describes the development of traditional science (the Newtonian–Cartesian paradigm) and the emergence of the modern organization from the upheavals of the Industrial Revolution. It also considers the relationship between science and organizations, and particularly the powerful role played by classical science in influencing the development of organizations and organization theory.

3 Organizations and the long shadow of scientific tradition

> With a mere three laws of motion and a universal law of gravitation in hand, Newton not only derived tides and orbits, but unleashed on the Western mind a clockwork universe.
>
> (Kauffman 1996: 6)

What evidence is there that organizations have been influenced by science and scientific thinking? How far have the major organization theories been influenced by the dominant scientific paradigm? How far has interpretation of these theories and management practice been affected? This chapter considers some theoretical evidence of the influence of science and the scientific tradition in organization theory and the development of modern organizations. I use the term 'modern' to refer to organizations in the late nineteenth and twentieth centuries and today – since the rise of the complex, large-scale industrial and technological societies of western Europe and north America.

This chapter commences by reviewing mainstream developments in science and the scientific tradition in the west over the last 300 or so years and briefly considers the influence of science and the scientific tradition on society and thereby organizations. It then considers some of the major theories on organizations and organizational processes and takes a roughly chronological route. Pugh (1990) defines organizational theory as the study of the structure, the functional activities and the performance of organizations, including the behaviour of the people who work in them. I have not broken down my review into categories of structure, function, etc., but rather try to give a picture of the prevailing view or the dominant approach and include reference to any significant aspects of structure, functioning and so on as seems appropriate to my purpose. Pugh also observes that managers are the practitioners of theory, considering theory and practice as inseparable. I, too, take this view and include some evidence from significant trends in management practice and some of the popular influences.

It is easy to follow the thread of the development of organizations and organization theory through the first half of the twentieth century. However, in the second half of the century things began to speed up and diversify until by the 1980s and 1990s there was an overwhelming spread of ideas and theories about organizations and management practice. It is not possible to review them all, so my selection will inevitably be influenced by my own experiences as a manager and as a training and development specialist.

In referring to modern organizational development (in the western world) I not only explore the nature of the relationship between scientific thought and discovery and organizations, but in so doing set the context for organizations today. This I believe will provide insights into the relationship between organizations, society and the developments in ideas and insights derived from complexity science.

This chapter also includes some observations on the use of language in organizations and management, including metaphors, for they offer significant pointers to the flow of dominant influences and tell us much about our attitudes towards organizations and organizational life.

Classical science and the scientific tradition

For over 300 years science as practised in the western world has been dominated by a powerful paradigm whose influence extended far beyond the thoughts of the scientific community. A world view arose in the seventeenth and eighteenth centuries that saw the universe and all it contained as some giant machine that operated according to a set of universal laws and principles. The image of the world as a gigantic piece of clockwork made up of sets of predictable cause and effect components shone in the minds of the educated classes and dominated language and thinking. It was believed that the key to understanding our universe lay in breaking it down into small pieces, and analysing each piece in a rational, logical way. How did this view come about?

The birth of classical science

The seventeenth century is often referred to as the Age of Reason and described as the 'century of genius' by the great modern philosopher Alfred N. Whitehead. It was a time of great discovery and experimentation. A time when the foundations of modern science and philosophy were being constructed and laid down for future generations to follow. It was a century which saw the foundation of the Royal Society with a membership that included such distinguished names as the architect, Christopher Wren, Robert Boyle, the founder of modern chemistry, Samuel Pepys, the diarist, John Dryden, the poet, John Locke, the philosopher and Robert Hooke, the mathematician, physicist and surveyor. It was a time which saw the rise of the physical sciences and marked the end of the medieval world and the decline of medieval notions of knowledge based upon Aristotelian methods. There was a gradual transition from Latin as the language of the learned world to the use of English and French as the language of learning. This meant that philosophical writings became more widely accessible and the exchange of ideas was more easily facilitated. During this period and the century which followed, the basic pattern of thinking developed upon which the modern world, as we know it, was based.

The seventeenth and eighteenth centuries saw the spread of learning and learned views across Europe. The writings of the Frenchman, René Descartes and the German, Gottfried von Leibniz became well known. Both were philosophers but also distinguished mathematicians and scientists, as there was no clear distinction between philosophy and the physical sciences. At the time a powerful symbiotic relationship existed between physics, mathematics and philosophy and they exerted a strong effect on each other. Further, as Hampshire (1956) notes, the seventeenth century is referred to as the Age of Reason because almost all the great philosophers of the time were trying to introduce the rigour of mathematics into all areas of knowledge including philosophy.

Descartes is regarded by some as the founder of modern philosophy and his book *Discourse on Method*, published in 1637, was to have a profound effect on learned thinking and on society as a whole. Descartes set out to construct a new method of thinking which was based on breaking problems down into small parts and using reason and logic as the tools of analysis. Descartes was inspired by mathematics and the discoveries of his day, and claimed that the human body could be explained by the same laws that ruled the planets. Descartes was fascinated by the study of automata and mechanical toys, and considered plants and animals to exist like machines. Humans were thought of as machine-like but with special capacities for speech and reasoning. Descartes' mechanistic view of life has had a profound effect on all aspects of life, even up to the present day. For example, in the field of medicine there still exists the idea that the body is a kind of machine and that the task of the doctor is to repair it when it breaks down. Furthermore, Descartes saw a huge gap between the mind and the body and argued that they should be treated as separate entities. Again, this is a view which is reflected in many approaches to activity even today, as witnessed by the very different roles of blue (body) and white (mind) collar workers.

As regards science, the work of Copernicus, Kepler, and Galileo transformed mankind's view of itself and its place in the universal scheme of things. Our understanding of earth's situation in space was dramatically changed by Kepler, who demonstrated that the planets move in an elliptical orbit, and Galileo, who confirmed Copernicus's theory that the earth travelled around the sun. Galileo, with others, considered that the key to understanding the natural world lay with mathematics and quantitative, precise systems of measurement. With this approach they made stunning discoveries about the world we live in. However, their approach included the rejection of the Aristotelian view of nature and the importance of qualitative differences and distinctions. Further, the world of the senses was considered unimportant or even irrelevant, as demonstrated by the following extract from Galileo's *Il Saggiatore*.

> I find no need to apprehend it as accompanied by such properties as to be white or red, bitter or sweet, sounding or silent, pleasant or evil smelling. ... Therefore I hold that these tastes, odors, colors, etc. of the object in which they seem to reside, are nothing more than pure names, and exist only in the sensitive being; so that if the latter were removed these qualities would themselves vanish. ... But I hold that there exists nothing in external bodies

for exciting in us tastes, odors and sounds but size, shape, quantity and slow or swift motion. And I conclude that if the ears, tongue and nose were removed, shape, quantity and motion would remain but there would be no odors, tastes or sounds, which apart from living creatures I believe to be mere words.

(Hampshire 1956: 33)

Thus the stage was set for the dominance of the intellect. This attitude united with the approach of the philosophers and reinforced the development of the detachment of the logical, rational tradition.

Prior to the 'century of genius' the medieval world view was built upon Aristotle's notion that a natural order existed which was everywhere maintained in a system of subtle and complex hierarchies. This concept was built upon and developed into the Great Chain of Being in which all living things had a place on an ascending scale. The universe was viewed as a living, spiritual being. But during the sixteenth and seventeenth centuries the mediaeval world view changed significantly. The development of new instruments, new methods of experimentation and major scientific discoveries weakened the spiritual view so that notions of a spiritual universe declined and eventually faded away. Thus the work of Copernicus, Galileo, Descartes, Bacon, Newton and others led to a radical shift in world view during the period known as the Scientific Revolution. Galileo in confirming Copernicus's hypothesis that the sun is the centre of our solar system destroyed the Aristotelian notion of the earth, and therefore man, as the centre of the universe.

Galileo believed that the natural world, apart from our perception of it, is exactly as described in the laws of physics and mechanics and in the language of mathematics. Thus a great early-seventeenth-century scientist prepared the way for the domination of the language of mathematics and science as the prime language with which to explain our world.

Another great man who also profoundly influenced the development of science and the scientific tradition during the seventeenth and eighteenth centuries and beyond was Isaac Newton. Newton, who was born in 1642, was a great mathematician and a man of incredible genius. He is most remembered for his theory of gravitation and his three laws of motion, but he also invented calculus, developed a theory of light, founded tidal theory, created hydrodynamics and developed the theory of equations. Newton's work is considered by many to be the most outstanding achievement of seventeenth-century science. His *Principia Mathematica* published in 1686, has been described by some as:

the greatest scientific book of all time, a jewel in the crown of scientific literature. Built on the sturdy foundations laid by Galileo, it has been likened to a great edifice soaring about the ramshackle and temporary constructions around it. ... This magnificent work was rooted in a distant past, but even today is used to calculate the trajectory of various objects lofted into the heavens, from space shuttles to missiles. Its influence will undoubtedly extend far into the future.

(Coveney and Highfield 1995: 22)

The mechanistic view has always been with us and has influenced scientific thought from the days of the Greeks, Democritus and Leucippus, through to the twentieth century. But Newton's view of the universe as a giant machine, combined with Galileo's thinking and Descartes views on scientific method and the nature of man, all combined to reinforce and reintroduce this view. This powerful synthesis of ideas and approaches forms the basis of classical science or what is sometimes called the Newtonian–Cartesian paradigm. It is a view of the world that has had far-reaching effects well beyond the bounds of science and the seventeenth century. It is a view characterized by materialism and reductionism and a belief that things can be taken apart and examined without causing any real harm.

The challenges of the nineteenth century

There was strong opposition to the Newtonian–Cartesian world view in the late eighteenth and early nineteenth centuries when it was challenged by the Romantic movement in the arts and philosophy. The Romantics saw the earth as a living, spiritual being and so revived ancient traditions. One renowned scientist, Alexander von Humboldt, the German naturalist rejected the world-as-a-machine view. He recognized the unifying global features of climate and the co-evolving, living nature of the earth. Humboldt's influence was limited, however, and by the mid nineteenth century the Cartesian, mechanistic view of the world once more held sway.

Darwin's *The Origin of Species*, published in 1859, which described his theory of evolution, was to make an astonishing impact on scientific thinking. Kauffman (1996) claims that Darwin's ideas completely upset the biologists of the day by demonstrating that species are not fixed by the squares of the Linnean chart, but rather evolve from one another. The new theory of evolution challenged the traditional, Newtonian view of the world as a machine fully developed and created by God, and showed that the world is an evolving, ever-changing, place. In spite of this scientists did not abandon their reductionist approaches, instead they focused on fitting Darwin's theories into the existing traditional framework. Mendel's work on hereditary mechanisms and the emergence of the new science of genetics, in Capra's (1983) view, reinforced the Cartesian approach. It did so by concentrating on fundamental building blocks and ignoring the properties of the whole entity.

The nineteenth century saw the establishment of evolutionary science, the emergence of the new fields of microbiology and biochemistry and the first understandings of hereditary mechanisms. Louis Pasteur laid the foundations for the new science of biochemistry and demonstrated the links between bacteria and disease. By the end of the nineteenth century Maxwell's work on electrodynamics and Darwin's theory of evolution had severely challenged the Newtonian model of the universe. Scientists had developed new mathematical models to solve scientific equations, but they still relied on linear components or linear approximations if difficult non-linear equations arose.

The twentieth century – other scientific revolutions

In the view of Briggs and Peat (1989) reductionism and the mechanistic view of the world still held sway at the end of the nineteenth century. Then during the twentieth century discoveries in the world of atomic and subatomic particles shook the traditional views of physicists and seriously challenged the dominant scientific paradigm. Quantum theory or quantum mechanics was developed in the early years of the twentieth century by an international group of scientists including Einstein, Planck, Bohr, Schrödinger, Heisenberg and others. Briggs and Peat describe quantum mechanics as one of the most successful scientific theories ever put forward. It made valid and useful predictions about a wide range of atomic, molecular, optical, and solid-state phenomena. This ushered in the technological advances of the modern world and enabled the development of nuclear weapons, lasers and computer chip technology. Einstein's work on relativity and his progress on quantum theory brought together and advanced the structure of physics, but his radical new views on the concepts of space and time severely undermined Newtonian notions. All these developments led many scientists to question existing theories and to consider the universe from a less orderly, less predictable, less machine-like perspective.

Cybernetics in the 1940s and 1950s recognized the importance of both negative and positive feedback loops and today the existence of both kinds of feedback everywhere at all levels of living systems is acknowledged. Recognition of the ubiquitousness of feedback and of its many properties prepared the way for many of the discoveries in chaos and complexity.

The 1960s and 1970s saw advances in physics and chemistry with Haken's developments on laser theory and Prigogine work on dissipative structures. Both were working on systems in far from equilibrium situations and their explanations were to recognize the amazing properties of self-organizing systems. Scientists were beginning to make significant discoveries in a world far from the ordered, predictable paradigm of classical science. Advances in mathematics and the arrival of high-speed computers made a significant impact and further opened up the non-linear world. These explorations contributed to the emergence of the new science of complexity.

By the 1980s the physicist David Bohm (1980) wrote that existing, analytical, reductionist approaches did not work for modern physics and that scientists were now looking for a newer and more integrated view of the world. Gleick (1993: 6) writes that the most passionate advocates of the new sciences believe that the twentieth century will be remembered 'for just three things: relativity, quantum mechanics, and chaos'.

There is much evidence to suggest that the classical, Newtonian, approach to science still dominates, but major challenges threaten. I am of the opinion that a new world view is emerging based on complexity science, supported and encouraged not only by thinking scientists but by researchers in business, healthcare and a range of university disciplines.

The relationship between science and society

Toffler, in Prigogine and Stengers (1984), sees it as no coincidence that concepts of a mechanistic universe were welcomed and reinforced during the emergence of the machine age which accompanied the rise of the Industrial Revolution. In his view, the spread of factories and industrialization, the advent of the railways, and the building of steel, textile and car plants all confirmed the prevalent notion of the world as some kind of giant Meccano set. Furthermore, he suggests that the notion of a simple, uniform, mechanical universe influenced many other areas of life not immediately associated with scientific ideas. He gives examples to support this: the machine-like construction of the American constitution and the concept of the balance of power in European politics.

Wheatley (1994) recognizes the powerful relationship between science and society and the influential role science plays in society's collective unconsciousness. In her view concepts from science and notions of scientific method are buried deep in society's collective subconscious. They are so deeply imprinted on us that it is impossible for anyone to ignore their influence, particularly as they have created the way we think. Wheatley sees science as having a powerful influence on many of our business operating principles and lists as examples planning, measurement, motivation theory, business management and organization design. Morgan (1986) too believes that the dominant world view has pervaded the world of organizations and radically transformed the nature of work. This he sees reflected in the way managers believe modern organizations should be run, that is, in a highly structured routine and regular way.

Scientists, philosophers and psychologists have all been influenced by the classical scientific tradition and even the newcomer, social science, has been heavily influenced by the idea of man as a machine. Modern psychology and the behavioural sciences having been influenced by the work of philosophers such as Hume, Locke and Bentham.

The scientific notion of the world as a machine encouraged a disregard of the natural environment which resulted in the creation of vast industrial waste lands, the eradication of age-old landscapes, polluted waterways and atmospheric degradation. This thoughtless destruction is only now being addressed by the ecological sciences. This disregard for the natural world was encouraged and reinforced by the traditional approach to scientific enquiry which set aside human and moral sensitivities in the pursuit of rational explanation.

Traditional science emphasized stability, order, uniformity and equilibrium and was concerned with closed systems and linear relationships. Thus people have been encouraged to see the world as normally an ordered, predictable place, a view often at odds with their own experiences. But it is a view which satisfies people's needs for stability and certainty. This view of the world has become so deeply embedded and mainstreamed in our social, political, judicial and educational systems and in our culture too, as to be inseparable from the way we think and view the world.

Bohm (1980) is concerned with what he calls the 'fragmentation' of human thinking whereby people are divided into different groups for consideration. Thus people are categorized according to race, nationality, profession and so on. It is a view which sets human beings apart from the rest of the living world. Bohm advocates that all these aspects are brought together into a coherent whole when considering human thinking and thought. He also advocates that scientists and philosophers overcome the prevalent tendency to ignore the role of emotions, relationships and the social and physical aspects of life.

How our values have been influenced by science is considered by Capra (1996), who alleges that during the seventeenth century values and facts were separated, and that today scientific facts are still divorced from actions and values. Does this explain why scientists are expected to focus on their research, ignoring any of the social or moral implications that may arise, and leaving such questions to politicians and others to address?

Descartes' argument that the mind and the body, and subject and object, should be separated in the pursuit of reason has had far-reaching consequences affecting all aspects of society. His ideas have been used to justify and reinforce the class structure, and the different systems in schooling and education.

The importance of cultural and religious influences in reinforcing the scientific traditions should not be overlooked. Pugh and Hickson (1996) suggest that Weber was influenced by protestantism and the work ethic, whereby industry on earth implied salvation and spiritual riches in the afterlife. Thus the technology of the Industrial Revolution along with the popular scientific view of the world enabled the successful manifestation of the Protestant work ethic which powerfully affects western society even today. Many people work exceptionally long hours, often when unwell, and often at the expense of relationships and family life.

There is also another influence at work shaping society's attitudes towards science and the traditional scientific world view. The rational empirical tradition has been the keystone of science and technology in the west for centuries and has successfully demonstrated its effectiveness, particularly in the hard sciences (Winograd and Flores 1991). Thus, most significantly:

> The rationalistic orientation ... is also regarded, perhaps because of the prestige and success that modern science enjoys, as the very paradigm of what it means to think and be intelligent.
>
> (Winograd and Flores 1991: 16)

Organizations and the influence of classical science

The notion of the organization as an orderly machine with a hierarchical structure is one that has been both widespread and potent for many years. How did this view of organizations arise and why has it been such a powerful perception in the western world for so long?

It is a long-held assumption that organizations need a hierarchical command structure if they are to work. But:

there is no logic which says that this horizontal decision sequence needs to be turned into a vertical ladder so that those who take the necessary earlier decisions are higher in the hierarchy than those who implement them. That is where history comes in, for those who got there first obviously set things up this way.

(Handy 1993: 350)

Industrialization and early organizations

So who got there first? Until the spread of the Industrial Revolution in the eighteenth and nineteenth centuries most people were occupied in some kind of agrarian activity and most were self-employed. Large organizations, apart from the church, the state and the army, were virtually unknown. Thus when early entrepreneurs first set up their enterprises they followed the hierarchical, command and control structure models of these older organizations. They believed that centralized production with division of labour offered more control over their workers, and enabled them to promote improvements in production methods (Salaman, 2001).

During the seventeenth century, at the same time as the rise of this new scientific paradigm, there was in the UK a major increase in coal production encouraged by a shortage of wood. The coal industry was to become one of the earliest forms of modern enterprise. To mine coal involved expensive underground engineering and the transportation of coal from the pits to the customer. All this resulted in huge expenditure and large and heavy investments were needed to support such enterprises. Thus coal mining and other fledgling industries such as iron mining and foreign trade were financed by a rising capitalist class. Thus the stage was set for the Industrial Revolution and the rise of the industrialized nations at a time when ideas from science and philosophy were grabbing the public imagination as well as convincing the educated classes of their validity.

An important factor in the design of early industrial organizations was the predominant classical scientific view of the world. It envisaged the world as a giant clockwork machine operated by a series of predictable universal laws. It extolled the virtues of the intellect, logic and reason over intuition and the senses, and advocated an analytical, empirical, reductionist approach to understanding the world. This powerful paradigm encouraged the development of linear structures and reductionist thinking. It underlined the importance of the division of labour and encouraged an organization structure made up of layers of separate neat compartments. It was a way of thinking reflected in the physical architecture of the early textile mills which rose up floor upon floor, with the machinery laid out in both horizontal and vertical linearity.

The development of new technologies and new machinery for production further influenced the design of early businesses and the way they were expected to function. The view advocated by the new scientific philosophy was that non-material structures were not considered of value. Thus, machines were all important. Keeping the machines running was considered far more important, for example, than the welfare and needs of the workers, even the children. Many of these early workers were agricultural workers making the transition from one working lifestyle to another. They were unused to factory life. Whole new sets of rules and disciplinary procedures (punishments) were set up to control these people and to ensure they conformed to the requirements of the production process. Control was seen as essential. Most workers became machine operators or hands, with the result that individual skills and traditional ways of working were replaced and lost.

As Burns (1963) explains, many of the early entrepreneurs considered that Newtonian science offered not only an interesting set of ideas that explained the world but also a set of laws which could equally apply to other processes, that is, the production process. This is particularly evident in the way the new factory system modelled itself. Burns points out that the factory system emphasized the importance of the machines and the need for a strictly controlled hierarchy of workers to support them. As it developed and became the norm for productive activities so the organizational structure to support it evolved. For example, the eighteenth-century iron master's role was broken down into more jobs and new, larger, organizational structures emerged which were patrimonial and hierarchical in nature. The number of administrative employees rose as the size of the enterprise increased and Burns identifies this with the emergence and growth of bureaucracy.

During the second half of the eighteenth century Frederick the Great of Prussia streamlined and reformed his army using as his inspiration the machine models of the day. He introduced ranks and uniforms, a range of rules and regulations, precise procedures and practices, and specialized tasks in order to create the perfect fighting machine (Morgan 1986). His successful army was also to provide an inspirational model for early businesses.

Classical science called for the separation of the head or the intellect from the hand or the senses and this led to the emergence of white collar workers and blue collar workers and their separate cultures. These distinctions are now ingrained in our working culture. Thus in the eighteenth and early nineteenth centuries the design model of a factory organization emerged. It was one based on division and control and heavily influenced by the Newtonian–Cartesian paradigm.

Bureaucracy

In the beginning of the twentieth century many of the ideas that emerged from the Industrial Revolution were brought together to create a comprehensive theory of organization and management. Max Weber, the German sociologist, is credited as a major contributor to the development of this theory and, especially, the theory of bureaucracy. Weber noted the similarities between the use of machines in industry and the widespread use of bureaucratic types of organization and in his work we find the first full definition of bureaucracy.

Many bureaucratic organizations have stood the test of time and it was Weber's analysis of the organization and structure of the church, government, the military and other long-standing organizations that led him to believe that hierarchy, authority and bureaucracy are at the roots of all social organizations.

Weber's theory was primarily a theory of organization structure, and he saw clearly defined roles, a stable hierarchy and written procedures as the ideal. Efficiency was achieved through the fixed allocation of tasks, hierarchical supervision and a system of rules and regulations and military style discipline. He believed that the rational use of authority and control was highly desirable for an organization. Further, in his view, the bureaucracy was the most efficient form of organization possible as it worked like a modern machine. Here are strong echoes of early organizational forms and the long shadow of the logical, rationalist tradition and its continuing influence. Further, the manifestation of linear thinking is clearly apparent in the bureaucratic organization with its linear, hierarchical, compartmentalized structure.

Pugh and Hickson (1996) point out that Weber's model bureaucracy had a set of rules and procedures which aimed to cover every possible situation that might arise within the organization. Here one encounters a view of the world that believes that events that may be predicted and planned for with a large degree of certainty.

During the mid-twentieth century large bureaucracies still abounded. These were often made up of different businesses, for example, the Hanson Trust, Trafalgar House, Unilever, and GKN in the UK and General Electric in the USA (Mabey *et al.*, 2001). In the public sector too, huge bureaucracies were created with the nationalization of the public utilities after World War II and the creation of the NHS in 1948.

> Tall structures were created with as many as 20 plus levels between the chief executive and the shop floor operative. Managerial control of employees at all the multiple levels was based on a mixture of direct command and budgetary responsibility. Hierarchy, command and control were the governing principles of employee management.
>
> (Mabey *et al.* 2001: 157)

Classical management and scientific management

Henri Fayol is credited by many as being the founder of modern management theory and practice. Writing at the beginning of the twentieth century he advocated an organization structure that was centralized, functionally specialized and hierarchical, in which everything had its specific place. As far as he was concerned the specialization of tasks reflected the natural world where in his view the higher the species the more specialized they were. Management was viewed as being all about planning, organizing, forecasting, coordinating and controlling. Sanctions and close supervision were considered necessary to control the workers and to ensure that work was properly carried out. Human emotions or passions were seen as weakness and had to be subdued because they could hinder the work of the organization.

The principles of classical management theory are derived from the principles developed by Fayol and they reflect an approach dominated by linear thinking, reductionist principles, and cause and effect arguments. One could consider that the classical organization is built upon a blend of military and engineering principles, underpinned by classical science. Others built on Fayol's work, which Morgan (1986) claims provided the foundation of management theory in the first half of the last century, and which is still much in use up to the present day.

Also in the early twentieth century Frederick Taylor drawing on his understanding of traditional science and scientific method devised a theory of management – scientific management. Taylor believed that work could be studied scientifically and through the application of scientific method it was possible to increase efficiency and productivity. For him scientific method meant the use of systematic observation and measurement and his approach extended to all tasks however menial or small. At no time did he allow for the use of guesswork or intuition.

Taylor's ideas came in for considerable criticism at the time over the way in which they appeared to treat people, but they brought about great increases in productivity albeit at the expense of reducing many workers to little more than automatons. Taylor's approach to work design fitted very well with the development of assembly manufacture in the early years of the last century and his ideas were most famously embraced by the US car maker Henry Ford.

Scientific management as advocated by Taylor lost sight of the complex, living aspects of human beings and in many ways continued the trend begun in the eighteenth century of treating men and woman as mechanical objects or operating parts of some larger machine. Another significant result of Taylor's thinking was the division of workers into those who thought and those who acted, which again shows the influence of Descartes and the traditional scientific paradigm. Winograd and Flores (1991: 16) also see management science today as the modern embodiment of the rationalistic tradition and a 'field concerned with mathematical analysis of decision making and with behavioral analysis of human conduct'.

Taylor's ideas were taken up and developed by other practitioners and thinkers, most notably Henry Gantt, and Frank and Lillian Gilbreth, and in turn they developed Work Study or Industrial Engineering. Kakabadse *et al.* (1988) point out that Gantt and the Gilbreths further advanced understanding of the manager's role in an organization. As they saw it, this was to organize activities, while the role of the worker was to carry them out. Kakabadse *et al.* write admiringly of this approach as in their view it showed that an organization could be more efficient if it used a scientific approach to job design and maintained a manager's legitimate role in the hierarchy.

Gantt according to Morgan (1986) carried the vision of the world as a machine to extremes in his proposal for an organization called *The New Machine*. His idea was that all organizations should be managed by engineers, who would design and run them with machine like efficiency. Gantt's planning charts are still used widely today and are founded on linear notions of predictability, thus encouraging managers to develop performance expectations that are often unrealistic and fail to take into account the unpredictable nature of organizational life.

There has been much criticism of the early management theorists, and their view of the organization as some kind of machine. They viewed the organization as a closed system, discounted environmental influences, and relied on rules and close supervision to the extent that often the rules became their *raison d'être*.

Behavioural influences

In the first half of the twentieth century other theorists and practitioners were contributing to ideas on organizations and organizational life as well as major figures like Taylor, Fayol and Weber. Hugo Munsterberg a German psychologist is credited by Koontz and Weihrich (1988) with being the founder of industrial psychology. Pugh and Hickson (1996), however, remind us that Elton Mayo is often referred to as the founder of the Human Relations Movement and industrial psychology. Both men demonstrate a direct link between the spread of the new science of psychology, the emergence of social science and their applications to people in organizations.

The Hawthorne studies carried out during the 1920s and 1930s demonstrated that organizations were not just about the use of machinery and working methods but also about their interaction with human social systems. Kakabadse *et al.* (1988) claim that the Behavioural School took off as a result of this work and led to research and interest in management styles, behaviours and morale. The behaviourists and the social and organizational psychologists saw the organization as an organism and a natural system, and not a formal mechanism. They suggested a radically different kind of organization to the one recommended by the traditional theorists. They envisaged a more 'organic' organization which was less rigidly controlled, more adaptive and less rule bound. In the 1950s and 1960s organizational psychologists such as Argyris, Herzberg and McGregor showed how it was possible to integrate the needs of individuals and organizations and as a result of their influence new models of organization began to appear.

Even so the work of many of the behaviourists shows the influence of the classical scientific paradigm. For example, it is interesting to note the influence of the notion of a linear hierarchy in Maslow's 'hierarchy of needs theory'. This was to recognize human needs on an ascending scale, rising from the fulfilment of basic physiological needs to the final need for self-actualization. Maslow's approach was modified and followed by Herzberg and his 'two factor theory' which explored notions of motivation and job satisfaction. In some aspects their ideas demonstrated a simplistic cause and effect approach and linear thinking which oversimplified and attempted to rationalize the complexity of real human behaviours.

Psychology was not the only major scientific influence on the behavioural theorists, for according to Morgan (1986), biology had also influenced the development of organizational theory since the nineteenth century. He sees the influence of ideas from organic biology in the Hawthorne studies of the 1930s, and in the work of Maslow, Argyris, McGregor and Herzberg.

The early 1960s to the early 1980s

By the 1960s theorists were becoming aware of the importance of organizational appropriateness, and the environment both inside and outside an organization. Tom Burns and G.M. Stalker based on research in the 1950s, developed their ideas on two important types of organizations, each at the edge of a continuum along which most organizations could be placed. One type was the 'mechanistic' organization which was particularly suited to a stable environment. This type of organization had a clear and defined structure which was hierarchical in nature. All tasks were broken down precisely and strictly allocated within a command and control framework. Essentially the mechanistic organization is a classical bureaucracy.

The other organization, the 'organic' or 'organismic' one, was flexible in structure and attitude and better able to adapt to changes in its environment. The command and control structure was missing, and instead management relied on the use of information and advice to achieve results. Also the rigid and precise definitions of roles and responsibilities were missing. Interestingly, Burns was of the opinion that a mechanistic organization could not consciously develop into an organic one. This he believed was due to the commitment of people to their place in the hierarchy and to career and sectional interests. Morgan (1986) considered the notion of the organization as an organism as drawing on ideas from biology, with the organic organization having much in common with an amoeba. As a result of Burns and Stalker's work the term 'mechanistic' has now become more clearly identified with traditional approaches to the management of organizations rooted in the work of Taylor, Fayol and Weber.

Burns and Stalker emphasized the importance of the relationship of an organization to its environment and showed how successful firms were appropriately suited to their external conditions. In Morgan's (1986) view, their work together with the findings of Joan Woodward, who researched the relationship between technology and organization structure, laid the foundations for contingency theory which was further developed by Paul Lawrence and Jay Lorsch.

The systems approach to organizations which developed during the 1950s and 1960s took a more holistic approach to organizations and built on the notion that organizations, like organisms, are open to their environments. Resources are taken in, worked on and then pushed out again. Priesmeyer (1992) attributes this approach to a developing awareness of the organization's relationship with its environment. During this period Henry Mintzberg's research discovered that managers worked in an entirely different way to the neat, functional model prescribed by Fayol and he constructed a model which broke the managers' role down into ten roles in three categories: interpersonal, informational and decisional (Kakabadse *et al.* 1988). It was a move to recognize the human behavioural factor but it still promoted the notions of authority and control and the chain of command.

Peter Drucker devised the concept of 'management by objectives (MBO)' in the 1950s and it was seen during the 1960s and even in many textbooks today, as an ideal way to plan and control activities in an organization. In Morgan's (1986) and Koontz and O'Donnell's (1955) view MBO was a reinterpretation of classical management theories as are other current management systems like management information systems (MIS) and planning, programming, budgeting systems (PPBS).

The 1980s saw many western organizations enthusiastically embracing Japanese management ideas such as total quality management (TQM). People were encouraged to think for themselves, to work in teams, to develop themselves and to seek for continuous improvements. Many aspects of the Japanese approach were Taylorist but, unlike the west, the Japanese combined thinking with doing, which may explain why about 80 per cent of TQM initiatives in the UK were unsuccessful (Wickens 1995).

The end of the twentieth century

Between 1985 and 1993 some 40 per cent of the companies in the Fortune 400 disappeared, either through merger or failure (Handy 1993). Thus the end of the twentieth century saw the rise of a range of organizational preoccupations concerned with adaption and survival that come under the blanket title of change.

By this time the trend for larger and larger structures was over. Almost every organization experimented with some kind of structural change process (Ashkenas *et al.* 1995). Large conglomerates were broken up and large bureaucracies slimmed down as organizations sought to become more effective and flexible. Companies merged and demerged, made acquisitions or sold them off and experimented with a range of approaches designed to make them more effective and responsive to a rapidly changing world. During this period organizations were awash with notions of delayering, right/downsizing and business process re-engineering, delayering and becoming 'lean' and for a time returns to shareholders were at record levels (Willis 2001).

Many companies chose downsizing as a way of adjusting their structures in order to be fitter and more effective. Large organizations with many bureaucratic features like Kodak, IBM and General Motors restructured in this way (Mabey *et al.* 2001). Coulson-Thomas and Coe (1991) reported that all was not well with many of these new style organizations. There were problems of work overload, increased work stress, lack of vision, poor decision making, corporate in-fighting and so on. Thus many of those forward-looking organizations which had dramatically responded to the challenges of the 1980s had created a new set of problems with which to survive the 1990s.

Further, this approach proved to be an unsatisfactory one, not only because of the immediate social costs and the loss of experience and valuable skills, but because many organizations failed to capitalize on the restructuring and implement new supportive systems (Mabey *et al.* 2001). The structure of the organization had changed but not in such a way as to improve its overall long-term effectiveness.

Business process re-engineering, for example, was enthusiastically embraced by many organizations in the early 1990s as a way of improving efficiency and profits by streamlining or removing bureaucratic systems. Mumford and Hendricks (1996) observe that in the rush to save costs many companies did not seek to improve by reorganization and rethinking about work processes, but rather by drastic staffing reductions. Many organizations saw re-engineering as a form of downsizing and as an exercise in cost reduction. Some chief executives had used the process to rid themselves of weighty bureaucratic chains of command but still held on to the controls. There were many critics of the concept and by the mid-1990s it was being described as a management fad that had failed because it had been misunderstood. Mumford and Hendricks ascribe this partly to a cultural change and write:

> It seemed that there had been a cultural change. During the 1980s, Deming and the socio-technical arguments were influential. ... Their idealism was seen as both possible and necessary if company relationships were to be positive and creative. However, during the recession ... the quality and socio-technical movements lost influence. Quality became control, and managers fired employees who had poor quality measurements.
>
> (Mumford and Hendricks 1996: 24)

The 1980s and 1990s also saw decentralizing as a key trend for many large organizations who set up divisionalized structures and strategic business units. Corporate roles and responsibilities were devolved out to the individual divisions or units, with strategic business units having more autonomy and less centralized features than divisional structures. As a result of these approaches many of the synergies and advantages of a large company were lost and the new structures often failed to build in strong links across units so that core competencies were shared and corporate cohesion maintained (Mabey *et al.* 2001). Decentralization appears to be a continuing process but as Mabey *et al.* (2001: 158) observe, a process which appears to be made possible 'by a series of moves which amount to increased centralisation'.

The end of the twentieth and the beginning of the twenty-first century saw a wide range of new organizational forms emerge which Mabey *et al.* describe as 'de-structured'. This definition covers a wide range of organization structures 'variously described as high performance organizations, knowledge creating companies, empowered teams, ad hoc, boundaryless, and process-based' (Mabey *et al.* 2001: 164). There is a strong similarity about these organizations in that they have endeavoured to break free from the traditional bureaucratic form.

> the new watchwords are teams (preferably cross-functional), lateral communications, the minimization (if not outright removal) of hierarchy, and the sparse use of rules. Informality and the exploitation of expertise, wherever it may lie in the corporation, are the essential idea. With some variance in emphasis, the same basic tenets can be found underpinning the so-called 'high performance work systems' and the 'knowledge creating companies'.
>
> (Mabey *et al.* 2001: 164)

Thus many managers faced with increasing upheavals and fresh situations had tried to find new ways of doing things. Yet in many respects the influence of classical management theory is so pervasive that even as organizations attempted to update their ideas and approaches to organizational life many were hampered by a subconscious mind set. All too often many of the ideas of classical management were reinforced under the guise of modern management and those attempting to devise new systems for organizations were only able to think mechanistically.

Yet alongside the gloomy picture of old mindsets and the adoption of a number of harsh processes there are new concepts of organizations emerging that recognize organizations as complex systems full of human potential. One of the most notable of the new ideas is the concept of the 'learning organization'. It is not a new idea as Garratt (1995) points out. After World War II there was a major rethink about the nature of organizations and their role in a democracy. At the same time the disciplines of psychology, sociology, cybernetics, economics and ecology came together with existing notions of finance and production and combined to create the roots of management education. Thus preparing the way for the modern learning organization.

A learning organization is continually developing its abilities in order to flourish and survive. Learning organizations are about creative as well as adaptive learning; they have an evolving shared vision; they use systems thinking; and they spend time challenging their mental models (Senge 1994). These are organizations which facilitate the learning of all their members, who constantly reframe their view of the world and continuously adapt and transform themselves. Here are ideas drawn from cell biology, evolutionary biology and new understandings about brain functioning and living systems.

The notion that there could be many forms of organizational form: clover leafs and federalist structures (Handy 1990) networks and virtual organizations, each adopted for its suitability to organizational purpose is now gaining ground. There is recognition that organizations have to be more flexible and suited to their own particular role, location, situation in the market place and so on. Here are influences of the new scientific approaches along with practical recognition that old models no longer work as well because the conditions they were created for no longer exist.

Old influences run deep?

Since the 1970s there has been a deluge of studies and resultant theories and ideas on how to design, develop and run organizations. However, in spite of this tide of new ideas many of the traditional attitudes still seem to run deep. Outwardly things may appear to be different but the traditional scientific paradigm often operates, albeit frequently at a subconscious level. Handy (1990) points out that the Newtonian view of science is manifest in organizations in the use of sets of rules, and planning and prediction activities. Many organizations are intent on collecting huge amounts of numerical data, on making decisions using sophisticated mathematical models and developing more and more advanced forms of business analysis (Wheatley 1994).

Many modern writers and theorists continue to be affected by Taylor's ideas and the work of Fayol. Wheatley (1994) refers to William Bygrave (1989) who noted that many management strategists from Chandler to Porter were originally engineers or physicists or admirers of those disciplines and comments on the close connection between their scientific training and their work in creating systematic and rational approaches to strategy.

Both Handy (1990) and Morgan (1986) refer to the common perception of organizations as machines which are expected to operate smoothly. The huge, impersonal, factory is perceived as an old model of how to establish and run a productive enterprise. But as Morgan (1986) reminds us, today's large paper processing offices set up to deal with insurance, tax or banking returns, are designed to operate like machines and the staff are in many ways expected to behave as if they were part of a machine. How much has really changed ?

Fowler (1997) calls for an end to the inequality of status endured by blue collar workers and writes:

> Distinctions between manual and non-manual employees are ingrained in the UK's employment culture. They have historic roots in the different patterns of factory and office work that evolved during the industrial revolution, and in related perceptions that link occupations with social status.
>
> (Fowler 1997: 21)

Here are echoes of Descartes.

Even some of those writing on learning organizations reveal influences from the past. Garavan (1997) refers to Pettigrew and Whipp (1991) who describe the notions of single/double loop learning as mechanical. Garavan also refers to Jones (1994) who comments that many organizations are unable to understand and to measure the learning that has taken place and employ measures that are essentially a controlling device.

Many organizations are experimenting with new structures and new concepts about organizations and organizational life but how radical and deep rooted have these changes been? I would contend on the evidence in this chapter that a major shift in thinking is needed before we shall *fully* be able to develop organizations that are not rooted in the Newtonian–Cartesian paradigm and are more appropriate to working life in the twenty-first century.

Language and metaphor

Language and its use of images can tell us a great deal. A dynamic, living language evolves and adapts to mirror exactly every nuance and facet of the world it seeks to interpret and describe. It can also enable us to re-visualize our world, for if we can develop a new way of speaking then we can develop new ways of thinking too. New thinking then in turn leads to new behaviours. If, however, a language fails to adapt then it may serve as a mirror to a society that is over attached to the past and reluctant to move into the future.

It is interesting to note that many writers and management specialists continue to use a language derived from technical or hard scientific terms. For example, in February 1997 I received unsolicited details of a conference on 'knowledge management'. The event was designed for 'senior level professionals in knowledge intensive industries involved in quantifying, leveraging and encouraging growth of intellectual capital'. Here is language with built in inferences of traditional scientific respectability. Key phrases describing one of the sessions read as follows:

- identifying the four levels of professional intellect
- deep knowledge of the web of cause and effect relationships underlying a discipline
- models and techniques of measurement
- incorporating critical success factors as quantifiable ratios
- measuring the speed of competence development and sharing intellectual capital ratios.

This suggests that the classical, linear, logical, rationalist approach is very much alive. Sadly the proponents of these ideas believe at the conscious level that they have discovered new ways of thinking and behaving yet, in my view, their language indicates quite the opposite.

Many organizations are still viewed as machine-like and their language with its talk of inputs, outputs and control devices is that of engineering. Thus the heartfelt nature of the common expression: 'I'm only a small cog in a big wheel'. The language of the military machine devised by Frederick the Great still exists in terms such as force, officers, ranks and so on. Wheatley (1994) tells how many activities are described as campaigns, skirmishes, and wars. She describes how many organizations have chains of command and how rules and regulations are used as a defence against employees. Capra (1996) reminds us that computer scientists often rely on old traditional, militaristic, language, derived from the traditional world view, for example, in the use of such terms as command, escape, fail safe, target and so on.

Senge (1992) recognizes the powerful influence played by language in the way we perceive the world and points out that its structure and development in western cultures has encouraged linear thinking such that people think in a linear fashion and tend to see the world in linear terms. This creates real difficulties for managers as they try to deal with complex, dynamic realities with a language designed for simple non-complex, problem solving.

If organizations today are to be fit enough to survive and prosper in turbulent times then they will need to find new ways of thinking, and doing. There are some signs of changes taking place in the way organizations think and behave that is demonstrated through their language. Handy (1990) refers to the use of terms such as cultures and networks, teams and coalitions, of team leaders, or co-ordinators. Kanter (1990) describes how a mould-breaking company like Apple Computers uses the language of vision and values rather than traditional terms. The language organizations use and create can give us an indication of how far we are moving towards developing new ways of thinking, new ways of envisioning, designing and experiencing life in organizations. Thus today new words and new images have crept in, but the trickle has yet to turn into a tide which will dramatically change things.

Gareth Morgan

Gareth Morgan has used the notion of metaphor as a way of exploring and understanding organizations and their complex character. He developed this approach to organizational analysis based on his belief that organizations are usually complex, ambiguous and full of paradox. Interestingly, this belief accords with one of the basic tenets of complexity: that life and living systems are complex, often ambiguous and frequently paradoxical. Morgan explores a range of eight different metaphors that might describe organizations and one of them, the notion of organizations as machines I have already discussed earlier in this chapter. He also refers to organizations as organisms, as brains, and as psychic prisons. In considering organizations as organisms the links with biology and biological thinking are very clear. He points out that:

> Biology classifies vital organisms into species, inquires into their geographic description, their lines of descent, and their evolutionary changes. What better description could there be of organization theory since the 1950s?
>
> (Morgan 1986: 352)

Further, he adds that biological thinking has influenced social theory and organizational theory since the nineteenth century or earlier. This thinking too has influenced the work of Mayo, Maslow, Argyris, McGregor, Herzberg and other leading psychologists and behaviouralists. Morgan suggests that the influence of biology and biological approaches has also affected the development of open systems theory, which in turn influenced social psychology and organizational studies. Notions of organizational health, the life cycle of an organization, and the affect of environmental factors all reflect the image of the organization as an organism and the influence of biological thinking. Morgan also suggests that ideas of competition and collaboration are derived from different interpretations of the theory of evolution.

The image of the organization as a brain is still in the very early stages of development. Yet, here again one may trace the scientific influences, in this case, they flow from cybernetics, biology and particularly brain research. Morgan writes that an organization can be conceived of as a brain in that it has its own cognitive system as well as its own behaviour patterns. The notion of the organization as a brain fits well with ideas of organizational learning and the concept of the learning organization.

The image of an organization as a psychic prison draws heavily on traditional psychology and particularly Freudian theory and the work of the Tavistock Institute. It also suggests some reasons why so many organizations find it so difficult to change. People have become so trapped in the traditional view of organizations and organization processes that they cannot easily escape, even when an opportunity presents itself.

Conclusion

Why has the classical, traditional scientific approach to the world been so powerful and for so long, such that it is now embodied in the rationalistic tradition of management theory? Winograd and Flores (1991) offer an explanation in describing how modern science is associated with high level thinking and high intelligence. However, there are challenges to this view emanating from concerns about aspects of the new bio sciences. These raise important moral and ethical dilemmas as they sweep unhesitatingly into new territories involving genetics and novel uses of DNA. Is modern science too sure of itself and too unthinking regarding all the serious issues that such explorations can raise, such that there is a growing level of public unease and even mistrust? Science appears to have failed people in that it has made serious errors and failed to live up to its promises. One can think of, for example, the areas of drug side effects, with the tragic case of thalidomide and more recently some severe reactions to antidepressants. Recent episodes such as the instance when scientists spent years mistakenly researching sheep's brains instead of bovine ones have also undermined public confidence and the status of science and scientists.

There is much evidence to show that in the world of organizations the old models, derived from the scientific thinking of the seventeenth and eighteenth centuries still exist. Most have been modified, often structurally, or functionally, but their origins may still be recognised in aspects of predominant theory, nuances of language and in particular behaviours of some of the people in organizations. Many managers continue to manage by using reductionist approaches (separating things into parts); by devising complex planning activities based on the notion of a predictable world; and in believing that cause and effect processes produce fairly foreseeable results. Thus in spite of the modernization programmes of recent years a considerable number of managers appear to have a mindset similar to the Taylorist model developed at the beginning of the last century.

Yet during the last century there was a shift away from the mechanistic, reductionist approach in science towards a more holistic, organismic one as the notion of the universe as a giant clockwork mechanism was challenged, particularly by biologists and quantum physicists. However, as with any period of upheaval and challenge the change is unlikely to be a smooth one.

New notions are continuing to sweep in, however, as the end of the industrial era is also marked by serious challenges to the Newtonian–Cartesian view. Toffler in Prigogine and Stengers (1984) argues that we should not be surprised if the transition from an industrial society to one based on innovation and information produces a new scientific world view.

If the scientific paradigm is shifting, and making way for a richer, more complex, more realistic view of the world – what of organizations? Wheatley (1994) can already see some of the new scientific ideas percolating into management theory, although the process has only just begun. A number of writers on organizations, notably Ralph Stacey in the UK and Pascale and others in the US are using ideas and concepts derived from the new science of complexity to propose new organizational forms and behaviours in keeping with the present turbulent and demanding times. Many thinking managers too are seeking new ways of doing things, recognizing at both the conscious and subconscious level that current approaches are full of shortcomings and often very inadequate in today's business environment. The next chapter discusses current approaches to organizational change and some of the thinking on how to achieve this.

4 Plus ça change ... the more it stays the same?

Change in this view, does not occur as a consequence of some force but is a natural tendency, innate in all things and situations. The universe is engaged in ceaseless motion and activity, in a continual cosmic process that the Chinese called Tao – the Way. The notion of absolute rest, or inactivity, was almost entirely absent from Chinese philosophy.

(Capra 1983: 37)

The world of the early twenty-first century is being experienced by many as a period of massive change and upheaval brought about by increasing and parallel advances in technology, science and global communications. Thus the topic of change is high on most organizational agendas. But, as shown in Chapter 3, far too many organizations and management theorists are still influenced by the old scientific paradigm. As a result they have a tendency to view change from a perspective that emerged centuries ago. It is a view and a consequent way of thinking that does not reflect modern realities. It is a perspective which, in my view, hinders the development of organizations more attuned to the times.

I would argue that if we are to renew and recreate our organizations ready for the upheavals of this new century then we should beware of old mindsets. Most importantly we need to start exploring other notions of the nature of change, particularly those drawn from the new science of complexity. I believe we should also consider the insights they offer us into the realities that surround us, and use them intelligently to see the world anew and to devise exciting and radical ways of designing organizational life.

This chapter briefly considers abstract notions of change and some of the prevalent, mostly popular, views of change and associated organizational theories. The latter are briefly discussed in order to compare and contrast them with the newer approaches and theories which are emerging, including some references to the complexity perspective. Some fresh ideas have arisen from dissatisfaction with the traditional approaches and more up-to-date understandings of the nature of change are influencing theory and practice. I consider some of these and, in particular, ideas and notions of change that are an essential, integral feature of learning organization approaches. The work of Mintzberg and Waters, and Quinn is discussed as they provide an invaluable framework within which to consider approaches to strategic change, both espoused and real. The review of strategic approaches to change is concluded with reference to work by Carlisle and McMillan (2002) to compare strategy from both a classical, Newtonian–Cartesian perspective and from a complexity paradigm perspective.

Considering change

With very few exceptions, there appears to be little discussion in modern UK management texts of the notion of change as an abstract concept or a universal phenomenon. The focus is on explorations of change in relation to some particular management theory or practice. Discussion tends to concentrate on the content of change, the process of change and contextual and environmental factors. This is, of course, entirely appropriate given the context. However, I would suggest that explorations of our ideas on change, that embrace a much wider perspective, even considerations of philosophical or scientific notions, would enrich and make more realistic people's understandings. This in turn might help managers to recognize their current mindsets and to develop even more effective and realistic practices.

What do we mean when we talk and think about change? We frequently refer to changes in our lives or lifestyle but how often do we consider it as an abstract concept or a universal phenomenon? I have come to consider change not as a single event, nor a series of events but an ever-flowing, ever-present part of reality. It is the underlying essence of life.

A number of writers point out that the ancient Chinese saw change and transformation as an endless flow and an essential feature of our universe. Everything was viewed as being in the process of changing and becoming something else. Here is a view of change which was held many centuries ago yet it resonates very clearly with modern notions of change and transformation, particularly those associated with complexity. The Taoist philosophy considers that the natural world is created by a cyclical pattern of comings and goings, of growth and decay. This arises from the dynamic interplay of the complementary opposites of yin and yang. The yin of night and the yang of day, of winter and summer, moisture and dryness, coolness and warmth.

The ancient Greek philosopher Heraclitus, who lived circa 540–480 BC, speculated on the nature of change and came to think that change was an inherent characteristic that flowed through the natural world. Thus he saw the nature of the universe in a similar way to the Taoists. In about 500 BC he wrote:

> Everything flows and nothing abides; everything gives way and nothing stays fixed. ... Cool things become warm, the warm grows cool; the moist dries, the parched becomes moist. ... It is in changing that things find repose.
>
> (quoted in Morgan 1986: 233)

Heraclitus' notions of change contained paradoxical elements, whereby different and even opposite things were the same. For example, he described how different waters or flow stayed the same. In other words, the flows, within flows, that create a river are always changing, but they are still the same river. Thus although everything is always changing and there are always differences or opposites, this continual process creates the ever present structure whereby everything exists.

Heat and cold are opposites, as are dry and wet. Heraclitus, in considering these opposites, considers that in the ongoing flow of change they come to replace each other. Thus they are not really opposites but part of a universal transformation process. Thus things are not fixed, and nothing exists forever in a fixed state of being. In another use of paradox he concludes that the only permanent thing in the universe is change. Through observation, reflection and deep thinking Heraclitus came to many of the conclusions reached by the Taoists and by chaos and complexity scientists today. He believed that the universe is in a constant state of flux. Within the ancient philosophies are echoes of Prigogine's dissipative structures.

Heraclitus' view of the universe as existing in unending flux resonates with the view taken by the physicist David Bohm. Bohm (1980) puts forward the theory that the universe is a flowing whole that is in a continuous process of flux and change. Further, there is an underlying process or reality which he calls the implicate order. This flowing order unfurls endlessly and creates the hidden dynamics from which arise the explicate order, or manifest forms of activity or change which we observe. In many ways his theory of these two kinds of order, the implicate and explicate, goes some way to explain why from many aspects the world appears to be stable when it is actually in a state of permanent change.

Morgan (1986) suggests that until fairly recently science focused on understanding the explicate or manifest order and has sought to explain it in linear cause and effect terms. This approach may explain why so many organizations hold traditional views of change. Unfortunately, too many people consider change as a series of discrete events breaking a stable unchanging reality, and not as a never-ending process. Traditional science's concentration on the parts may explain why individuals and organizations have failed to understand and see the nature of the whole woven into the implicate order, as an eternal, creative process.

If one considers change from a complexity science perspective then one thinks of change as forming patterns and of flowing through time. Like a giant stream flowing forever, within the flow of change there will be flows, and flows within flows, and eddies and ripples within these, all interweaving to create an overall dynamic whole. These flows could well form repeating fractal-like patterns over a long time period. Wille and Hodgson (1991: 9) remind us that the philosopher Alfred N. Whitehead referred to us as 'human becomings' in a reflection of the perpetually changing nature of our being.

Types and degrees of change

Within the flow of change there are many different eddies and effects, as already described, and there is a general recognition that the nature of what I would call observable change, may vary and its effects can vary in impact, magnitude and time span. A number of writers on organizations have sought to describe these different types of this change. They write of first- and second-order change, or first- and second-degree change, of transformation and self-renewal.

First-order change tends to change things on the surface or in a limited way. For example, an organization introduces some new process or procedure to improve things, but the total or overall way of working is very little changed. A very common example of this type of change is found in customer care and the service sector. Consultants come into a company and suggest that service to the customer may be improved by introducing a more friendly telephone greeting. A customer making an enquiry is thus answered in a new way. Very commonly, the mantra is something like: 'My name is … How may I help you?' The response to the customer may have changed, but how much has their attitude or degree of helpfulness changed? How different will be the back-up services required? In reality very little may have changed. Sometimes an organization changes from a manual system to an automated one. This is a more significant change than the customer service example, but it is a limited change unless it involves other major differences in procedures and behaviours. The receptionist has learnt a new telephone greeting but perhaps little else. It is the kind of change also referred to as superficial change or single loop learning.

First-order change was particularly suited to the early years of this century when organizations moved from periods of apparent change to periods of relative stability and the bureaucratic organization was well adapted to this situation. But many writers would argue that organizations involved in the turbulent, fast-moving world of today need second-order change, deep-level change, or a sea change, if they are to survive. The term 'sea change' is used to describe a major transformation and is derived from the verse in Shakespeare's *The Tempest*.

> Full fathom five they father lies;
> Of his bones are coral made:
> Those are pearls that were his eyes:
> Nothing of him that doth fade,
> But doth suffer a sea change
> Into something rich and strange.
> (Shakespeare 1960: 7)

Here the human male has changed from a recognizable human shape into a sea creature made of pearls and coral. It is a complete transformation. The man that existed before has vanished and been replaced by 'something rich and strange'.

Dale's (1994) definition of a sea change is not quite so transforming as Shakespeare's. She writes that a sea change requires people to see the world differently and she defines it as a change where the structure or basic shape stays the same but the fabric changes. Thus in organizations that have experienced a sea change people do things differently and also see the world differently. She likens this to many of the public sector organizations where the same people work in the same place, providing similar services but work in very different ways and for new reasons. She notes, however, that in many organizations the notion is limited to a one off major change event or process. It is important to note that major structural change may also be a factor in accomplishing second-order change, but it is unlikely to achieve it without other significant changes taking place. Major changes are also described as evidence of double-loop learning taking place. When double-loop learning takes place people undergo significant personal change. They change their mental models and shift their internal personal perspectives in such a way that important new insights emerge and significant new behaviours develop. This kind of change is truly transforming for the individual and through their changed behaviours the organization itself changes.

Richard Rumelt (1995) describes deep-level change as a transformation, a process which seeks to bring about fundamental changes in order to bring about dramatic improvements in an organization's performance. Transforming change may be described as self-renewal which Nonaka (1988), echoing Prigogine's dissipative structures, describes as a process whereby the existing organizational order is dissolved and a new one constructed. The organization has moved from one kind of existence or way of existing, to another. This has resonances with Shakespeare's sea change.

Stacey (1992, 1996a) sees three major kinds of change: closed, contained and open-ended. He describes closed change as a change or changes that are readily recognized and understood and contain a measure of predictability. For example, how the number of customers a company has had over a given period has changed, and how they may change in the future and how it will act accordingly. With contained change it is more difficult to understand evidence from the past and why, for example, a particular product has sold better than others, and how it will do in the future. Closed and contained change Stacey describes as developments that usually have short-term consequences. They are considered short-term in that they are more or less repetitions of previous events or activities. These, therefore, relate closely to notions of first order change. Open-ended change, however, is unique and has never happened in that particular way before. This is real change on a par with notions of second order change, transformation or renewal.

In Stacey's view (1992) managers need to consider all three forms of change if they wish to help their organizations survive. But, he points out, open-ended change is qualitatively different from closed and contained change and has to be handled in a totally different way. In his view there are obvious links between the causes and the effects of closed and contained change and therefore it is possible in a small way to predict some of the possible outcomes. This is the kind of change that is recognized and often looked for in most organizations as it still relates to a more traditional view of the world. In situations of open-ended change, however, Stacey claims there is no useful past experience to draw upon, no obvious links between cause and effect and lots of ambiguity – the future is unpredictable.

I would endorse Stacey's view and further suggest that organizations need all kinds of changes to be constantly flowing through them if they are to be responding to events, creating events, and inventing their own futures. Organizations need to be constantly adapting intelligently and resourcefully to the flows of activities in their own world and connecting worlds, and they need to be learning as they go. In other words, they need to behave as truly complex adaptive systems.

Change and transformation in organizations

A number of writers on management and organizations observe that many western managers have mind sets derived from the traditional scientific world view. This is a view which itself provides the foundation for vast numbers of management textbooks and education programmes. Further, some of the research presented in this literature is based on contexts which were highly controlled, sometimes unrepresentative and the results viewed from a linear perspective. Thus, in spite of the turbulent environments in which many managers operate, many have failed to grasp the true nature of the reality in which they work. There is a tendency to believe that if an organization is to be successful it must be stable, function smoothly and harmoniously, and that a manager must be able to plan and even predict for the longer term. They seek to create a niche for their organizations which in science would be called stable equilibrium. This is the stable, orderly zone, or frozen zone far from the edge of chaos. Their idea of change is a controlled move from one stable state to another. There may be difficulties and a short period of uncertainty as the change takes place, but handled properly, that is all. It is a view which tends to consider the world as essentially stable and orderly and change as a disruptive and temporary aberration in the scheme of things. Cooksey and Gates (1995) argue that this static snapshot style approach leads to the creation of static management approaches which hinder and even sometimes destroy an organization's effectiveness by restricting its ability to adapt to turbulent and chaotic events.

Many managers as a result of this mindset become worried and sometimes deeply upset if they feel that things are running out of control and not going to plan. They must be failing if they are not controlling events. Many senior managers, in particular, were brought up in an era when science and scientific method were held in high esteem. Thus many believe that a scientific approach will provide them with accurate tools and techniques for managing. Consequently they rely on logical analysis of data and other sophisticated pseudo-scientific techniques which have been created to help predict the future and to ensure that the right decisions are made at the right time. One would think sometimes that project management and business analysis processes have almost become sciences in their own right.

As a result of this mindset too many managers follow limited and repetitive strategies believing that success may be achieved through long-term planning, monitoring of progress, and tight control systems. Senior managers continue to encourage and endorse these activities while setting direction and staying in command. Many organizations attempt to cope with change by producing mission statements, strategic planning processes, and new (usually linear) organizational structures. Careful measurement processes, detailed graphs and charts and considerable statistical data are all used to try to capture the dynamic nature of organizations with a view to controlling them.

Walsham (1993) refers to a change process in a wholly-owned subsidiary of a large manufacturing company. His case study notes that informal systems were very much a part of the existing set-up and it was planned that the new systems with their increased regulations would reduce the need for such informal processes. Senior management saw the new system as a tool which they could use to increase their overall control of the business. So here in the 1980s we encounter the traditional mechanistic mindset whereby tools are used to increase control and thereby improve production. In reality the employees lost their responsibility for transport arrangements and the allocation of warehousing space. However, they adapted to the changes by finding ways of working around the new systems. So effective were they at this and at identifying cost-saving improvements that some years later a new management team came to recognize the value of their informal systems and practices. In reality, as this example shows, informal processes based on informal human networks often offer a more adaptive approach than formal ones based on traditional notions of command and control. The need to recognize the importance of such informal systems is explored in subsequent chapters when I consider the use of self-organizing principles in organizations.

Considerable attention has been given to the notion that organizations need to change in response to some external force, usually changes in the external environment. Kotter (1995) found that fundamental changes tended to be introduced into organizations as a response in order to help the organization cope with a different and challenging environment. All too often when an organization is impelled to introduce changes by some major outside event it does so as a crisis response. Managers seek a range of rapid responses to the current situation, often relying on past approaches. The aim is to overcome the present difficulties or threats as quickly as possible and to get the organization back on an even keel. By comparison much less attention has been given to the notion that organizations themselves should constantly be seeking change in an active way, such that changing is an organizational way of living. Kotter also observed that few of the corporate attempts to introduce change during the ten-year period of his studies were very successful. There were a few complete failures but most attempts at introducing major organizational change on a success – failure scale tended to be at the failure end of the scale.

Some authors write of using the 'levers' of change and in so doing use a machine metaphor that betrays a mechanistic view of things. Managers are advised to seek out and use the 'levers' that will impel an organization and all its individuals to change according to a predetermined plan using a predetermined process.

Considerations of management science approaches to change are still found in the literature. Walsham, for example, suggests that management science would benefit from more formal methods of analyzing organizational change drawn from organizational theory. He describes management science as being concerned with intervention in an organization in order to bring about beneficial changes. This interventionist approach to change implies that an organization can be fixed or tuned to operate better. Here are shades of the machine metaphor which ignore the dynamic, living complexities of organizational life and take a simple, linear cause and effect approach. Walsham points out that many management scientists have tended to concentrate on the content of change rather than on context or process and suggests that they also focus on analyses of environment and the process of change projects. The focus on context and process is helpful but I would suggest that the emphasis on analysis implies the influence of traditional scientific methods. Walsham points out that recently there have been moves towards considerations of context and process although many traditional management scientists have still not adapted their approach. Johnson (1993) while recognizing that scientific management approaches to strategic change can provide helpful models also makes it clear that they alone will not make change happen. In his view change is brought about by the action of managers and not by rational planning techniques. He argues that strategic management relies on the cultural and cognitive processes in organizations which shape managers' thinking and activity. In his view over reliance on traditional, rational approaches to strategic change is at best unsatisfactory and at worst possibly dangerous.

Change is still regarded by many managers and writers as something that may be stopped or started at will. Notions of the importance of consolidation are also popular, encouraging a perception that change is a process whereby something moves in a linear fashion from one state to another state. A major example of this approach is Lewin's (1951) renowned model which is still taught in many business schools and still held in the heads of many managers. A number of writers still consider Lewin's model as a very useful one and still use it both as a model for action and for analysis. His model advocates that change is introduced as part of an unfreezing process and then later refrozen in a stabilizing process. This is based on the notion that organizations like living systems have homeostatic tendencies and therefore are always striving to maintain a steady state. This view of living systems is at odds with Prigogine's dissipative structures and concepts of ongoing self-renewal. Living systems are constantly adapting to their environments in order to survive and a steady state of existence is likely to be very transitory unless the system is in decline. The model is essentially a linear one and views change as an input and output process. There is recognition of the many complex and dynamical factors that make up an organization and its environment, but stripped bare this approach tends to view an organization as a mechanism that takes in resources, transforms them and outputs or produces them in another form. Again the change process aims to move the organization from one state to another. Further, although there is recognition of the human factor and the many problems that may arise during such a process there is still enormous consideration and confidence placed on planning and control. Thus there are assumptions being made about cause and effect, the value and necessity of control, and the possibility of accurate predictions of the future.

Durcan *et al.* (1993) consider this movement from one state to another state approach as very misleading, yet it is still not uncommon and to support their view they cite two examples in different organizations. For some twelve months a large engineering company had undergone some substantial changes. The production manager felt that the workers on the shop floor now needed several months in which to settle down and embed the many changes. His unit was subsequently closed down as it was unable to make all the changes needed to meet the pressures of increasing competitiveness. In the other example a staff attitude survey in a multinational showed that staff felt that the pace of change was too much and probably not necessary. Many wanted a period of stability. A senior manager with the company agreed that having undergone substantial structural change the staff of the company did now need several years for things to settle down. When considering these examples it is worth bearing in mind that both managers and those managed shared similar views on the nature of change and change events. Both sought stability and bedding down.

Durcan *et al.* further describe the mechanistic approach to change as one which manages change in an incremental way within an existing organizational framework or mindset in order to achieve a 'deliberate strategy' (Mintzberg and Waters 1989). They list four assumptions that they consider reflect the mechanistic approach to change:

1   Time is viewed as linear and sequential. Thus many theories show organizational change as a series of logical, sequential steps which take place within a specified time period. The overall process is viewed as a progressive one leading an organization from an unhealthy condition to a healthy one.

2   That change is an incremental process of adjustment. Periods of transforming change are seen as abnormalities which are not part of the normal incremental process. This notion leads to the belief that it is possible to intervene in the organizational processes and produce the changes desired. Step-by-step change is, however, possible in a relatively stable environment.

3   The concept of 'fit' is all important. This is whereby an organization's structure and strategy match the external environment. Management's role is seen as ensuring that the organization always matches its environment and this is the reason for introducing change. This assumption also requires that an organization not only fits its external environment but also that its internal processes also match. This reflects 'a semi-concealed Darwinian concept of gradual evolution and survival of the fittest' (Durcan *et al.* 1993: 6).

4   There is an assumption that the direction the change has to take is clear and that by using specific and appropriate skills the required destination will be reached. This is a view of change that assumes that the future is predictable and that the organization has enough information about itself and its environment to make predictable and effective plans.

This mechanistic approach detailed by Duran *et al.* neatly reflects the traditional scientific paradigm and the notion of controlling change in order to determine future outcomes.

Other writers too point out some of the drawbacks to considering change in organizations from an exclusively Newtonian–Cartesian perspective. They recommend moving away from narrow linear approaches and a rationalist mentality which over relies on logical, analytical processes. Stacey (1992) suggests that interpreting the world and organizations as being inherently stable (in the classical sense) is unhelpful in dealing with real change issues and that managers need to explore and understand the nature of ceaseless creativity and natural systems if they are to successfully support their organization. Morgan (1986) suggests that we will better understand the dynamics of change if we think of change in a new way. He refers to change as flux and suggests that we will better understand this if we consider it as part of the unfolding nature of the explicate and implicate order.

Figure 4.1 illustrates the major differences between approaches to change derived from the traditional, classical, mechanistic view of change and those associated with a more modern view of change. The new radical, dynamic approach mirrors the new ideas emerging from the changing scientific paradigm influenced by quantum physics and chaos and complexity.

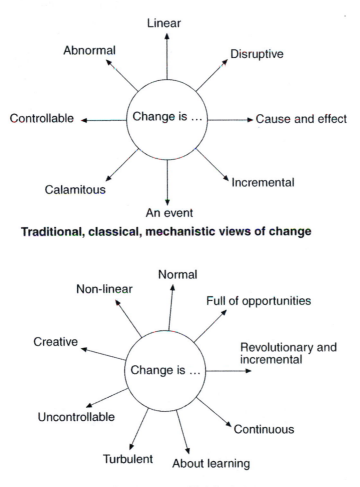

Traditional, classical, mechanistic views of change

New, modern, dynamic views of change

Figure 4.1 Perceptions/views of change

Strategy and strategic change management

Strategic planning, in Priesmeyer's (1992) view, was developed in the 1970s primarily as a tool for senior management. The standard strategic planning approach was basically an analytical process which was carried out annually. It examined the organization's mission, carried out internal and external analyses and a review of strategic issues in order to develop a strategic plan. In Priesmeyer's opinion this took an over-simple approach and suffered from too narrow a focus which did not look carefully at patterns of change.

Moncrief and Smallwood (1996) agree that the 1970s was dominated by a planning style of strategic management which gave rise to a range of analytical and planning tools designed to predict the future. Organizations believed that companies, markets, customers and competitors behaved in a logical and predictable way. Thus the development and use of tools for strategic analysis and planning would ensure that the future could be handled effectively.

During the 1980s the traditional rational, sequential approach to management was adopted and included the visioning approach to strategy. Visioning the future inspired many organizations to let go of some of the old tools, but too often the new visions were indistinguishable from the old mission statements and organizational processes were hardly touched. During this period the notions of incremental and emergent strategy developed by writers like Quinn and Mintzberg began to challenge the established view.

Mintzberg and Waters, Quinn and others

Mintzberg and Waters (1989) developed the concept of 'deliberate' and 'emergent' strategies based on years of empirical research. Their model offers a range of approaches to strategic change each of which embodies different amounts of what they call deliberateness or emergentness. It is important to recognize that they define strategy as the pattern which emerges from the flow of decision making. They identify these different patterns or streams of behaviour in order to investigate and explore the relationship between top-level planning and intentions and what organizations actually do in reality. Deliberate strategies are those strategies which were planned and intended, whereas emergent strategies are those patterns of activity which emerged or became real whether intended or not.

Mintzberg and Waters list eight main types of strategy, but are careful to point out that in reality a strategy may not belong purely to one type but will have an overall tendency towards being deliberate or emergent. They list: planned; entrepreneurial; ideological; umbrella; process; unconnected; consensus; and imposed. In Eccles (1993) view imposed strategy was a strategy imposed from outside the organization and therefore not the organization's own. Deliberate strategies are more widespread but perfectly deliberate strategies are rare because they rely on predictability and order to proceed. According to Mintzberg and Waters most real-world strategies fall somewhere along a continuum between deliberate and emergent.

The planned strategy is highly deliberate and relies on authority, elaborate and detailed planning and powerful controlling mechanisms. Here is an approach to change and to the future heavily influenced by notions of the organization drawn from classical and scientific management and the bureaucratic organization. Notions of control are present in the entrepreneurial strategy which is very much driven by the vision of a leader who exercises personal control. The ideological strategy also has controlling elements as strong shared beliefs are shaped by indoctrination or strong socialization processes. The umbrella strategy relaxes some of the tight controls over people in the organization used by the more deliberate strategies and intentionally creates the conditions for strategies to emerge. Here is recognition that responding rather than attempting to totally control is more effective. Similar to the umbrella strategy is the process strategy. Here the leadership controls the strategy-making process while leaving the content to others.

Unconnected strategy tends to be found in organizations such as universities or hospitals where individual units have sufficient autonomy to pursue their own strategic change activities without reference to any central vision or plan. The consensus strategy is of particular interest too for it is not driven by top management but rather evolves as a result of a range of individual actions. It is a strategy evolving from learning.

> In our view, the fundamental difference between deliberate and emergent strategy is that whereas the former focuses on direction and control – getting the desired things done – the latter open up this notion of 'strategic learning'.
>
> Defining strategy as intended and conceiving it as deliberate, as has traditionally been done, effectively precludes the notion of strategic learning. Once the intentions have been set, attention is riveted on realizing them, not on adapting them. ... Adding the concept of emergent strategy, based on the definition of strategy as realized, opens up the process of strategy making up to the notion of learning.
>
> (Mintzberg and Waters 1989: 17)

The concept of organizations learning from their actions as a strategic notion is a very powerful one which resonates with ideas developing from complexity and the underpinning concepts of the learning organization. Strategic learning suggests that an organization is constantly aware of its own actions, reflecting upon them and learning how to do things differently. This is a significant shift away from the more deliberate strategic approaches which tended to focus on central direction and hierarchy towards the more emergent ones which create the space for collective action and supportive behaviours. These more emergent approaches suggest that organizations are complicated, complex, interactive systems that are not so easily directed and controlled. They go a significant way towards recognizing that they are not machines but are made up of complex, living systems. •

Most organizations, Mintzberg and Waters point out, have aspects of both deliberateness and emergence and they conclude that organizations need both. Thus an orderly framework is needed that draws on planning and thinking ahead but not one that constrains spontaneous and learning behaviours. Organizations should expect the unintended and the unexpected.

When Mintzberg and Waters talk of emergence do they mean the same thing as the notion of emergence spoken of by complexity scientists? The answer is yes and no. Yes, in the sense that something unplanned and unintended arises. No, in the sense that something greater than the sum of the parts arises. They are not talking of all the 'cells' in an organization interacting spontaneously in order to carry out their functions and in the process creating something greater, an organizational 'consciousness'. It is important to understand this distinction. Mintzberg and Waters' definition is not that of complexity science – but the interesting question posed is do organizations if they are complex, adaptive, systems manifest 'emergence' as understood by complexity science?

Another significant point to note is the observation by Mintzberg and Waters (1989: 17) that 'emergent strategy means, not chaos, but in essence unintended order'. What do they mean here? I believe that they use chaos in the sense of uncontrollable happenings or changes which is very much the popular understanding of chaos. Interestingly, the 'unintended order' they speak of is the kind of order that clearly resonates with self-organizing systems.

Quinn (1989) considers that change is introduced into organizations not by the use of recipes from management books and long-range planning techniques but step by step in a way he describes as 'logical incrementalism'. This notion of change being introduced step by step suggests the influence of the Darwinian concept of gradual evolution. It is now thought, however, that changes also occur in major, random shifts. Goodwin (1997a) points out too that Darwinian evolution explains the adaption of a species but not the creation of a species. In other words, it explains micro evolution but not macro evolution. Does this mean that the changes observed by Quinn are changes of the first-order, minor adaptions only?

Quinn believes that managers actively work to bring about change and he sees a number of patterns as being dominant where change is successfully managed. These include a step-by-step approach that builds awareness, through the development of informal networks, the testing of ideas, creating support for changes, high-level tactical shifts, widening political support, and overcoming opposition. He suggests too that progress is solidified in a step-by-step way. Throughout Quinn argues in favour of small step-by-step activities and the need for logic and also control. He suggests that managers wait until they have all the right bits in place if they want to be successful in bringing about change. But this ignores the fact that the world will not stand still and wait while they do it. Quinn's reliance on approaches rooted in authority, complex analysis and planning suggests that logical incrementalism follows a linear, sequential approach.

● Eccles (1993) argues that notions of strategy as emergent or incremental have led to confusion between planning and action among the strategists. He states that the traditional view of strategy saw formulation and implementation as sequential. Whereas the emergent and incrementalist views suggest that the two phases are concurrent. This symbiotic relationship clearly reflects the interwoven complexity of real life events. Eccles proposes that strategic change can take place quickly, especially when top management has considerable power and that planned, sequential change is more common than has been acknowledged. Change is seen as developing in a linear fashion and organizations as led by the head with a dependent body obediently following. Here one detects Cartesian influences.

Eccles' own model of the stages of evolution and implementation of strategy incorporates five elements: formulate, plan, assemble, implement, endorse. He recommends that these five elements are not just put together randomly but are included in an approach to strategic change that is designed and controlled by senior management. He seems unaware of the patterning, order and forms that arise spontaneously from self-organizing systems and his five elements sit very comfortably with logical, rationalist traditions.

Comparing paradigms – Carlisle and McMillan

models

Carlisle and McMillan (2002) consider that many existing theories on strategy have failed to address major concerns about strategic thinking and strategic events. In their view many of the current theories put forward fail to match up to the rigours of reality because they draw on a view of the world that is essentially Newtonian–Cartesian. Researchers have sought for universal prescriptions but have found that these are not applicable in all organizational situations.

In Carlisle and McMillan's view the search for an effective approach to strategy produced three major content-based theories over the years. In the 1960s and 1970s, the strategy–structure–performance model derived from the work of Alfred Chandler was prominent. In the 1980s, Michael Porter built on this model to create his market-product positioning theories. In the mid-1980s, the resource-based view emerged. During the 1990s it overtook the market-product positioning perspective as the dominant framework to be represented in the literature. Carlisle and McMillan consider that all three of these strategy content theories have been developed in the image of Newtonian science in which economic rationality, linear causality, stable conditions and equilibrium points are unquestioned assumptions.

Prior to the 1980s, rational top-down strategic planning was seen by many as the route to potential organizational success. From the mid-1980s onwards, the accelerating pace of environmental change led strategy scholars and managers to call into question the efficacy of existing models as a means of dealing adequately with environmental change. By the end of the twentieth century many writers and managers had begun to recognize that in the rapidly changing world of modern organizations not all cause and effect relationships are constant. Sometimes, small changes will have major consequences over time. Also small changes in the environment may produce large variations in outcomes and such outcomes and effects are often unpredictable.

Capra (1996) has categorized a number of broad dimensions along which he compares the Newtonian–Cartesian world view with that of the complexity paradigm. He shows clearly the differences between the two and the implications they have for the thinking that underpins strategic theory and practice. Carlisle and McMillan build upon this comparison and expand Capra's work to construct a more comprehensive categorization for use in organizational analysis than currently exists. See Table 4.1.

Carlisle and McMillan argue that the bulk of established strategy is founded upon the Newtonian–Cartesian paradigm. On its own, this paradigm had been found to be an inadequate framework for developing twenty-first century science and they suggest that it is an equally inadequate paradigm for the development of twenty-first century strategy. They suggest that considerations of the complexity paradigm offer a promising way to consider some of the issues facing both theorists and practitioners of strategic change. Some of the possibilities offered by a complexity approach are discussed further in the next chapter

The learning organization

In recent years there has been considerable interest in the notion of the learning organization or learning company as a way of achieving organizational change. The essential tenet on which many interpretations of the learning organization is based is that through learning an organization is able to adapt, develop, transform and change to meet the needs of itself, its people and society. Here learning is the key to transformation. This is very much a holistic approach to strategy and to learning which sees learning linking individuals and groups in an organizational web that responds, reacts and transforms in an ongoing process. As Leonard Barton (1994) points out, any manager considering establishing a learning organization will need to adapt a holistic, systems thinking approach. This means focusing less on specific events and more on the ongoing and underlying patterns and movements for change. This is very different to previous notions of change and of organiza-

Table 4.1 Strategic comparisons

Newtonian–Cartesian paradigm perspective	*Complexity science paradigm perspective*
Essentially mechanistic	Essentially dynamic/self-organizing
Linear	Non-linear
Controllable	Uncontrollable
Centralized	Networked
Hierarchical	Non-hierarchical
Limited connectivity	Highly connected
Uniformity	Diversity
Cause and effect	Effect and effect
Predictable	Unpredictable
Reductionist	Holistic
Objective focus	Subjective and objective foci
Entity focused	Process focused
Correlation	Patterning
Highly preclusive	Highly inclusive
Evolutionary	Revolutionary and evolutionary

Source: Adapted from Carlisle and McMillan (2002: 3).

tional learning. Then learning was mainly undertaken in discrete chunks related to specific organizational skills, tasks and processes and only indirectly connected to the overarching structure of the organization. Further, once the skill was acquired or the task learnt then the learning process was deemed to be over. Learning was seen as a neat, controlled, self-contained entity not as a continuous, stimulating, enriching, flow of experience. This attitude very much reflects the traditional approach to employees discussed earlier and traditional notions of change and the world order. Durcan *et al.* (1993) contend that the mechanistic approach attached value to accumulated learning arising from an organization's experience whereas more recent models of learning stress the importance of stimulating the organization's capacity for learning, learning from new experiences, its own and others, on the need to experiment and to reflect, in order to speed up the learning process.

Peter Senge (1994) has taken a leading role in developing the notion of the organization as a learning organization considering that traditional, controlling approaches are not sufficient to cope with the uncertainties of the modern world. Senge advocates individual lifelong learning; the creative use of mental models; the building of shared visions; learning in teams and systems thinking. Many organizations have been inspired by Senge's model or parts of it and have used it with varying degrees of success. There are obvious difficulties in trying to introduce new concepts into large organizations, particularly if the existing organizational framework is not supportive and if the underpinning design principles are essentially hierarchical and linear. These themes are explored in later chapters.

Merry (1995: 142) refers to Montuori who considers that most learning that takes place today is non-reflective, 'maintenance' learning'. Montuori writes:

> It is incapable of questioning its own assumptions and of engaging in change but 'more of the same'. Unable to question its own origins and guiding framework, maintenance learning allows us to learn only within a pre established framework, but does not allow for free enquiry.
>
> (Montuori 1993: 189)

This is akin to single-loop or surface learning whereby learning is limited and routine. It is learning which is about coping not adapting. This kind of learning resonates with the traditional view of training within organizations where all training activities tended to focus on the solution of particular problems and the acquisition of specific skills. Training was viewed as a tool for managers that 'fixed' the organizational machine or tuned it up so that it ran more efficiently. Many notions of learning were skill based, task orientated and routine. People did not learn to learn nor to challenge their own mental models. This kind of learning is unlikely to introduce any real deep seated change and it represents an attitude that is deeply ingrained in many organizations.

The learning organization, however, contains not only single-loop or maintenance learning but also Morgan's (1986) 'double-loop' learning whereby people are able to question their own assumptions, where they learn to learn and to self-organize. People develop the skills of reflection and inquiry and are encouraged to develop new mental models of the world, to become creative as well as adaptive.

Within a learning organization there is a fresh approach to strategic change. Management recognizes that the achievement of strategic objectives may be less important than the learning, or the learning process, that takes place. Here change is viewed as a continuum and learning as an ongoing process that is valuable in its own right. Organizational transformation is achieved by a continuous process whereby changes in individuals and groups that arise from individual and group learning experiences change the culture and behaviours of the organization. These are changes developed from within rather than being the result of external intervention. Further, a number of writers contend that a learning organization learns most effectively and creatively when it is going through a period of major upheaval or drastic change. This fits well with the notion that creativity flourishes at the edge of chaos or in conditions far from equilibrium.

Many of those who support the notion of a learning organization do so because they believe it will prove an effective way of meeting corporate objectives. By adopting learning organization principles a company can search for new ideas that may give it a competitive edge, come up with clever ways of solving problems and create new business opportunities for itself.

It is important to note that organizational transformation is different from organizational development which was a common term in the 1960s and 1970s. Organizational development was used to describe a range of processes and activities designed to improve the way people worked together and handled change – and usually involved the intervention of external consultants. Organizational development focused on identifying corporate or team goals, exploring roles and relationships and understanding group dynamics. All these activities and interventions were aimed at achieving a particular change in process or procedure. They were not concerned with learning in its own right, but rather on achieving the task in hand. There was little or no recognition of the importance of learning and the learning process and the role it could play in transforming a company.

Overall the underpinning philosophy of the learning organization fits well with notions emanating from complexity. There are, however, some examples which do not, for some writers on the learning organization still talk of the need to control change.

In conclusion

Organizational change is a hot topic and there is widespread recognition amongst management that being able to change and adapt to changing circumstances is necessary for organizational survival and that facilitating or enabling change is a key management skill. In spite of this, however, there is evidence to suggest that many organizations find it really hard to make major changes even when their survival is threatened. Richard Rumelt's (1995) research shows that, in spite of all the literature on managing change, many organizations still struggle to do things differently. It is as if there is an in-built resistance to change which emerges as a kind of organizational inertia. Some of this Rumelt attributes to human factors whereby people in the organization refuse to acknowledge and act on any external threat, or where the current situation feels fine and changes seem unnecessary and uncomfortable. These responses to change have a psychological feel to them. They may well be founded on our human needs for comfort and security but they also ignore our needs for novelty and stimulation. Traditional views on change as an unpleasant and disruptive upheaval are likely to strengthen this response.

Rumelt also describes how sometimes an organization is unable to be decisive and fails to decide how to act and what direction to take. This suggests a linear approach to change and a view of change as a cause and effect process. Thus the importance of making sure that the right approach is taken, for if it is not then the effects could be disastrous perhaps. Rumelt also describes how political deadlock can lead to inaction, as can other forms of behaviour. These may be due to an inactive leadership, attachment to the status quo or a past failure to reward people for changing their way of working. I would suggest that a contributing factor to this inability to act might be due to the traditional structure of the organization. If it is highly compartmentalized then managers will defend the territory of their individual functional patches and fail to co-operate with changes that they perceive might threaten them. Further, a hierarchical structure by its very nature suggests that the further down the layers you travel the less important are the employees, and so the lower you go the more likely it is that you will encounter a weaker commitment to the organization.

In recent years a number of writers have challenged the mechanistic approach to change. They refer to Tom Peters who challenged the notion of change as gradual and incremental, and Massarik (1990) who also finds the old approaches inadequate and who criticized Lewin's Force Field Analysis. The notion that a significant planning phase has to proceed an action phase has been challenged. It has been replaced by the view that planning and action should proceed side by side. The incrementalist approach has been criticized for being too linear and essentially reactive. Strategic change approaches which assume a predictable future have been shown to be less than adequate. The concept of linearity has come under attack because it oversimplifies the complexities of organizational life and leads to unhelpful assumptions about the nature of change and of reality. There has also been criticism too of the dangers of 'excessive fit'. Pascale (1986) argues that change should be envisaged as something that is revolutionary and is often accompanied by a paradigm shift. This moves away from earlier Darwinian analogies, for Pascale argues, that notions of 'fit' can leave an organization too vulnerable to major environmental shocks – shocks which can move an organization from a position of complete fit to one of total lack of fit in a very short time.

Some writers have developed anti-rationalist models which emphasize the roles of ambiguity and chaos within organizations. Nonaka (1988) refers to Weick (1987) who argues that organizations may have to devise strategic change processes wh' become chaotic in order to accurately reflect the chaotic nature of their envi ment. However, Nonaka does not consider that the anti-rational theorists ha' fully developed and explored the concepts of the turbulent dynamics which lead them to consider the more radical notions of self-organization and self-renewal which are emerging from complexity.

In spite of the challenges to mainstream thinking on organizational change and strategy there are still many writers and managers who believe that rational decision making, defining and setting long-term goals and making appropriate long-range forecasts and planning assumptions are what is needed. Here is the influence of the old, classical scientific tradition with its emphasis on the rational logical processes and its belief in predictability and a predetermined outcome. In reality, however, most people have only half an eye on the written documents of prediction and muddle through as best they can. Theoretical beliefs do not match the reality of practical, day-to-day behaviours in organizations creating a kind of organizational cognitive dissonance. In the next chapter I continue to consider the theme of organizational change by looking at some of the ways in which insights from complexity may be used to transform and redesign organizations.

5 Transforming organizations using complexity

> The lessons of complexity are simply too important to be lost or frittered away. We have seen how they can transmute the most leaden of organizations into the gold of a flexible, fast-reacting, innovative enterprise.
>
> (Pascale *et al.* 2000: 15)

This chapter describes how the ideas and principles derived from complexity (incorporating chaos theory) described in Chapter 2 may be used radically and realistically to transform and redesign organizations. It considers in general terms the new thinking about organizations in the light of complexity science, referring to some of the key ideas, key writers and interpretations of a number of key concepts. It describes how they challenge our existing notions and what complexity may mean in terms of organizational renewal. It also looks at the application of specific notions such as the butterfly effect, strange attractors and notions of order and disorder. New approaches to organizational order and strategic change are also considered. Complete sections are dedicated to particular aspects of complexity in order to explore new ways of thinking about organizations and how they are managed. New ways that, if enacted, should change and transform organizations and our perceptions of them. These include sections on the edge of chaos, self-organizing systems, fractals and complex adaptive systems. There is also a short review of some of the arguments that undermine or inhibit the use of complexity concepts in an organizational context. Throughout this chapter case studies and examples are used to flesh out the real-life possibilities that the use of complexity science can offer.

It is important to recall the new understandings of change as discussed in Chapter 4, where life is seen as a never-ending, unfolding flow of events. As organizations are made up of dynamic living systems then they too are part of the natural order and always unfolding and changing. But how well do they do this and how well do they adapt to this unceasing flow with its many turbulent eddies? Do management and strategic approaches based on a more static and stable view of the world impede or weaken an organization's ability to adapt or renew? I believe that they do and that it is only through a better understanding of the 'real world' that organizations will evolve to a higher level of adaptability and survival. This is another reason why this chapter takes a closer look at the interpretations and insights complexity science can offer us into the 'real' organizational world.

Challenging our perceptions

A number of writers are now looking to the new science of complexity for ways of better understanding the structure and the dynamics of modern organizations. Some of these writers who had a good grounding in organizational systems and theories like Stacey, Wheatley, Nonaka and Pascale did not develop their ideas just from existing organization theories but drew on principles emerging from the new sciences. Nonaka, for example, draws on the work of Ilya Prigogine and his work on dissipative structures and the notion of order out of chaos. Stacey, too, refers to the work of Prigogine when he explores systems dynamics and the nature of self-organization in organizations. He also draws on the writings of Kauffman, Gell-Mann and Madelbrot. Pascale refers to Kauffman, Langton and others.

Wheatley (1994) considers the discoveries made in quantum physics, biology and chaos theory and the radical suggestions they make for the way we think about people and management in organizations. Her book weaves together a synthesis of these new sciences including references to self-organization. She refers to the work of a number of distinguished physicists including Albert Einstein and David Bohm, the writings of Eric Jantsch and the work of Benoit Mandelbrot and Ilya Prigogine. Wheatley believes that understanding of the new sciences reminds organizations of some key guiding principles that are perhaps overlooked. These are the importance of shared visions to guide an organization and shared values to influence behaviours. The new sciences challenge the rigid mechanistic models of management and encourage managers to search for new forms of order, which recognize the connected wholeness of all human experience.

Merry (1995) writes on the social sciences and organizations and the insights complexity offers into these fields of study and activity. He asserts that all human and social systems are open, far-from-equilibrium systems, and that to try and understand them in a mechanistic way is bound to fail. He suggests that all living systems and societies are in a never-ending process of change and, like chemical dissipative structures, a new order emerges out of internal turbulence. Living systems are constantly dissipating energy in order to retain their integrity, but at some point a critical period is reached and there is a period of great change and instability. Everything then breaks down and then self-organizes into a new order. He gives as examples the disorder in the Middle East and the break-up of the Soviet Union.

McMaster (1996) considers that understanding complexity science and its applications can enable us to develop simple rules or principles with which to interpret and understand living systems, including organizations. He also considers that developments in the new sciences are suggesting new ways of looking at organizations, at structures, communications and creativity.

Battram (1996) points out that the implications of complexity science for organizations are huge because complex systems are unpredictable and because the old command and control approaches to management are no longer valid. Turner (1996) writes that complexity theory challenges existing views of strategy and emphasizes the value of process and dynamics rather than content and analysis.

Berreby (1996) talks of the attraction of chaos theory being the way it mirrors real life and reflects the complexity, the uncertainty and the paradoxical nature of life itself as well as the new realities of today's organizations. He quotes Chris Meyer, a partner at Ernst & Young, who believes that complexity points the way to how we will view the management of organizations in the future. In Meyer's view the current way in which most businesses approach their operations by attempting to control a number of key variables is an enormous oversimplification of reality. Further, manufacturing resource planning (MRP) and strategic planning approaches have been unsuccessful because they do not reflect the ways in which people really behave.

Other writers too point out the flaws in current management approaches that an understanding of complexity can help address. Cooksey and Gates (1995) write on how human resource management, as a sub-discipline of management science, is over-reliant on systems and processes that are inherently linear. They cite such human resource management theories as those on job satisfaction, motivation and work performance. All too often, in their view, working realities fail to match the theoretical models. These are inherently flawed as they tend to be based on non-representative contexts and simplistic linear interpretations. In their view, considerations drawn from chaos theory and non-linear dynamics (complexity) offer a better model of observing and understanding the complex and unpredictable aspects of human behaviour. They consider it folly for human resources managers to believe that they can fine tune an individual's performance or that they can manage that performance in such as way that it reaches a steady state.

> It lulls management into a fall sense of security and control with regard to expectations of HRM policy impacts and outcomes, and it contributes to the continuation of management 'fads' where dissatisfaction with one set of policies and practices (because the policies fail to meet predicted outcome expectations) leads to their displacement by another 'more modern' set of policies and practices … replacing one equilibrium-orientated linear approach to management with another merely perpetuates the problems and the unrealistically high expectations.
>
> (Cooksey and Gates 1995: 35)

Pascale *et al.* (2000) recognize the powerful influence that science has on society and the role traditional science has played in establishing the current machine model which they describe as being essentially about taking raw materials, making them into goods and in the process breaking important social and ecological balances. In other words, an approach to business was constructed that was essentially destructive. Complexity science, however, which is strongly influenced by biology and understandings of the living world offers a radically different model. It has fostered interest in the natural world and how species survive and endure by competing and collaborating in an endless cycle of change. It has also, in their view, encouraged some managers to seriously challenge the machine model of management and to look for other ways of realizing the potential of people and organizations. They offer a new management model derived from complexity science which is based on four core principles. These are as follows:

1   *'Equilibrium is* a precursor to *death.'* When a living system is in a stable state then it is not readily responsive to changes and so it is placing its survival at risk.
2   When faced with either an opportunity or a threat living systems move towards the edge of chaos. This is because here they are able to mutate and experiment and so fresh solutions to these challenges are more likely to be discovered.
3   When living systems do this they undergo a self-organizing process and new forms and new behaviours emerge from the upheaval.
4   You cannot direct living systems in a linear fashion as unpredictable consequences are inevitable. The challenge for organizations is to disturb these systems in a way that is similar to the outcomes desired.

(Pascale *et al.* 2000: 6)

Nonaka (1988) suggests that an understanding of chaos science widens the spectrum of options and forces the organization to seek new points of view.

It is not my intention to explore and review the literature that is critical of complexity science and its application in domains outside the scientific arena. However, some writers and researchers have pointed out that not enough serious research has been undertaken to validate these applications and thus, most importantly, there is not enough empirical evidence to support such claims. I would suggest that one of the difficulties in finding supporting evidence in the literature is that it is spread across many fields and is not confined to mainstream management literature, much of which is still predominated by modifications of ideas emanating from classical management sources of thinking. However, the complexity and organizations and management literature is growing, and more articles are finding their way into the prestigious journals. Further, if one considers the history of science and the development and acceptance of new theories and ideas then it becomes apparent that new concepts, especially ones that challenge the existing order, have an uneasy journey to acceptance. There may well be a shortage of empirical evidence and examples of successful application, compared with other established schools of thought – but I would argue that is only to be expected in the circumstances. To take a theory, or a number of interrelated theories, and apply it, or search for evidence of application, when the theory is relatively unknown, in order to provide empirical evidence, is difficult and time-consuming. In spite of this, however, considerable evidence is emerging in a variety of non-scientific domains (healthcare, social sciences, organizational studies) which demonstrates the usefulness and applicability of complexity in offering valid and valuable explanations of many real-life processes and in suggesting new ways of doing things. I shall describe some of these as I proceed through this chapter.

Some writers argue that a convincing case has yet to be made that organizations can be studied from a complexity perspective, other than in the metaphorical sense. Fuller and Moran (2000) cite Rosenhead (1998) who in a critical review of texts on complexity and management claims, that there is no properly validated evidence to support the notion that complexity ideas when used in organizations and management are as effective as claimed. Fuller and Moran point out the difficulties of providing such evidence from large, complex and complicated organizations and instead offer evidence from studies of small firms. They point out that empirically the populations of small businesses have the characteristics of complex adaptive systems. Additionally,

> evolutionary and ecological metaphors of emergence, fitness, and mimicry resonate with observations of the large number of smaller firms in the economy. Small businesses are not a homogeneous population. They vary considerably in size and sector activity, in their ownership, their location, the markets served, and so on. Each business is different. Each has its own 'initial conditions', and each incurs a number of 'accidents' in its temporal path. Given that entre-preneurs are 'innovative', many businesses will operate with their own 'rules', as well as complying (more or less) to more general rules.
>
> (Fuller and Moran 2000: 3–4)

Evidence for the application and applicability of concepts derived from complexity to small–medium-sized organizations, is provided by Stewart *et al.* (2000). Stewart *et al.* describe their research on three different organizations and their use of a model derived from complexity which they call the 'conditioned emergence' model. The model offers a prescriptive approach to organizational change and embraces three strategic stages.

> An initial re-configuration of order generating rules creates a subsequent period of instability within which new order is created, and then finally reinforced through successive applications of positive feedback.
>
> (Stewart *et al.* 2000: 468)

The organizations that were the subject of their research included a Scottish bakery, the Scottish Advisory Health Service and the Estates and Building Division of the University of Glasgow. Briefly, the model was used in an interventionist mode with the bakery. New forms of order were created using the model and the organization did change, restructuring its operations. However, disequilibrium was only obtained when there were pressures from major external factors. Only after this happened were the people involved able to reflect and redesign their rules in order to change the form of their organization. It succeeded in increasing its turnover whilst lowering its production costs. The Advisory Health Service project followed a different route where ideas from complexity were used as a metaphor

for understanding emergent developments. The development of these new understandings driven by communications processes in the organization ultimately led
to a shift in understandings and changes being made.

The third project encompassed aspects of both the other projects. The
researchers experienced difficulties in using their model in a prescriptive way and
came to recognize the power of existing internal networks of influence and control.
However, they discovered that instability did emerge as anxieties and tensions
were surfaced. Changes in the communications structure amplified the emerging
instability which led to the emergence of new meaning for the management team.
The project was still under observation when Stewart *et al.* wrote their paper, but
there were signs of 'emergent properties acting as causative phenomena' (Stewart
et al. 2000: 472).

As a result of these three research projects Stewart *et al.* are rethinking the use
of their model of 'Conditioned Emergence' and moving away from interventionist
approaches to notions of complexity as a sense-making tool. In their view this
notion has particular value in bridging the Cartesian split between thinking and
activity and also offers a theoretical approach that assists sense making in organizational conversations. Further, they aver, this has potential for strategic change
programmes which are still largely predominated by rational planning influences.
Stewart *et al.* write:

> In applying complexity theory within live organizational research, we feel
> our experience has demonstrated that such concepts are of critical value in
> helping those organizations involved in transformation efforts, to secure lasting
> business benefit.
>
> (Stewart *et al.* 2000: 474)

Stacey (1992, 1996a) is quite clear about the contribution an understanding of
complexity notions can make to organizations. He asserts that notions from
complexity apply literally to organizations and business and are not simply to be
considered as useful analogies or metaphors. In his view, if managers want to
adopt a scientific approach to management then they need to understand the
behaviours of non-linear feedback systems in unstable or far-from-equilibrium
situations. This is because, in his view, organizations are just such systems.

Lewin and Regine (1999) support Stacey's view and write that if the scientists
are right about the nature of complex adaptive systems in the natural world, then
there are important implications for business and organizations. In their view,
organizations are complex adaptive systems as they have all the properties of these
systems. Additionally:

> the science offers something that most management theories do not. The
> argument here is that most management theories are not really theories at all,
> merely techniques for managing in a certain way. Complexity science is still
> nascent as a theory, but it has determined certain fundamental processes and
> characteristics of complex adaptive systems. In other words, when we speak

of businesses as 'complex adaptive systems' we are not speaking of a metaphor or a technique: rather, we are saying that by understanding the characteristics of complex adaptive systems in general, we can find a way to understand and work with the deep nature of organizations.

(Lewin and Regine 1999: 7)

Stacey (1996a: 349) has developed a theory of organization using complexity which is based on nine propositions. They are as follows:

1   All organizations are webs of non-linear feedback loops that connect to other people and other organizations by webs of non-linear feedback loops.
2   These non-linear feedback systems are able to operate in conditions of stability and instability, or in the areas between these conditions, in the area far from equilibrium, in 'bounded instability at the edge of chaos'.
3   'All organizations are paradoxes.' They are pulled towards stability by control processes, human needs for security and stability, and adaption to the environment. But they are also pulled to the opposite extreme of instability by the pull of organizational divisions and decentralization, human needs for excitement and innovation, and remoteness from the environment.
4   If an organization is pulled into stability it will fail because it will ossify and be unable to easily change itself, but if it is pulled into instability it will disintegrate. Success lies in sustaining an organization in the borders between stability and instability. This is the edge of chaos.
5   'The dynamics of the successful organization are therefore those of irregular cycles and discontinuous trends, falling within qualitative patterns, fuzzy but recognizable categories taking the form of archetypes and templates.'
6   The successful organization because of its internal dynamics faces a completely unknown future.
7   Agents (people) within the system (organization) are unable to control the long-term future. They cannot successfully apply traditional, analytical, long-term planning methods and controls to the long-term future, only to the short term.
8   Long-term planning and development should be a spontaneous self-organizing process out of which new strategic directions may arise. Spontaneous self-organization arises from political activity and group learning situations. Managers need to operate by considering similar or parallel situations.
9   This is how managers should create the long-term future of their organizations.

Stacey's theory of organization provides a valuable theoretical framework with which to consider organizations and organizational transformation. It is a framework to which I shall refer again.

It is worth noting that Stacey writing more recently (Stacey *et al.* 2000: 121) has further developed his views on the use of complexity science in organizational thinking. He argues that the views of a number of complexity scientists (he cites as an example the work of Gell-Mann) do not advance our thinking 'because the theory of causality remains unquestioned'. However, on the other hand, the work of scientists like Prigogine, Kauffman and Goodwin tend to support the assertion that complexity science has much to offer management thinkers, and offers real challenges to predominating views. He envisages this leading to a paradigm shift. In this new paradigm the organization emerges as a result of the relationships of all those within it. He writes that, where complexity challenges the established thinking about organizations, it does so by recognizing that organizations are paradoxical entities where predictability and individual choice are constrained; where difference, spontaneity and diversity are important; and where there is a close link between destruction and creation. An organization is a place in which

> self-organizing relating between people in which power, politics and conflict of ordinary, everyday life are at the centre of co-operative and competitive organizational processes through which joint action is taken.
>
> (Stacey *et al.* 2000: 8)

Creating a new order without control

Complexity suggests that scientific chaos is not as disorderly as first appears. It has an order and a structure of its own and even within the chaos zone there are also patterns of order or stability. These may be irregular patterns of behaviour but they share recognizable similarities. Many phenomena that were once considered chaotic are, in fact, part of an ongoing process of transformation and renewal. The living world may appear to be disorderly but it is inherently ordered. These notions have major implications for the way we view change and our understanding of order and disorder and the need for control. Complexity suggests that managers need to think about change and transformation in new ways.

Instead of trying to control the unexpected or the disorderly, managers should think more about how to understand such situations or events. Durcan *et al.* (1993) suggest that we need to understand organizations in terms of order and disorder as something that cannot be controlled but is often created. In some extreme situations, they argue, any attempts to control or create will inevitably fail. What is needed is new thinking and fresh approaches based on the realities of the real world and not on some textbook model. Disorder or chaos has its own kind of order, and recognition of this paradox can be a useful way of thinking about organizational upheaval.

Wheatley (1994) makes a very important distinction between our notions of order and our notions of control in organizations. We have, she avers, confused control with order. Organizations have sought to create order with the kind of buildings they have designed and erected, by using plans and organization charts, job descriptions, detailed procedures, and so on. Much of this is due to the fact that in the management literature there has been a heavy emphasis on the controlling functions and the need to control people to be successful. Wheatley refers to Lenin and his dictat that: 'Freedom is good, but control is better' and considers that the management search for control has been as destructive as Lenin's controlling political processes. Of course, if organizations are machines, then exerting a machine-like control would make sense, but complexity reminds us that organizations are made up of living human beings. Unfortunately, too many managers still consciously or unconsciously subscribe to the machine model and exhaust themselves and their colleagues trying to oversee and control all the dynamical and unpredictable aspects of these living systems. If only, as Wheatley points out, they could see the inherent orderliness that exists in the natural world about them.

The emphasis in the management literature on control and mechanistic interpretations of order has been closely linked to notions of stability and equilibrium. Stablity was the holy grail for managers, for stability meant order and certainty and long-term planning success. Stability comforted and assured managers that they lived in a stable, predictable and therefore, manageable world. These notions were underpinned by classical science and the Newtonian–Cartesian belief system. Unfortunately life and living systems did not always conform to these models and often even more controlling devices would be needed. It was, up to a point, still possible to live in a world where order and equilibrium were the expected norm until the end of the twentieth century when massive changes in technological, scientific and economic systems created waves of organizational uncertainty. The world was changing, had changed. It was the end of equilibrium as we knew it.

One organization which was prepared to experiment with the prevalent notions of order and control was the Danish company Oticon. Oticon, which was founded in 1904, manufactures hearing aids and provides hearing care. Today it is one of the market leaders. Yet in the late 1980s it was struggling to survive. A new chief executive, Lars Kolind, was appointed and made a number of improvements that put the company back on its feet. However, the company still faced fierce competition from much larger players such as Philips and Siemens. Kolind decided that small changes to the company were not enough if it was to survive and prosper. In 1990 Kolind 'disorganized' the company and created a new form of order. The formal organization with its complex hierarchical structure, controlling layers and separate functions was dismantled and people began to work in self-managed project teams. The new organization came to be described as a 'spaghetti' organization. The term captures neatly the complexity and informality of the new order introduced by Kolind. A few years later Kolind sensing that the company was returning to former behaviours and that departmental structures more reminiscent of the old order could be emerging decided to disorganize again. He created turbulence in the organization by physically moving the project teams around the company premises and unsettling everyone. He deliberately created disorder so as to create a new kind of dynamical order that would help the company to reinvigorate itself and flourish.

In the final decades of the last century a number of writers were pointing out that chaos theory and complexity science challenged old notions of an equilibrium based world. Chaos theory shifted expectations away from the idea that it is possible to achieve a stable or change free state of existence to the notion that continuous change is the norm we should expect. But with what should we replace the dominant theories of equilibrium? Nonaka (1988) suggests we replace them with the concept of self-renewal derived from self-organization which arises from upheaval and dissolution. Further, he believes that if an organization wishes to transform or renew itself then it must keep itself in a non-equilibrium state or unstable state. This is a new notion of order. Instability equals order. The new stability is instability. These strange and paradoxical notions of order and stability are further explained when one considers the webs of order created by strange attractors and looks for the calm of non-linear patterns rather than linear sequences. In Nonaka's view the paradoxical nature of chaos in relation to order and disorder has long been ignored by the management theorists.

The butterfly effect

The butterfly effect, or sensitive dependence on initial conditions, has clear implications for meteorology, but what of organizations? It is often the small changes in our lives which make the biggest differences and this can be the case in organizations too (Handy 1990). It is possible for the actions of one individual to make a significant difference over time. Indeed, it is possible for one individual or one or two small actions to significantly change an organization. Battram (1996) tells of a manager who introduced a small range of changes in her area which were so well received and so successful that they were later adopted by the whole organization.

Organizations are highly complex, highly interconnected dynamical systems and one small fluctuation or change in the system will reverberate throughout. Such a vibration in this highly responsive and interconnected web of feedback loops is amplified over time. Usually this happens in such a way that completely unpredicted and unexpected behaviours emerge. Further, the source of the original 'vibration' or fluctuation is often lost. This often makes standard notions of cause and effect irrelevant in trying to understand the origins of the change. It also challenges many of our notions of the need to set up large programmes to engineer organizational change. A complexity approach would suggest that encouraging and empowering people to make small changes in their own spheres of influence and activity can be a highly effective way of transforming an organization. However, it is worth bearing in mind that, while some people welcome empowering processes, others do not. They find the old controlling order familiar and in an odd way comfortable. Often they are afraid of change. As Cooksey and Gates (1995) point out, many large-scale empowerment programmes fail because they do not recognize the possible range of responses. They treat everyone in the same way and do not recognize individual differences and the effect this will have over time.

The butterfly effect explains how so many energetic new leaders are able to create wholesale changes in an organization. The explanation offered suggests that the changes may have more to do with the dynamic feedback web of the organization than the energies and charisma of a new leader. One person can affect the life of an organization and that person does not have to be in a position of formal authority or leadership, but if they are then they are especially able to make an impact.

The linear, simplistic, approach to organizational issues sometimes leads to an assumption that the same methods and approaches will work with everyone more or less effectively. In other words, that a successful model of organizational change may be used in a number of organizations with very similar results. But understanding of sensitive dependence on initial conditions suggests that this is most unlikely. Every organization is unique with its own culture, its own environment and its own complex web of living individuals. Thus each organization has its own unique set of initial conditions. Thus it is not possible to transfer a set of organizational initiatives and successful models from one organization to another and expect similar results. The differences in initial conditions are likely to lead to widely different outcomes.

Strange attractors

In this section I briefly consider how strange attractors may be used in organizations by referring to a particular example. However, it is important to remember that strange attractors are powerfully bound up with notions of order and disorder and sensitive dependence on initial conditions.

Cooksey and Gates (1995) have suggested that it is useful to think of work performance as behaving like a strange attractor. It will constantly change as it is observed over time. For most people it never follows the same path twice and tends never to settle down to a fixed level. According to Cooksey and Gates all employees are affected by sensitivity to initial conditions. They illustrate their idea by using the notion of a marble in a bowl, which was the example used in Chapter 2. In this case the marble represents the individual and the rounded bowl the interactive nexus of organizational, social, and work systems. The surrounds of both the marble and the bowl equate with the surrounding environmental system. They then illustrate several trajectories which the marble might take as it rolls around the bowl, having been released at a point at the top edge. The marble's path is highly sensitive to initial starting conditions and to its own changing conditions. It is also highly sensitive to the bowl, the surrounding atmosphere and other environmental factors which may influence the state and location of the bowl and marble.

Cooksey and Gates map out four possible models of performance behaviour. Each shows a range of responses or patterns which behave as strange attractors as they interact with the different conditions in and around the theoretical bowl. They conclude that each is different as each trajectory responds to small changes in initial conditions. For example, one model shows moderate levels of chaotic behaviour. Paths are never retraced and no fixed point arrived at, but overall it is constrained by boundaries. This they considered is analogous to the work performance of a fire officer, a police officer or a sales person. In other words, workers whose jobs make their 'paths' sensitive to the environmental systems they are surrounded by and by the social components of their roles. Another model shows considerable amounts of chaotic behaviour as the trajectories move across large areas of space and display major shifts and changes. These shifts may be responses to changes in individual, internal and external systems which individuals are highly sensitive to when compared with individuals in other professions. This may be due to the cognitive and highly social aspects of their work and would be considered analogous to the work performance of a politician or an academic. The marble and the bowl analogy serves to illustrate the complexity of each individual's relationship with an organization and how this affects attempts to bring about predictable changes in processes and behaviours.

Understanding of the principles and behaviours of strange attractors may also prove to be very useful in business if companies want to avoid business failures (Willis 2001). Complexity has important implications for current mainstream notions of leadership including the idea of leadership as a strange attractor.

Fractals in organizations

A number of writers believe that fractals have a direct application for the management of organizations, and that the best organizations have fractal qualities. It is suggested that these are organizations that have strongly shared guiding principles and shared codes of behaviour and practice which appear at every level. In a fractal organization employees throughout may exhibit similar behaviours although these may have different degrees or levels of emphasis. If, for example, the organization has a shared ethos of trust and openness then it is likely that these values will be apparent in everyday activities and reflected in formal systems. Examining an organization from a fractal perspective encourages one to look for repeating patterns and their evidence on different levels and on different scales of space and time. It provides a way of discovering, representing and interpreting the complex non-linear dynamics of an organization in a way that is not achievable by current linear approaches.

Using fractal principles it is possible to see an organization's communications system afresh and to re-energise its flows. Wheatley (1994: 114) gives an example of how to do this when she describes the 'Future Search' conferences she was involved in. Some fifty to seventy people from different areas of an organization were brought together with people from outside groups connected with the company in some way. The delegates to the conference were put into groups and encouraged to create shared visions of the organization's past, present and future. At first lots of information was generated and many rich pictures and scenarios developed as delegates exchanged information on all aspects of the organization's life. Through the conference process new connections and new flows were encouraged. After a few days the delegates self-organized 'weaving all that information into potent visions for the future'. Rather like a fractal where information fed back upon itself creates 'elaborate levels of definition and scaling', the conference needed only some information to feedback and generate richness.

One organization which has made extensive use of fractal concepts is SENCORP. This is a private company, based primarily in the USA, which was founded shortly after World War II. It has three main operating companies. The founding company had its origins in the car industry but now produces pneumatic fastening systems. The second company, which emerged from a collaboration with Johnson and Johnson in the late 1970s and 1980s develops products and services for the medical industry. The third company set up in the late 1980s offers financial services. The company was very successful until the late 1970s when it started to face a range of challenges emanating from uncertainties in the world's economy. The management of the company decided that in order to sustain its success it needed to develop new insights and processes. Thus during the early 1980s it began to experiment with a range of ideas as it looked for a new management model.

The new model emerged over time from years of discussion and reflection and was based on three distinctive characteristics, which are as follows:

1   The development of a management model that could apply to the whole organization and which was based on analyses of the behaviour of individuals in the company. This aspect of the model draws on concepts of autopoiesis and complex adaptive systems.
2   The integration of everyday operational activities with the management of knowledge development. This approach makes it possible for individuals to learn more and build their knowledge base while at the same time handling and improving upon everyday operational activities. This is achieved by ongoing discussions and decision-making concerning a wide range of matters from routine concerns to strategic issues. These take place at all levels of the company.
3   The importance of all employees being able to partake in the dialogue process was considered essential, therefore adequate resources to enable this to take place had to be provided. This ensured that everyone was able to bring their own knowledge and experiences to the process of creating better business practices.

After considerable discussion and experimentation the fractal management model emerged. It is a model based on fractal patterning based on three interacting areas or 'realms'. See Figure 5.1. The A realm is dedicated to decision-making, the communication of these decisions and the equal allocation of resources. All without any controlling mechanisms. The B realm is concerned with thinking and the development of new ideas, new knowledge and new options using discussion, analysis and communication. The C realm is the activity or 'doing' realm. This is the implementation zone where the person responsible for the implementation of new ideas or options decides how best to make them a reality. As Slocum and Frondorf (2003) point out, in traditional organizations most prominence tended to be given to the C realm. Employees were given explicit targets or goals and

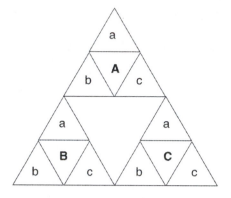

Figure 5.1   Fractal management model at SENCORP (adapted from Slocum and Frondorf 2000: 239)

were monitored for progress by the use of quantitative performance measures. The management of SENCORP considered that thinking time or realm B was neglected in traditional organizations and needed to be given equal prominence with C and A activities. This it was felt would go a long way to engaging employees more successfully in decision-making. Their model provided employees with the time and the resources to think about some of the options presented to them by higher management. The A realm was given the responsibility of ensuring that the balance between realms B and C was maintained.

The model and the reality in which it works uses multiple organizational scales. For example, each of the different realms focuses on different responsibilities in the company, on different levels of detail and on different time frames. C is focused on the short term, whereas B focuses on the medium term and A on the longer term. This basic pattern is repeated throughout the organization from day to day, from on-the-job activities to long-term strategic approaches. Slocum and Frondorf (2003) describe how a president of the company could make a decision that sets a new direction. This is passed on to an employee who has agreed to implement it at the next scale down. This person will create a project designed to think about how best to implement things. This could lead to another project to consider the decision further, or it could lead immediately to an implementation process. Thus the model works at all levels throughout the company. And as Slocum and Frondorf point out, an employee could be involved in a range of projects at different levels and scales. The whole system is based on the activities of individuals and depends for its effectiveness on the free flow of information through all the scales.

The model is based upon describing, and therefore improving, individual decision-making in a business setting. We have identified three distinct respon-sibilities that each individual carries out: to think, to decide, and to act. These are the basic nodes of a system and the information flows between these nodes are the linkages. Therefore, since an organization is an aggregate of individuals (agents in a complex adaptive system), an organization must have the same basic set of responsibilities. Hence the fractal nature of the model.

(Slocum and Frondorf 2000: 238)

SENCORP over a number of years experimented with a range of ideas and activities. All of these were designed to impact on the company and to introduce changes that would facilitate its successful survival in the business world. It was in effect a major strategic change programme but it was developed in a novel way that drew on ideas recognizably based on complexity. I have chosen to discuss it in most detail in the section on fractals as the structure and processes that emerged from these changes is powerfully fractal. It should not be forgotten, however, that it provides a good example of how to consider an organization as a complex adaptive system and how to take a fresh approach to strategic change.

New approaches to strategic change

There are major implications for strategic change and strategic activities when one considers them from a complexity perspective. The traditional view of organizations tends to see them as machine-like, if not exactly machines. They are viewed as entities that are controllable, or, if not controllable, then 'directable', if the right systems and procedures are in place and being correctly practised. It is a view that is strongly held, even in many modern and apparently progressive companies. Strategic planning is seen as a key way of preparing for the future and of delivering a series of expected outputs and outcomes. Huge amounts of time, effort and expense goes into the collection of data for analysis and interpretation in order to produce plans and forecasts for the future. Further, strategic planning and strategic activity are often separated out from each other and become only loosely connected exercises. Complexity sees organizations as dynamic, unpredictable and non-linear. Therefore a complexity perspective suggests that many of these current approaches have little real value.

In Chapter 4 reference was made to the work of Carlisle and McMillan (2002) who point out that a number of strategy researchers have begun to recognize that many approaches to strategy are at odds with the world of modern organizations. There is recognition that small changes in organizations can, over time, be highly significant and produce large variations in outcome, and that not all cause and effect relationships are constant. They make a comparison between a traditional Newtonian–Cartesian paradigm view of strategy and a complexity view of strategy. This was summarized in Table 4.2 which listed some of the stereotypical approaches of both views.

Carlisle and McMillan propose that a Newtonian–Cartesian perspective considers organizations as being essentially mechanistic with controllable moving parts that may be 'fixed' or replaced as needed. A complexity paradigm perspective, however, sees organizations as dynamic, living systems with self-organizing attributes which are not controllable. The classical model is essentially a linear one which is reflected in the use of hierarchical layered structures. Dynamical systems, however, are seen as essentially non-linear and non-hierarchical. Carlisle and McMillan consider that the machine model is essentially an artificial construct that does not mirror the realities of a complex, complicated, constantly changing world. In their view, it can only exist in theory whereas complex, dynamical, living systems are real evolved systems.

In Carlisle and McMillan's view a complexity perspective would suggest that there are many advantages to being highly networked and highly connected. Complex adaptive systems, such as ant and termite colonies, are highly connected working together in a networked fashion. This gives them an in-built flexibility and adaptability that centralized and loosely connected organizations find difficult to achieve. It also enables them to be very effective at handling a variety of situations without any central controlling mechanisms.

Table 4.2 also compares the Newtonian–Cartesian desire for uniformity with the complexity desire for diversity. It is common practice that when organizations merge or are taken over then the dominant one expects the lesser one to conform to its organizational norms. One common example of this is the wearing of the company uniform, whether informal or formal, and the use of strong pressures to merge cultures. From a complexity perspective, diversity is absolutely necessary for survival as it facilitates and encourages learning and adaption. All too often changes are planned on an $A + B = C$ basis, as classical notions of cause and effect mislead managers into thinking that changes can be made and outcomes predicted in a simple linear fashion. A complexity perspective suggests that managers should instead consider the range and pattern of the effects that are taking place and try to work with them rather than trying to predict events. Understanding of sensitive dependence on initial conditions and the behaviours of strange attractors could prove very helpful in this.

● A complexity perspective believes that it is important to consider the organization as a whole. Thus strategy and strategic activities should take a holistic approach that embraces all aspects of an organization including its underpinning design principles, it values and core belief systems. Thinking and action should be as one and not put into separate structural functions or distinct and different processes. The phenomenon of emergence suggests that an organization operates best as an emergent whole. ●

The complexity paradigm takes a much broader strategic perspective than the one suggested by the typical Newtonian–Cartesian world view. It acknowledges that it is not possible to offer objective explanations for all the phenomena observed. Not everything can be precisely measured nor quantified. It suggests that, alongside the seeking of objective explanations for events in organizations and business, less tangible and more subjective explanations should also be considered and valued for the insights they may offer.

> Strategy with a focus on 'entity' tends to concerns itself with tangible, concrete, discrete attainments. A complexity perspective considers strategy as a constantly unfolding, flowing process that is not content or output driven.

Influenced by fractal geometry, it seeks to understand and explain things by looking for and interpreting patterns rather than seeking for matches and correlations. •

(Carlisle and McMillan 2002: 4)

The classical scientific perspective on evolution viewed it as a gradual incremental process and this has had a major influence on the thinking on strategic change. Recent evolutionary research, however, has discovered that there were massive explosions in the number and range of species on earth and also massive extinctions. We now know that life on earth developed both incrementally and also with huge and unexpected leaps. This has important implications for strategic thinking and contrasts sharply with many conventional approaches.

Stacey (1992) suggests that successful and innovative organizations adopt a different approach from the dominant ones. These organizations develop a strategy for change which draws on what is currently happening in the organization and what has happened in the past. They focus on irregularities in the present in order to create fresh perspectives on the past and the present. This means exploring problems and opportunities in a new way – a way that looks for potential and possibility. According to Stacey (1992) it was this approach that enabled Federal Express to develop a more effective delivery system.

Nonaka's (1988) ideas on strategic change are based on his observations of transformation or self-renewal in Japanese firms. He suggests how an understanding of chaos theory may be used to transform an organization. Scientific chaos may be created by events in the external environment or intentionally by the organization itself in order to renew it. An organization using chaos to transform itself deliberately generates internal chaos but linked to the external environment. This approach is a far cry from traditional incremental processes.

Nonaka proposes the following actions to generate such self-renewal:

1   The creation of chaos: this may be generated by the presentation of a strategic vision that is deliberately ambiguous. This offers broad direction and plenty of scope for many different interpretations or ambiguity. This then encourages creativity within the organization and the more passionate and aroused people are by the strategic vision, then the longer they will be energized to create ideas and information designed to solve the ambiguities. Additionally, managers should ensure that new information is continuously entering the organization. This will create fluctuations, as will the use of new technologies and networking with customers and other organizations. Thus the two chief ways of creating chaos or fluctuations are essentially strategy driven, but Nonaka considers that an organization by its structure, design and processes can encourage and allow managers to be challenging and creative. It should aim to encourage movement between areas and roles, involve everyone in discussions and dialogue throughout the organization regardless of status, and allow experimentation.

2   Amplification of fluctuation: this process seeks to stimulate the creative activities of an organization by the creation of a crisis. This should stimulate new ideas and approaches though in some cases it can lead to a company's disappearance. Nonaka quotes a manager from Honda who states that such an approach is like putting the people on the second floor and telling them to jump, or else. This example seems to be pushing the concept to an unacceptable extreme. It may work in the Japanese context but would it transfer successfully to the Western World?

3   The stimulation of problem solving by encouraging vibrant co-operation within the organization: this process encourages employees to change their point of view and when this happens dynamic co-operation can emerge. The key to encouraging this co-operation is the use of self-organizing teams sponsored and protected by senior management.

4   The first three processes were designed to promote active information creation. The fourth process is concerned with changing accumulated information into knowledge. In Nonaka's view if an organization is to evolve and change then it must continue to learn.

The edge of chaos – the edge of innovation

It is important to understand that the edge of chaos is not an exact spot or an edge like the edge of a cliff. It an area composed of flows of order and disorder. It is rather like a vibrant planetary sea that is influenced by the gravitational forces of two large planetary neighbours. One is the planet of Far from Equilibrium where all is utter confusion and disorder. The other is the planet of Equilibrium where the order is so complete that nothing disturbs it. It is a lifeless planet. The sea of the edge of chaos is influenced by both these powerful planets but is never pulled into the gravitational 'tide' of either. What does this mean for organizations?

Complexity considers that organizations are complex adaptive systems thus notions of the edge of chaos are highly relevant. When a system is poised on the edge of chaos it is neither too rigid so that is ossifies and dies, nor too chaotic such that it disintegrates into disorder and anarchy. When a system is in this situation its systems are neither coupled too tightly, nor too loosely. This is highly important, for if a system is too tight then any major change in one part of the system will impact significantly on the rest of the system. This means that any perturbation or major event anywhere in the system, or even outside it will have a profound effect on the whole. This can be so profound that it could lead to an over random, over dynamic, deeply turbulent state. On the other hand, if couplings in the system are weak then there is little chance of change and the whole system is unable to respond when necessary.

Waldrop (1994) reports on a conversation with Doyne Farmer on the notion of the edge of chaos. Farmer cites some examples. He refers to the Soviet Stalinist system which was so rigid and so tightly controlled that it became too stagnant and locked in to survive. Similarly in the 1970s the big American car manufacturers had become so large and were so locked into doing things in certain ways that they failed to see the challenges coming from the Japanese, less still respond to them. Thus to be located and behaving as an organization or a system too close to equilibrium is very unhealthy and survival is hazardous. On the other hand, to be located too close to non-equilibrium is equally threatening and unhealthy. Farmer states that anarchy and laissez-faire approaches are not likely to work either and cites the anarchy in the Soviet Union after its break up and a savings and loan disaster in the US:

> healthy economies and healthy societies alike have to keep order and chaos in balance – not just a wishy-washy, average, middle-of-the-road kind of balance, either. Like a living cell, they have to regulate themselves with a dense web of feedbacks and regulation, at the same time that they leave plenty of room for creativity, change, and response to new conditions. ... The dynamics of complexity at the edge of chaos ... seems to be ideal for this kind of behavior.
> (Waldrop 1994: 294)

In designing organizations and organization systems complexity suggests that we need to learn how to balance them on the edge of chaos. Merry (1995) also suggests that if things are too tightly controlled then an organization does not benefit any more than if it is too loosely connected. Should an organization go into a chaotic state then people work at cross purposes and the organization fails to be effective. In Merry's view an organization balanced on the edge of chaos has sufficient freedom for creativity, entrepreneurship, experimentation and risk taking to emerge. There is ongoing change, but there is a dynamic balance so that the organization does not tip over into massive confusion and uncertainty.

When Ricardo Semler (1989) created a new set of values for his company to work for they led to an experimental and challenging way of running an organization. Thus he encouraged his company to move closer to the edge of chaos. As a result of this complex, interactive, new cycle of activities an innovative company emerged. Gareth Morgan (quoted by Pickard 1996) comments: 'Innovation emerges. ...You cannot create innovation by having an innovation programme. Semler recognizes that, and what he has done is a good example of a new order emerging out of chaos – none of that was planned.' The inference is that innovation is not something that one can readily bring about in a preconceived way. Rather it is one of the properties that may emerge from a complex range of activities that unsettle traditional norms.

Complex adaptive systems learn to live on the edge of chaos by constantly learning, exploring and adapting to changes in their circumstances. This means that learning has a major role to play in enabling a system to exist successfully at the edge of chaos. Thus if an organization wants to exist at the edge of chaos and enjoy the rewards that this may bring it needs to be a stimulating, challenging and constantly changing environment. It needs to be a dynamic environment where learning is encouraged, but where there are strong frameworks to ensure that there is not too much novelty and surprise. These frameworks may be strongly shared organizational values, or human resource systems that underpin personal development and employee support. Other frameworks might include recognizable management structures that are effective, flexible and responsive and which play an integral role in the organization's dynamics.

There has been recognition of the importance of an organization existing on the edge of chaos outside complexity writing. Kanter (1990) writing on Apple Computers and Kodak in the 1980s, describes two very different companies, almost at opposite ends of a spectrum of organizational difference. Kodak was mature, traditional, hierarchical and very large. It lacked energy, flexibility and responsiveness. Apple by way of contrast was very new, very confident, very dependent on its bright ideas. It lacked a clear organizational structure resulting in poor decision making and unclear lines of responsibility. Kodak was too tightly constrained whereas Apple was a free for all. Neither would have flourished as they were without massive changes. As Kanter points out, an approach was needed that married the best aspects of the two ways of organization. This approach would keep the best features of the entrepreneurial and creative spirit but blend it with discipline and teamwork. As Kanter (1990: 32) writes, something was needed, 'something that helps loosely managed companies get a little tighter and tightly controlled companies loosen up'. This was a recipe that maps onto complexity notions of the edge of chaos.

One way to encourage an organization to live on the edge of chaos is to focus on individuals and their need to be working in the edge of chaos 'sea'. What does living at the edge of chaos mean for the individual? It is well known that lack of stimulation and activity can lead to mental and physical decline in a person. Too little activity can lead to apathy and lack of real interest. A good example of this is someone who is retired and who lacks a range of interests and a supportive network of friends and relatives. At the other extreme an individual who has too much going on in their life is also at risk. There are many well-documented sources of stress and not all are negative. But if a person has too much happening in their life such as overwhelming problems at work and family or personal problems too, then it is a recipe for breakdown. The happy, well-balanced individual who has supportive moral and ethical frameworks, good personal relationships and a challenging and fulfilling range of activities is living in the 'sea' of the edge of chaos. Occasionally a traumatic life event may push him or her towards the far from equilibrium zone and nearer to disintegration. But useful life skills and helpful people support will enable them to return to the edge of chaos again.

Knowing this managers can be aware of how much stimulation is needed in the workplace to keep creativity and interest levels high. A manager who sets impossible and unrealistic deadlines in working situations that are already in danger of overload stands a good chance of pushing the employee into a highly stressed and ultimately unproductive state. People in such situations may make serious mistakes, fall back on old routines, and make poor decisions. In such situations there is very little chance of any innovation emerging. However, the proper use of project work and the setting of realistic yet challenging tasks allied to realistic but challenging deadlines can stimulate real creativity and bring out the innovative imagination in people.

Living at the edge of chaos has many advantages for an organization for it is a good position to be in when the world is always changing. This is because it can always experiment with different ways of doing things and try them out, and so avoid becoming stuck in one particular way of being. Organizations that become too formalized and too rigid struggle to survive in a changing world, as did, for example, the large bureaucracies at the end of the twentieth century. Similarly those organizations that were too disordered and had too little structure or under-pinning processes, like many of the dot com companies, also failed to survive. Oticon the Danish hearing care company, mentioned earlier, had all the typical strengths and weaknesses of a well-established hierarchical organization when Lars Kolind became chief executive in 1988. Its top management had been in control for some thirty years and was typically reactive, concerned with maintaining the status quo and dedicated to stifling disagreement and differences of opinion. Engineering was the dominant ethos and technology was paramount. It had three major functional areas and there was limited contact and communications between them. They were operating as an organization close to equilibrium. The result was that the company's research and development activities were not flourishing and it was focusing too much on the traditional, 'behind the ear' hearing aid market, when the growing market was for 'in the ear' hearing devices (Larsen 2000). First Kolind introduced a range of traditional changes to improve things. He cut costs dramatically and took all power in his own hands. These were necessary but short-term measures. Then in 1990 he announced that the company had to: 'think the unthinkable'. He dramatically restructured, introduced project team working on which the whole organization became based, empowered his employees and gave them increased responsibilities. His radical restructuring and new thinking moved the company away from equilibrium and more towards non-equilibrium. As a result the organization turned around very quickly.

> Thus, it demonstrated its innovative potential by re-vitalizing important, but 'forgotten' development projects, that, when implemented in the production of new hearing aids, produced significant financial results, essentially saving the firm from bankruptcy, as well as by turning out a number of new strong products.
>
> (Foss 2000: 10)

Pascale *et al.* (2000) describe how British Petroleum's exploration unit (BPX) was moved to the creative edge of chaos by a new managing director, John Browne. Browne came into an organization that was very low in the league tables. It had failed to find any major new oilfields in the last twenty years, was overstaffed, under-energized and full of unco-operative groups. When Browne was appointed in 1989 there had been a series of important changes in the global oil exploration field and there was everything to play for. The winners would be those with the best diplomatic and negotiating skills, the best technical expertise and the best business skills. BPX was not well placed to achieve this as every aspect of the organization was working in a way that was contradictory to what was needed.

First of all Browne brought a hundred of the top managers together to announce that he was to carry out some standard cost-cutting and slim down the unit. Then he divided the managers into groups and had them explore the current situation in relation to the Seven-S framework. As the day progressed the discussion became more intense and more involving. More time was allocated so that people had to rearrange journeys home, change appointments and so on. Browne was sending an important message – that things were going to be different from now on. In other words, he was starting to push against equilibrium and bring in new norms. At the end of this session there was recognition that every aspect of the BPX way of working was contradictory to what was needed if the unit was to be successful. Things had to change. Browne continued to turn up the heat and brought his top eight officers together to distil the issues down to nine major challenges. Then he arranged for 120 staff to assemble to discuss how they would address these problems. This was an organization that worked to very long time scales. Browne gave them six weeks' notice of the meeting at a very busy time of year and in so doing was challenging and disturbing the normal balance or pattern of the organization.

The groups who came together to address the issues came from all sections of the unit and all roles. After three days they presented their findings and Browne told them to proceed with their ideas and to produce their recommendations within ninety days. This dictat seriously disturbed the organization as managers unused to working on such issues struggled to create the time and space to do so. In order to meet Browne's deadline they were forced to re-examine their own roles and to consult and delegate to more junior staff. This involved people at more junior levels in the heightened activity. The papers were presented and discussed, debated and chewed over six weeks later. As a result of his turning up of the temperature at BPX Browne was able to turn the unit around.

> Utilizing the simple devices of (1) overloading the organization beyond its business-as-usual carrying capacity, (2) using deadlines, public scrutiny, and other action-forcing events to sustain disequilibrium, and (3) identifying adaptive challenge (but not stepping in to save the organization from it), Browne amplified disequilibrium and moved his organization out of its frozen state. Damping mechanisms such as milestones, resourcing, and deliverables brought closure at the end of the process.
>
> (Pascale *et al*. 2000: 101)

Using self-organization to free up people and energies

As already described in Chapter 2, living self-organizing systems are ubiquitous and highly effective in the natural world, but how can notions of self-organization and the use of self-organizing principles assist organizations especially in transforming themselves?

Morgan (1993) considers the random way in which termites self-organize to build their complex, free-form nests offers inspiration for developing a new approach to strategic management and change. The termites do not work to any predetermined plan, but are opportunistic and spontaneous, guided by an overall sense of purpose and direction. In Morgan's view the behaviour of these termites suggests that managers leading a change process should have clear visions of what it is they want to achieve, but should not try to attain them by the traditional methods of directing and controlling people. Instead managers should encourage and allow people to find their own ways of making the visions real. They should wait for positive and useful outcomes to emerge from the changing situation.

The way in which insect societies self-organize to their advantage has been used in a number of organizations to great effect. Anderson and Bartholdi (2000: 92) point out that insect societies are 'just as much an economy as any factory and importantly, face the same logistical challenges'. Just like human organizations they have to compete for resources and live and work in an environment that is unpredictable and subject to great changes. Anderson and Bartholdi provide a number of examples of how organizations have successfully adopted the self-organizing techniques of social insects.

One example describes how Revco Drugstores (now CVS) achieved a 34 per cent increase in its order-pickers' throughput at its national distribution centre by using self-organizing principles. They did this by changing from a centralized scheme to one based on bucket brigades where the work is shared on a self-organizing basis. This removed the need for planning and management controls. Bucket brigades follow the same principles as social ants when collecting food. For example, an ant furthest from the nest finds a source of seeds and carries a seed in the direction of the colony's nest until it meets another ant closer to the nest. The seed is transferred to this ant while the first ant returns to the seed source. The second ant carries the seed towards the nest until it meets another ant. The seed is again passed on with ant two returning towards the seed pile. The third ant carries the seed towards the nest until it meets another ant, and so on, until the seed arrives at the colony's nest.

This method of working also has been observed at work on assembly lines and 'it can be shown empirically, and proven mathematically, that workers spontaneously gravitate to the optimal division of work so that throughput is maximized'. Additionally, 'production is more flexible, agile, and robust than other forms of work organization, ... because the assembly line spontaneously rebalances itself to account for disruptions or changes in work' (Anderson and Bartholdi 2000: 94).

The use of self-organizing principles has been used effectively in other industrial situations. Berreby (1996) describes the paint-spraying operation at a General Motors (GM) plant in Fort Wayne, and cites it as a way in which complexity theory is being effectively used in business. The booths which are set up to spray the trucks different colours as they roll off the assembly line, are not centrally controlled. Each is allowed to bid for each painting job as it comes up. The bids they put in reflect their availability and the associated costs of carrying out a particular painting job. By using an approach which reflects the way in which complex self-organizing systems work GM has saved some $1,500,000 a year.

John Deere, in the USA, is the world's largest manufacturer of farm machinery. It too uses some ideas from complexity to organize it assembly lines. It does so in order to offer its customers a greater variety of products while keeping costs down (Roberts 1998). Roberts describes how the assembly line system is divided into twelve modules or teams of workers, each responsible for building a particular part of the entire product. Each module leader is responsible for budgets, overseeing staffing and costs. There is a considerable flow of information on all aspects of the production process so that the team is able to plan ahead and anticipate how best to organize their work. Most day-to -day decision making is made by the assembly workers. They are given considerable authority, information and incentives to do this. The company remunerates its workers according to the number and the quality of the machines they produce. Thus each team has two guiding principles: to make as many machines as possible and to make them of a high quality. This ensures that members of the team self-organize in support of their guiding principles and to achieve a common purpose – a large pay packet.

Studies on the way birds self-organize into flocks have shown that they communicate by a method known as receiver-based communication or RBC. RBC means that individual birds let others in the flock know what they are doing in a very open way and the receivers of the information decide how to respond to it. Decision-making responses are all based on the group's shared purpose. This may be to return to their usual roosting site or to look for new food sources. The US Air Force, for example, has used this procedure to allow its pilots to co-ordinate their behaviour in situations where there was an absence of ground control. The pilots talked to one another and responded preferentially to those nearest to them. Thus they achieved a collective co-ordination similar to that achieved by birds flocking.

Battram (1996) gives an example of how self-organizing principles can be used in an organization to great effect using RBC. He describes how Rank Zerox used this method to improve the service in their photocopier workshops. All the repair engineers were given 'walkie talkie' sets permanently open to receive messages. At first they tended to gossip. Then after some time they began to share problems and ideas and positive feedback loops were established. There were significant improvements in productivity because the engineers were able to self-organize and spread good practice. They did this by using their own informal network, and this was made possible by the use of RCB and their 'walkie talkie' communication system.

In Stacey's (1996a) view self-organization is a process whereby a number of individual agents spontaneously get together and co-operate in a co-ordinated way while at the same time sharing common behaviours. In organizations self-organization will often take the form of groups of people getting together and forming unexpected and unplanned groups. Often these groups will be formed as a response to a specific problem or issue. The groups will operate as teams communicating and co-operating with each other as they respond to the issue. A key word in this description is 'spontaneous'. Stacey's view of self-organization builds upon recognition that in human society all kinds of formal and informal groups spontaneously arise and organize themselves often creating a network of contacts. They do not arise as part of some thought out plan or process but as a kind of natural response to events in the world around them. The development of the internet is an example of this, as is the development of the high-tech industries in Silicon Valley and the fashion industry in north Italy.

Self-organizing principles may be used in a variety of organizational types as Pascale *et al.* (2000) point out. They refer to the self-organizing attributes of companies as different as the volunteer organizations like Greenpeace and The Sierra Club, and direct-sales organizations such as Avon and Tupperware. These concerns all use self-organization in practical ways in order to operate successfully. Pascale *et al.* cite how the US Army makes use of self-organization and how large multinationals like Monsanto and BP have harnessed effectively aspects of self-organization. In their view if an organization wants to use the twin attributes of self-organization and emergence then they need to pay attention to two points. First of all they need to increase the number of nodes in the organization's network. This they can do, as John Browne did at BPX, by having large meetings and involving many more people than would usually be involved in such discussions. Second, they should seek to improve the quality and number of connections in the organization. This would be achieved by bringing together people so that they gain a better understanding of the organization and by improving contacts across functions and across all levels.

The use of self-organizing teams is one practical way in which self-organization can be introduced into organizations. Nonaka (1988) sees the creation of self-organizing teams as essential to enabling organizational transformation and envisages members of these teams competing with each other in creating information and devising new concepts. It is important, however, not to confuse self-organizing teams with self-managed or empowered teams. Stacey (1996) lists seven ways in which self-managed teams differ from self-organized teams and these definitions are used to analyze the nature of the New Directions teams in the case study of the Open University.

Johnson (1996) provides an example which in his view illustrates the principles of self-organizing systems when he describes how staff at the Open University produce multi-media teaching and learning materials. He describes how academic staff usually self-organize into course teams to produce courses which they find interesting. The team usually starts out as the result of a chance encounter between two or three academics who become energized about shared interests and then invite other staff to join them in putting a course together.

Prahalad and Hamel (1990) describe how some self-organizing organizations have structured themselves around core competencies and so avoid rigid or permanent structures. Skills, tasks, groups and projects emerge in response to a need and when the need changes, so does the structure of the organization. Such an organization is able to respond more quickly to new opportunities and is guided by its own competencies.

One very early example of the use of self-organizing principles was their use by Dee Hock in the late 1970s. As chief executive officer of Visa, Hock used the principles of self-organization to revive its fortunes. Self-organization may arise in many forms in an organization, in temporary teams, or in underpinning and ongoing practical principles, or as part of strategic approaches and the deliberate creation of turbulence and the conditions for emergence.

> Visa represents self-organization in almost a pure form. Its decentralized structure relies almost exclusively on self-interest as the primary incentive. The transactional nature of members' relationship to the clearing center and to one another suffices to cause the right things to happen and the simplest structures to prevail.
>
> (Pascale *et al.* 2000: 129)

If we use ideas based on self-organization in organizations, then we should create organizations that are better able to deal with instability and uncertainty in creative and innovative ways that enhance survival possibilities. For example, the Ford Motor Company was changed from a loss-making one to a more profitable one and not by the implementation of some major strategic plan. The changes came about as a large number of separate initiatives for change came together and built up into a major movement The various initiatives included employee participation teams, multidisciplinary teams, and various informal groups set up to challenge the bureaucracy and bring down barriers to change. Various task forces were also set up and there was extensive use of training and development programmes (Stacey 1996a).

I would argue that the use of self-organizing principles instead of controlling ones frees people up to act in ways that are both creative and constructive. Instead of trying to inhibit and overly control natural self-organizing tendencies managers should try to work with these notions and create the right conditions for the development of self-organizing groups and the emergence of a self-organizing movement. These ideas are explored further in the next chapters when the New Directions Programme at the Open University is considered.

The organization as a complex adaptive organization

Complexity tells us that societies, organizations and individuals are complex adaptive systems and therefore have the ability to transform themselves in order to adapt to changing circumstances. This does not mean, however, that this transformational ability is always put to use. Certain environments can constrain and inhibit the use of the behaviours necessary for such adaption to constantly take place.

It is learning which sets complex adaptive systems apart from other complex and complicated systems. It is this aspect which determines their aliveness. Complex adaptive systems are self-organizing systems, but they are different. A self-organizing sand pile does not learn and adapt, but a human self-organizing team does. Here is a major difference. Stacey (1996a) emphasizes the importance of learning as a feature of complex adaptive systems and points out that human systems are adaptive because they engage in double-loop rather than single-loop learning.

In an earlier section in this chapter notions of how organizations might exist on the edge of chaos were explored with reference to complex adaptive systems. Complex adaptive systems are able to live on the edge of chaos and they do this by constantly learning, exploring and adapting to changes in their circumstances. This is where they belong and where they flourish. However, as this section explained, not all individuals nor organizations are able to constantly flourish on the edge of chaos. Certain conditions may help a complex adaptive system to fulfil its potential, others will not, and the system may move into many places on the spectrum between equilibrium and far from equilibrium during its lifetime. A complex adaptive system is only truly adaptive and creative when it is living on the edge of chaos.

Another important feature of complex adaptive systems is that they have emergent properties. These systems are able to create emergent outcomes through a process of spontaneous self-organization. As explained in the section on self-organization, a number of self-organizing interactions can produce a range of outcomes which together create something new and unexpected. Something which is not readily explained when its constituent parts are separately analyzed. Thus emergence is a feature of complex, adaptive systems and it often leads to the creation of new, often more sophisticated and complex forms which arise out of the myriad activities of complex systems.

Another highly significant feature of a complex adaptive system is that it can anticipate the future based on its own internal models. It suggests a complex, dynamic learning web linked to experience, the history of the individual or group or species, observation and reflection and imagination. Thus the development of a complex adaptive system in an organization is intimately linked to the organization's culture, values and history and its own internal view of itself. This may serve to encourage and facilitate further complex learning or to hinder it.

What does this mean for organizations? Lewin and Regine (1999) make it quite clear that they consider organizations to be complex adaptive systems and that, by understanding and learning all about these systems, organizations can learn a great deal about their own dynamics. Further, if companies are to survive in today's fast-changing world then they will need to be constantly innovating, constantly adapting, and continually evolving. In other words, they will need to behave as complex adaptive systems operating on the edge of chaos. For Lewin and Regine the issue is how to ensure that businesses are able to nurture the underlying processes that will enable them to fulfil their potential as complex adaptive systems. They acknowledge that sometimes the mechanistic approach to organizations can be appropriate in contexts where there is very little uncertainty and business destinations are clear and this model worked well in the industrial age economies. However, in the information age such approaches are likely to push an organization towards equilibrium or stasis so that adaptivity is impeded. Thus they suggest that organizations need to find ways of encouraging and enhancing their creative potential as complex adaptive systems. They list a number of ways in which organizations can seek to achieve this.

1   People interact and mutually affect each other and this leads to emergence. Thus businesses should recognize and look after relationships amongst individuals, groups and companies.

2   Practices in organizations tend to become rules. An organization's practices should be few in number and they should be guided by shared values.

3   The use of small-scale experiments is a better way to introduce changes rather than the introduction of fast large-scale interventions.

4   Managers should not try to plan strategic goals in detail but should focus instead on creating the right environment for emergence. To do this they should encourage the development of teams and encourage creativity with a focus on evolutionary rather than designed solutions to problems. Additionally, any existing hierarchical central controlling mechanisms should be replaced by a flat organizational structure and distributed influences.

5   People diversity is key to the creation of richer patterns of interactivity, leading, for example, to enhanced creativity.

They provide a number of examples of organizations which have managed to do this. One company that exhibits many of the features listed by Lewin and Regine is St Lukes the highly successful UK advertising and communications company. It is an organization, which has built itself on 'invisible' structures – values and moral principles, and it has abandoned the traditional linear organizational form and adopted a project team approach to delivering its services. The company is owned by all its employees, so that each is a co-shareholder. It has an organizational structure based on three core but interconnected notions. These are:

- Vision – The company's vision is 'to open minds' and this is explored by the chairman, the chief operating officer and the finance director.
- Value – The company is given value by creating imaginative products for its clients.
- Values – The company believes that everyone's values as well as the values of St Lukes need to be cherished and it is the role of QUEST trustees to make sure this happens.

QUEST is a key part of the company structure and it stands for Qualifying Share Ownership Trust. Its six trustees are voted in by all the employees on an annual basis. QUEST is not only responsible for the company's shareholding scheme but for overall policy guidance. The co-founder and chairman, Andy Law (1999: 133) describes how the trustees 'maintain the values of the company which are an aggregation of the personal values of everyone – freedom of expression and thought, lack of coercion and fear, and a determination to make work fun'.

Pascale *et al.* (2000) describe how Sears, the giant US retailer, lost its market share in the 1970s and 1980s and revived its flagging fortunes by moving nearer to the edge of chaos and enabling itself to operate for a while as a healthy complex adaptive system. A new chairman, Arthur Martinez, when he took over saw that the company was in an equilibrium state and set out to disturb things. He did this by using a wide range of approaches including moving responsibilities down the organization, challenging his top executives to face up to the company's failures, setting business targets that could not be achieved using traditional practices, and building teams of managers trained and energized to push through rafts of changes. He called big meetings of all the sales staff in the company's stores, involving some two-thirds of the company's 300,000 employees. Teams at these meetings were given the task of improving customer retention and asked to make suggestions as to how best to achieve this. By the mid-1990s the company's fortunes had revived and Martinez was awarded a gold medal by the National Retail Federation for his work at Sears.

But, as Pascale *et al.* point out, although Martinez acted in many ways that moved the company to the edge of chaos and enabled it to flourish for a time as a complex adaptive system, he and his senior team did not view the company as a living system. This meant that they did not appreciate that it could drift back towards equilibrium again. Further, although Martinez carried out a range of actions that resonate with living systems theory, he did not appear to see that ultimately he needed to extensively use the collective intelligence of front-line sales staff if the company was to remain successful.

> The Martinez era came to a close with more of a whimper than a bang. But this much is clear: Sears, whatever its future, is very much a complex adaptive system. It reflects (1) the ever shifting struggle between equilibrium and innovation and (2) the unending tension between the preserving forces of tradition and the transforming forces of change.
>
> (Pascale *et al.* 2000: 57)

Stacey (1996a) suggests that organizations operating as healthy complex adaptive systems do have a special kind of order which they create themselves. There is no mission statement nor a charismatic leader involved in achieving this, it arises spontaneously. These systems are spontaneous, emergent and creative and also very paradoxical. They are paradoxical because they are both competitive and co-operative. Self-organizing teams given the freedom to behave as they wish can explore areas normally that would be considered out of bounds as either too contentious, too politically sensitive or whatever. This enables them to explore a wide range of issues and to create and consider innovative and exciting options for handling them. This opens the windows to radical new visions of the future. As the teams explore options for the future in an unhindered way so they learn and adapt to the ongoing changes they have stimulated and those which have arisen from other sources within the organization. They develop into complex adaptive teams and out of all this emerges enormous creative potential for the teams and an organization. When a team is working as a complex adaptive system it works together so that something else emerges, perhaps what is often called 'team spirit'. These are themes that are further considered in the next chapters.

6 Changing the Open University – a case study

All these changes have brought a new style with them befitting an established institution. The links with the past are necessarily severed; and the memory of early struggles fades. This is as it should be, for there are new struggles to be faced, no easier and no less challenging than those that have already been met.

(Perry 1976: 287)

This chapter focuses on the detailed story of the main case study in this book: the New Directions change programme at the Open University (OU). The first section describes the UK's Open University which is the setting for the case study. Thus this section is primarily descriptive in order to provide background and context. It outlines the history, structure and culture of the University and sets the stage for the launch of the programme. The next section describes the programme, its birth and development, and the range of activities that it undertook or was associated with, within its organizational context. The chapter then moves on to consider the programme as an innovative learning process for change, reviewing some of the underlying processes and principles at work with particular reference to the 1994 conference, the work of the volunteer teams and the emergence of a democratic strategic action plan. It also reviews briefly the evidence presented in the light of the strategic change models discussed in Chapter 4, especially the learning organization model.

This chapter is a necessary stepping stone to Chapter 7 which looks at how the New Directions programme consciously and unconsciously used ideas from complexity science to disturb the equilibrium of the university and introduce flows of change.

The primary data in this chapter was derived from interviews, from two questionnaires, one a Likert scaled questionnaire, and two workshops. The secondary data for this chapter was drawn from a range of internal documents including records kept by the training and development unit in the University's personnel division, internal correspondence, diary notes, reports, formal and strategic documents, electronic messages, the conference report, *Open House* – the university newspaper, and various OU publications. Additional secondary data was provided by an Institute for Employment Studies (IES) study (Tamkin and Barber 1998) of the

New Directions Programme. This used interviews, a bipolar semantic differential questionnaire and focus groups.

The Open University

Walter Perry (1976), the university's first Vice-Chancellor, thought that the whole idea of the university was really a political gimmick and that even if it did succeed it would only ever produce a few graduates and they would be of poor quality. But subsequent events and his own energy and commitment were to prove his original views to be very wrong.

The OU was born during the Wilson Labour government and derived from Prime Minister Harold Wilson's notion of a university of the air. It was granted its royal charter in April 1969 and the first students were admitted in 1971. By the mid-1970s there were over 50,000 undergraduates and a wide range of courses of study on offer. It is now (2003) the largest university in the UK with over 200,000 students and customers and it ranks amongst the top universities for the quality of its teaching

The university offers its own high-quality degrees and is open to all adults regardless of qualifications. Its teaching is based on using distance methods that bring learning directly into the homes or workplaces of its students. The use of this approach has meant the development of a wide range of high-quality materials suitable for learning at a distance. These are further enriched by the provision of tutor support, face-to-face, on-line and by telephone, and residential elements.

The OU views research as part of its academic lifeblood and an essential basis for the production of excellent teaching materials. In the 2001 Research Assessment Exercise (RAE) the University achieved top of the scale ratings for international research excellence in four areas. Across another twenty-one subjects the university's profile was one of national excellence.

The university offers a wide range of undergraduate courses including BA and BSc degree programmes and a range of taught higher degrees as well as the research-based degrees of BPhil, MPhil and PhD. In addition to its graduate and postgraduate programmes the university provides professional training in the areas of business, manufacturing, computing, education, health and social welfare. A wide range of study packs and short courses are also available.

The university continues to expand its curriculum and, in 1995, modern languages were introduced; in 1997 the university launched it first courses in law. Further, it now offers teaching on an international basis.

Structure and culture

The university is governed by two main bodies: Council and Senate. Council has responsibility for all financial and employment decision-making, while Senate is responsible for all academic matters. The organizational structure is large and complicated with a series of complex sub-structures which continue on down through the layers – see Figure 6.1.

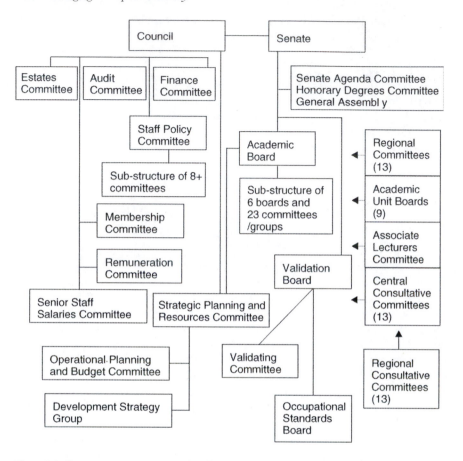

Figure 6.1 Government structure – the Open University (adapted from the *Open University Government Structure Handbook* 7/2000)

The chief executive of the university is the Vice-Chancellor and her senior management team consists of five Pro-Vice-Chancellors (PVCs), the Director of Finance and the University Secretary. The University Secretary heads the administration area of the University which comprises some eight main divisions, each with its own sub-divisions. There are eleven faculties or schools, a Student's Services Division and a huge Learning and Teaching Services division which has its own complex underpinnings that support media development, publishing, rights and warehousing facilities – see Figure 6.2. The university has thirteen regional centres in the UK each headed by a director. The centres are largely responsible for the admission, tuition and counselling of students. The centres appoint and supervise approximately 7,400 associate lecturers who provide tutorial and counselling support.

The organization structure is classical and bureaucratic in form. It is centralized, functionally specialized and hierarchical, and fits well with Fayol's classical

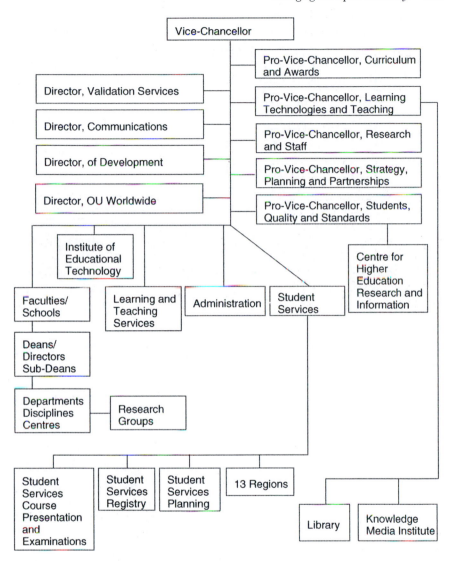

Figure 6.2 The Open University – organizational structure (adapted from the *Open University Government Structure Handbook* 7/2000)

management theory. This form works well in stable conditions, but it is slow to change and in the last decade of the twentieth century the university had to adjust to some major changes.

I have described the formal and official structure of the university, but as with many large bureaucracies there are a number of informal internal networks that survive and enliven the organization. They are often the lifeblood that keeps the organization productive and much of the business of the university is conducted outside the formal structures. Within the faculties the course teams that develop teaching materials are the creative engines for the production of new courses and teaching approaches. Likewise within the administration there are small groups that try to speed up the more cumbersome processes and invent new and creative ways of addressing old problems. There are strong personal relationships and alliances which ignore the traditional structure and oil the wheels of the organization.

The complex, hierarchical and linear nature of the governance and organizational framework of the Open University fits very neatly with Handy's (1993) model of the role culture which is typified by the image of a Greek temple. As Handy points out this type of organization is controlled by the culture of reason, and logic and rationality appear to prevail. This kind of organization can work very well in the right circumstances and it is particularly good where economies of scale are important, as is the case with the university, which needs to mass produce its courses in order to ensure their economic viability. It can also be very effective, as Handy (1993) points out, where the market for its products is stable and predictable and the product has a long life cycle. But the danger comes when the environment changes. Such organizations need stability to flourish. Handy notes too that this kind of organization is slow to see the need for change and slow at responding even when the need is perceived.

Costello (1992) sees the overall culture of the university as consisting of three broad but distinct sub-cultures. The academic areas he sees as the creative areas where small flexible teams usually work for a period of three or so years together to produce a course and then break up.

The second sub-culture Costello identifies is that of the operational and administrative areas. Both have strong bureaucratic structures and cultures. The need to get the job done is paramount and difficulties can arise between those who want to change things and those who have to deal with any consequent organizational implications.

The third broad sub-culture is the regions. Here staff from the academic areas and the administration work very closely. Each region aims to provide a service to the students and they, more than any other area of the university, come into close contact with the student body. The management of the regional centres is a complex one as many senior staff have a dual line of responsibility both to their regional director and to their faculty, and this leads to tensions and even conflict on occasion.

The culture of the Open University is difficult to define in a neat way. It is both complex and complicated, and is possibly even richer and more diverse than the three sub-cultures described by Costello would suggest, and it should be noted that Costello only included managers in his study. Inclusion of all the other many roles, categories and grades would colour even further this already rich picture. Overarching all this and at the same time threading through all aspects of university life are its long held values of openness and democratic participation.

Environmental changes

In 1993 the university's funding arrangements changed significantly when it became part of the newly integrated funding arrangements for higher education in the

UK. Whereas it had previously been funded directly from the Department of Education, from 1993 on it would receive its core grants from the Higher Education Funding Council for England. The HEFCE block grant of £104 million for 1993/4 represented 57.7 per cent of the university's total operating budget of £180.4 million. £58.8 million fee income from students represented 32.6 per cent of the total budget.

The change in the funding arrangements had major implications for the university. First, it meant that the OU was now in direct competition for funds with other universities and competition was likely to be high. Second, for the first time in its history the university was now able to build up some capital reserves. Previously any unspent monies had to be returned to the Department of Education. Under this system the OU had no capital reserves to fall back on in hard times and also no real incentive to save money or to create entrepreneurial income. The new arrangements changed all this. It would now be in the OU's favour to be more businesslike. Further, the way the funding system was now set up meant that if the OU expanded its student numbers then it would attract significantly more income.

The university's external environment had changed in many ways since the 1970s and early 1980s. In those days many higher education institutions had poured scorn on the idea of effective distance teaching. Now, however, their attitude was very different and very many of them, and also many local further education colleges, were offering substantial programmes of distance learning courses. Many potential OU students were being attracted away from the OU to other, often more local, providers. Further, many aspects of traditional distance learning delivery were under challenge from new developments in multi-media teaching and the use of the new technologies. As described in an earlier chapter, significant changes in the environment coupled with its own structures and attitudes resulted in the US shopping giant Sears being left behind its competitors. There was a danger that the OU was about to be left behind too.

Strategic plans

Recognition of all the changes in the OU's external environment was to be reflected in the university's new strategic plan of 1992. It identified the central purposes of the university and set down its strategic aims and goals over the next decade. In early 1993 'Plans for Change', the university's strategic action plan set out the major initiatives which the university would need to take over the coming five years in order to make its strategic plan a reality. It was the template which would guide all the university's departments and by which senior officers were to frame and prioritize their activities.

Most significantly 'Plans for Change' recognized that changes in working practices were needed on a university-wide basis. These were described as six 'new directions'. Each direction sought to change the cumbersome heart of the university's organizational systems and practice (see Appendix 1). Further, these changes required 'all staff to play a full part in the achievement of the university's strategic objectives'. Thus there was recognition at a strategic level of the importance of involving all employees in realizing the university's aims for the future. But how would it achieve this major undertaking? 'Plans for Change' provided an answer. It stated:

> It is intended that the full benefit of these changes of approach will be achieved through a process of awareness raising, staff development and management action at institutional and unit level in which all staff have an opportunity to participate.
>
> (McMillan 1999: 227)

Here lay the core tenets of the programme and its *raison d'être*. This was its legitimate purpose and its role as described by the formal systems of the university.

People

Costello (1992) points to the powerful roles played by the university's three Vice-Chancellors: Walter Perry, John Horlock and John Daniel. Under Perry the university sought to establish itself and to develop new conventions in education. Under Horlock it went through a period of consolidation when, in Costello's view, it became, in many ways, more conventional in its approach and when a more hierarchical system for the management of the university was developed. Then in 1990, after a ten-year period when the university had been experiencing a reduction in its resources, John Daniel was appointed. He brought with him an enthusiasm for distance education and a vision of a much expanded university. Thus there began in the early 1990s a major shift in the university's vision of itself in the future. This was further reinforced by external changes – the change in the funding arrangements, competition from other higher education institutions in an expanded higher education sector and the challenges posed by developments in the new technologies and the emerging notion of knowledge media.

In August 1991 a new Pro-Vice-Chancellor, Strategy, Geoff Peters, was appointed. His appointment coming so closely after the appointment of an energetic and dynamic Vice-Chancellor with a powerful and potent vision of the future for the OU was to have a major impact on the University. Geoff Peters is a key player in the New Directions story.

In 1993 the university had over 3,000 full-time staff. There were approximately 800 academic staff, 500 administrators and 1,200 secretarial and clerical staff. The term administrative staff is in some ways misleading, for as well as significant numbers of staff employed in typical educational administrative tasks there are other professionals. These include accounting, auditing and personnel professionals, computing experts, surveyors, editors, designers, print production and publishing specialists. The university also employs a number of technical staff who are highly skilled in their different fields and several hundred skilled and unskilled manual workers including warehouse packers, gardeners, electricians, plumbers, postal staff and porters.

The New Directions programme 1993–1996

Appendix 2 contains information on all the events and activities that took place in the programme. They are described in chronological order via a diary of events which lists the workshops, briefings and activities for the period concerned.

The story begins – 1993

In January Geoff Peters, PVC, Strategy asked the personnel division for its support in setting up a series of workshops to provide an opportunity for staff consultation over the new 'Plans for Change'. As head of training and development I was thus involved in the programme from the very beginning. This is how I became a participant–observer.

Geoff Peters described how the university needed to double its student numbers over the next ten years and how, at the workshops, he wanted people to explore both the real blocks and the real opportunities to change. He described two major outputs that he was hoping for from the workshops.

1   'People wanting to change, questioning the status quo'.
2   'Insight into attitudes and issues'.

Further, he was looking for feedback from the workshops which he would use to brief his own team, his task groups, and heads of units or divisions. The workshops were designed 'to give staff an understanding of the scope of the change needed, and for staff to tell the university about any problems which our plans pose for them and for their colleagues' (Geoff Peters quoted in *Open House*, April 1994).

It was decided to set up six two-day workshops as soon as possible and to invite some thirty staff to each. Staff from all categories and locations were invited to attend and their names were selected from the internal phone book. In this way it was hoped to have a representative 'diagonal slice' of staff at each workshop. Invitations were sent out and heads of units/departments asked to allow their staff to attend and also to brief them on the university's strategic plans before they attended. Furthermore, they were asked to follow up with a debriefing and to give their support for actions to be taken afterwards.

Six two-day workshops were held in the first half of the year. At first the design of the workshops varied but by the fourth workshop a pattern of process had emerged which was to become the model for later ones. This was follows:

* initial plenary introduced by Geoff Peters, PVC, Strategy
* work in small groups on visioning the OU of the future
* plenary discussion to share these visions and draw out key themes
* work in small groups to develop an action plan for each key theme
* final plenary to present action plans to the PVC, Strategy.

In his initial plenary session Geoff Peters described the current situation in which the university found itself, the need to increase student numbers and the need to change the way the university did things if 'Plans for Change' was to become a reality. He also made it very clear that he believed all members of staff had a part to play.

The design of the workshops may look similar to many of the 'away-day' type of events that managers attend from time to time. As Stacey *et al.* (2000) point out, typically when managers participate in these events they fail to properly address the real issues and to consider any ideas on a practical day-to-day level. Further, there is a strong tendency to continue doing what they have always done during and after these events and to avoid discussing why their controlling mechanisms so often fail. A number of factors made these workshops quite different, in particular, the mix of people, the facilitators and their approach and the interaction of all these things.

Each workshop consisted of a mix of staff, and this mix was replicated in the small groups. A group might contain a clerical worker, a warehouse worker, a junior administrator, a senior academic and a middle manager from one of the professional areas, say, a surveyor. Thus, each group had a range of perspectives on the organization, on what was needed and on how to make things happen. For example, in one group session several members discussed how to bring extra courses on line. Then a worker from the warehouse asked how they were supposed to do this when the warehousing facility was already at capacity. This stopped everyone in their tracks and they then discussed ways in which this problem could be sorted out. The warehouse worker was able to keep everyone focused on the practicalities of an expansion in teaching materials. People used to working in different theoretical and bureaucratic domains encountered staff used to working with hard-nosed, practical issues. It was an encounter that enriched the discussions and encouraged the development of multiple perspectives. People discovered that an idea that might have advantages for their area could pose real problems for other staff in other areas. The interconnected nature of people's activities soon became vividly apparent. In some groups departmental antagonisms emerged and the facilitator, along with other members of the group, would work to resolve things and find a way forward if at all possible.

Thus by the afternoon of the second day when the groups were asked to put plans for action together a rich learning interchange had taken place which ensured that the suggestions and recommendations made by the different groups in the plenary sessions were founded in fresh realities. Out of these realities came a variety of ideas and practical suggestions for changing many existing practices and introducing new approaches.

Skilled facilitators from the training and development unit played a key role in each group. They were there to encourage and ensure equality of participation and the resolution (if possible) of real issues. Equality of participation was seen as vital if the groups were to work. The university is a hierarchical institution and some members of staff see themselves as junior to others and so on. Further, some staff are used to discussing issues and exploring ideas with colleagues and others are not. Many of the manual, clerical, secretarial and technical staff were not at all used to this kind of activity and they were given support and recognition in the group via the subtle interventions of the facilitators. Additionally the facilitators were briefed to encourage their groups 'to let go', to experiment, to have fun and to see the future as wide open and full of many possibilities. Further, I had recently come across chaos theory and some of its core tenets and I had discussed many of these with the facilitators.

An important feature of the workshops which emerged during the first series was the notion of everyone being empowered to take action. The PVC, Strategy, the facilitators and myself encouraged people to consider what changes they could make themselves in their own areas, no matter how small. Many people were accustomed to being directed to do things, or to having to ask for permission. Thus for a lot of staff taking action on their own behalf and making a change, however minor, was a major step. Over time the programme came to be recognized for its action approach and for the importance it attached to individual action.

By early summer the workshops were beginning to generate interest across the university. Staff began to ask to come along instead of waiting to be invited. In the autumn two more workshops followed which concentrated on specific aspects of New Directions, such as short response times. There was also an effort to increase attendance by academic staff who had so far been under-represented, and also to include staff who were also students taking OU courses, in order to introduce a student perspective. Each workshop was unique in that it had its own mix of staff and thus its own internal dynamics, but they were all characterized by energy and engagement.

In the autumn a letter went out to all New Directions workshops participants asking for volunteers to form a committee to organize a New Directions conference for the coming year. This would provide an opportunity for participants to update themselves, review the outcomes of the workshops, network, celebrate changes and communicate directly with the Vice-Chancellor, and the Vice-Chancellor's top team.

By the end of 1993 there had been eight two-day workshops involving approximately 164 staff and reports/features in three editions of *Open House*, the university's staff newspaper.

1994

This year was to see a significant expansion of the programme and several important developments. Early in the year it was decided to continue the programme of workshops by offering workshops based on key themes which had emerged in 1993. These included considering the need to develop 'an electronic strand' to the university's teaching design and delivery; improving the way the university attracted its students; improving the joining processes and improving internal communications. Each of these workshops was attended by the PVC, Strategy and the senior manager with responsibility for addressing these themes. Some senior managers were more enthusiastic than others at having to share their 'brief' with a random selection of staff and to ask for their views. In the event, however, all these workshops were highly successful from the view of both the participants and the senior manager concerned. Following the model created by the PVC, Strategy, ideas and suggestions from the workshops were fed into the appropriate planning groups for consideration.

An event of major significance during the year was the New Directions conference in May.

The 1994 conference and conference planning team

Some twenty-three staff responded to the invitation to form a conference organizing committee. It was decided that twenty-three was too many to form an effective group. After a lot of thought eleven staff were chosen as a representative cross-section. In the event eight staff regularly attended. There were: two regional academics, two secretaries, a senior editor, a warehousing manager, an administrative assistant and a chief clerk and myself as facilitator and provider of developmental advice and training administrative back-up.

The group first met in March 1994. Its task was to organize the conference so that it represented all staff groups, to pull together all the ideas and experiences to date and to initiate further actions. A provisional date for the conference had been fixed: 18 May 1994. Thus the conference planning team had just over two calendar months to organize everything. The event was organized with five meetings between which there had been an email flow of ideas, discussion and decision making. The conference offered twenty workshops in parallel streams with a mix of internal and external speakers and an exhibition. It was a significant achievement.

> On the day, the University's Training Centre was filled to capacity with over 100 delegates (and there was a waiting list). Participants included secretaries, gardeners, academics, administrators, managers and technicians. The day culminated in the presentation of action plans to the Vice-Chancellor, Pro-Vice-Chancellors and other members of the OU's senior management team.
>
> (Parsons and Russell 1995: 2)

The conference was very successful, it influenced a range of activities and initiatives and was to make an important impression on those staff who attended. A formal report was written up and circulated to all delegates and senior staff.

The staff survey team

A few days after the conference it was decided to involve New Directions participants in organizing a staff survey for the university. The effective way in which the highly successful conference had been organized by a group of volunteers from the programme had impressed the group charged with delivering the survey. For almost two years the Staff Policy Committee of the university had talked of the need for a survey of staff, to find out what the various staff groups felt about working in the university, but nothing had been done.

A note went out to all the conference delegates asking for volunteers to work with the Director of Public Relations, Les Holloway, on the design and delivery of a staff survey for the autumn. Eleven people volunteered and in the event nine were able to make the first and subsequent meetings. The team consisted of one senior academic, two senior secretaries, one editor, one administrator from the Planning Office, a senior O&M officer, a course manager and the grounds superintendent. I, too, was a member of the team where I acted in a facilitative role.

During June a revised tender document was prepared and an invitation to tender went out to five companies. The tenders were received by the end of July. Next the team met to decide which company to recommend to carry out the survey and a revised timetable was drafted. In September the team met for a debrief on the qualitative stage of the survey and discussed the draft questionnaire. In October there was a briefing on the results of the pilot survey and discussion of next steps. The questionnaire went out to all full-time staff of the university on 31 October 1994. There was a very good return of 65 per cent.

Meanwhile the conference planning team continued to meet and 'reconstituted itself as a "ginger group" to facilitate, and if necessary carry out the follow-up work' (Parsons and Russell 1995: 2). It was a significant shift in the 'ownership' of the programme. I attended the meetings of this group and found its members had been highly energized by the conference and its success and were committed to building upon the enthusiasms it had aroused. They decided that more staff could become involved in New Directions if events took place in the lunch hour. Thus with the backing of the PVC, Strategy, they arranged a series of lunchtime briefings which took place in the autumn. These included a briefing on 'Plans for Change' by Geoff Peters, a session with the Director of Marketing and one with the Director of Personnel. The briefings proved to be very popular with staff and the rooms were usually filled to capacity with deeply interested employees. In a move to involve more regional staff inter-regional workshops were held in Birmingham and London. These explored how regional activities would look in ten years time and produced a wealth of new ideas for both course topics and better services to students.

The group also 'hit upon a novel way of spreading the *New Directions* message … they invited staff to enter a cartoon competition on the theme of "the OU of the future"' (Parsons and Russell 1995: 3). The entries were imaginative and amusing with innovative possibilities for the future. The winning cartoons were used to produce a New Directions Cartoon Calendar for 1995. A thousand calendars were printed and made available to all staff and the winners presented with bottles of champagne. The calendars were rapidly taken by staff and pinned up on walls in different parts of the university. Also in the autumn a simple leaflet describing New Directions what it was all about, its principles and practice was distributed to all staff.

In December the survey team met to discuss the follow-up to the findings of the survey including presentations to the staff and supportive action in relation to the findings.

Total attendance at the programme in 1994 was approximately 533. It is difficult to precisely quantify the figures as some people attended more than one workshop and no formal attendance records were kept of the lunchtime briefings. There were reports/features on New Directions in five editions of *Open House* in 1994.

1995

In January the first report on the staff survey was presented to the Vice-Chancellor's senior team and the staff survey team members. A series of presentations to different representative groups was arranged and an open presentation to all staff in the university lecture theatre. All staff received a summary report of the findings and all department heads were asked to discuss these with their staff and devise follow-up action plans. The survey team had completed its task and after celebrating over lunch the team disbanded. It had been a highly effective and successful team.

Also in January several members from the conference planning team (now the 'ginger' group) and the staff survey team got together and formed the New Directions 1995 action group. On an away day in January the new group brain-stormed a number of ideas which were picked up and taken forward during the year. These included a mistakes workshop, a visualization workshop, a workshop for OU students and series of communications workshops. The idea for a mistakes workshop arose out of discussions about experimentation and creativity. If people were to take risks to change things then the university would need to be a 'safe' place, it was argued. Thus a group of the volunteers got together and designed a 'Make Better Mistakes' workshop. The open invitation to staff to attend the work-shop was worded as follows:

> Change at the Open University is bringing new ways of working. Inevitably things will sometimes go wrong. How do you cope with mistakes? Does the University learn from its failures? Can one replace blame by objective analysis?

The two workshops offered generated enormous interest and were oversub-scribed. The visualization workshop arose from interest in conjuring up new images in order to stimulate new ideas and new ways of thinking. Two artists were employed to work with the staff at the workshop and to help them create vivid visual images of a changed university. The communications workshops were a direct response to the call for better communications which came out of the conference. These were organized in consultation with different departments of the university so that teams of staff from different areas got to together to explore how to improve things. Another calendar was also produced and distributed.

The number of attendees in the programme in 1995 was approximately 387. In 1995 there were reports/features on New Directions in four editions of *Open House* and one edition of *Sesame*, the students' newspaper.

1996

The programme was now in its fourth year. There were three communications workshops and a 'Making Better Mistakes' workshop and in the autumn another conference. This conference organized by the action group was not so ambitious as the 1994 conference, but it offered eight workshops in two streams. It also included a 'fair' element that comprised an OU horoscope, a picture gallery of New Directions artwork, a graffiti wall and the planting of a symbolic new mulberry tree by the Vice-Chancellor, Sir John Daniel. Thus in its own modest way it made a significant contribution. It showed clearly by the kind of activities it offered that conferences on important topics did not have to be serious events composed of lectures and 'talking heads' but that, by appealing to the senses as well as the mind, people could meaningfully explore strategic issues.

Members of the action group were now finding it more difficult to create the space needed to support the programme and enthusiasm was waning. Further, changes in the external environment were affecting people's workloads and most importantly their morale. In January 1997 the group decided it would take a break and review the situation at a later date to be decided. This was to be the last time that it met.

The New Directions 'volunteers' in the form of the 'ginger' group (some of the conference team) and the 1995 action group (the two teams plus a few others) had been active for over two years and had supported, suggested or helped to design and deliver some six lunchtime briefings; four regionally based workshops; three mistakes workshops; six communications workshops (one of these in Cambridge) two cartoon calendar competitions and a conference. I had worked very closely with the volunteers and provided developmental expertise and administrative support, but they had come up with the ideas and backed them with their energies and commitment. It was a significant achievement for a disparate group of volunteers with full-time roles in the institution – and a development that had not been expected at the beginning of the programme. It had been a totally spontaneous and unpredicted response.

In 1996 approximately 170 staff participated in New Directions events and there were items/features on New Directions in three editions of *Open House*.

Attendance was not recorded at all events in the programme so to arrive at an accurate figure for the number of individual staff who participated in the programme is impossible. But it is estimated that about 23 per cent of the full-time staff were involved. It is important to bear this in mind when considering the impact the programme made on the university and the extent of its influence. The records show that academic staff were in a minority.

An innovative learning process for change

The New Directions programme could be viewed as a consultative device that sought to enlist active staff support for a top-down approach to strategic change. It was one part of a university-wide strategic change process which included new unit planning processes linked to 'Plans for Change' with accompanying plans for management action, and an 'Investors in People' initiative. The first workshops and the staff development programme sought to enable staff to cope with the expected changes needed and to deliver them too. In this largely traditional way the university recognized and sought to handle the human dimension of change.

The New Directions programme in its early days, in as much as it reflects any theory or model of change, was a mix of partly 'emergent' and partly 'deliberate' approaches to strategy (Mintzberg and Waters 1989). The process of strategy making was controlled by the top management of the university, but with the conditions created for new strategies to emerge via a responsive and consultative approach.

Parsons and Russell (1995) point out that the workshops were used as part of a process of review as well as consultation. They were a way in which the senior team could check its strategic goals and performance indicators directly with those who were expected to deliver on them. Viewed strategically from the top the programme was a way of supporting other mechanisms for change and staff development. However, the ways in which staff responded to the programme were totally unexpected.

Feedback, strategic listening and the response dynamic

From the start of the programme several processes were created which were to help shape its future development. The original invitations sent out to delegates at random, regardless of status or role, pushed involvement in strategic activity down and around the organization. It also involved senior managers in direct discussion with more junior staff.

Feedback processes were set up by the PVC, Strategy which facilitated the involvement of all levels of staff and encouraged a response dynamic. For example, at the early workshops all the ideas and suggestions were recorded on flip charts. These were typed up and circulated to all those in attendance. These documents provided a text for discussion between workshop participants, their colleagues, and their senior managers. After each workshop these ideas were considered by the PVC, Strategy, who undertook to feed them into meetings of the university's top team. This was an overt demonstration of strategic listening intent. By acting as he did, Geoff Peters also ensured that ideas from the grassroots were fed upwards to the top levels. From the very beginning of the programme feedback loops with amplifying potential were created. In time it became clear that these were positive feedback loops.

Figure 6.3 was created by Geoff Peters in 1994 for an internal discussion paper. It shows New Directions' role in the larger change process that was taking place. Priorities and actions detailed in 'Plans for Change' fed through the university's management structure and were formalized via the unit/divisional planning process. Managers were responsible for translating the university's strategic plans into local plans for action and activity. These plans were then fed back into the formal structures.

It shows how the programme linked to other strategic processes and how staff in the university were part of a feedback mechanism that embraced planning processes, strategic thinking, strategic action and staff development initiatives. The model shows how it was possible to recognize and to use the human feedback loops as part of a strategic change process. Further:

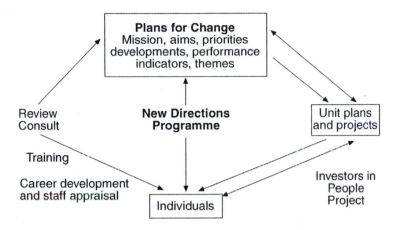

Figure 6.3 The role of the New Directions Programme (adapted from Peters, 1994)

Without the *New Directions* programme, this could have been consistent with a traditional 'negative feedback loop' approach – checking responses against targets and correcting to reduce differences. However, in bypassing organizational boundaries and formal procedures it set off some positive feedback processes. New ways of doing things encouraged further change.

(Parsons and Russell 1995: 3)

Feedback by the PVC, Strategy ensured that ideas from a wide range of staff were fed into some important strategy papers. Parsons and Russell (1995: 1) describe how senior managers met to discuss the programme and to hear reports from different departments that were bringing New Directions participants together to consider changes in their own areas. The overall process fed in fresh flows of information and ideas from a wide range of staff not usually involved in such dialogues. It was a flow that was essentially informal in nature, arising as it did from the relaxed and freewheeling approaches of the workshops, although channelled by formal frameworks.

A series of workshops originally planned for a six-months period was initially extended to a year and the pattern of response for the whole programme unexpectedly created. The staff responded to the workshops and the workshop organizers (the PVC, Strategy, and his office team) responded to the staff's response. This was the early dynamic of the programme and it continued through much of the lifespan of the programme (see Figure 6.4). This also shows how from 1994, after the conference, staff volunteers inherited the responsive mantle from the original organizers.

The programme in responding to the issues raised created its own dynamic which was energized by various feedback loops around the University. These were fed back via a number of channels including meetings, discussions 'along the corridor', further workshops and *Open House*, the staff newspaper, which played a key role in informing staff and also feeding back comments and views via its pages.

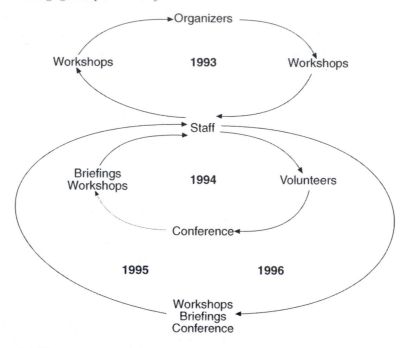

Figure 6.4 The response dynamic

Further, by responding to the response of those it sought to involve, the creators of the programme learnt how to continue to involve people and they did this by responding spontaneously and not by preplanning in any large measure. It was in this sense also that the initial programme can be characterized as a mixture of partly 'emergent' and partly 'deliberate' approaches. The programme was designed in a planned way to respond to the workshops and that was 'deliberate', but the unintended way that the response developed and the outcomes of the response were essentially 'emergent' (Mintzberg and Waters 1989) outcomes arising from a willingness to learn and let go.

Why did the staff who attended the workshops respond so positively? An important and in many ways typical insight is provided in a letter sent to Geoff Peters. It is from a member of the regional staff in Scotland who had attended an early workshop in 1993. She wrote:

> I felt that the informal atmosphere and the friendly welcome established a group environment which was totally unthreatening and which helped everyone to feel able to contribute freely. I came home refreshed, better informed and with the feeling that, however, lowly my position … I had been listened to. I was made to feel that I had something to contribute to the future of the OU.

Further:

I thought that it was a most creative and imaginative idea to choose staff at random from all grades and areas within the OU. ... I felt privileged to be asked to take part. It has increased my respect for the openness of the OU. ... From someone who never wins a raffle I felt this time, at least, I had won one of the major prizes.

(McMillan 1999: 260)

The letter conveys some of the enthusiasm that the workshops engendered in many staff, especially the more junior staff who were unable to participate in the university's consultative and decision-making processes. It should be noted, however, that not all members of staff who attended the workshops were so enthusiastic and one or two were unimpressed.

If, as Stacey *et al.* (2000) suggest, we think of organizations as processes then the emergence of the response dynamic and the creation of fresh webs of feedback loops added and enriched the flow of processes which are the institution.

Innovation – the New Directions way of doing things

It is one thing to set out to involve people in a change programme and another to make that participation genuine. The PVC, Strategy set up and supported listening and feedback mechanisms, but how else did the programme encourage people to become actively involved? Employees at the university cover a wide spectrum of roles, skills and abilities and as an institution it has many hierarchies. How do you appeal to a junior clerk, a warehouse packer, an editor, a computer technician and a social sciences lecturer, for example? Also, most importantly how would it not only appeal but also encourage active support for the change process?

New Directions sought to do things in a way that was described as informal, open, involving, inclusive and different. Thus aspects of the programme's style actively reflected the university's own key principles of openness and open access to all and thus the OU's espoused values gave a supportive cultural context to the programme.

Creativity

The programme encouraged the use of creative ways of presenting ideas and behaving at workshops in an attempt to stimulate new thinking. Group presentations not only consisted of the traditional flip chart lists but also drawings and on occasion a poem, street theatre or a skit on the News at Ten. In an article in *Open House* one manager describes how she had been inspired by a 'theatrical presentation' on the OU in the year 2005 made by 'a particularly creative bunch of people' on a regional workshop. She described how the use of drawing was also encouraged as one way of stimulating fresh ideas but also because the 'richness of an idea may get lost when it's put into words'. As Handy (1990: 20) points out: 'New imagery, signalled by new words, is as important as new theory; indeed new theory without new imagery can go unnoticed.' This notion inspired the action group to organize a visualization workshop.

Humour

Humour also played a key role in stimulating discussion and raising awareness of key issues. In one instance staff were asked to produce limericks for a Limerick Wall as part of the 1996 conference and fair. One manager interviewed described New Directions as 'sometimes a bit zany', another commented that it had 'a humorous style reflected in the calendars'. The New Directions calendars are a good example of the programme's approach to change. 1995 began 'with a significant number of the University's staff pinning up "new imagery" on their walls. Here was a message that the future would be different and might even be fun' (Parsons and Russell 1995: 3).

One senior clerk observed that New Directions used 'a sense of humour to get over the serious issues'. Everyone, she commented, could appreciate the joke and get the message. The Institute for Employment Studies (IES) study also notes that the workshops took risks with the use of unusual techniques and fun activities to explore serious high level issues. The study observes that the programme discovered that:

> the way to unlock people's creativity, to get them to speak openly and equally at all levels of the organization was through the use of unusual techniques, an informal atmosphere and creative facilitation. Individuals were encouraged to work with people they do not know, to have fun, to loosen up, to explore the use of metaphors.
>
> (Tamkin and Barber 1998: 18)

As Morgan (1993) points out, it is very difficult for people to shake off old ways of thinking about their organization and their role in it unless they are encouraged to use their imaginations and imagery to discover new interpretations and fresh ways of thinking.

Experimentation

The IES study reports that in the programme experimentation was key. This is crucial for innovation and a necessary activity in challenging the status quo in a learning organization (Leonard-Barton 1994). A report in *Open House* in May 1995 describes proposals for 'a revolutionary-for-the-OU workshop' (mistakes workshop) which will help staff 'to take more risks, make more mistakes, but learn from them'. Mistakes and the experience of mistakes are elemental features of development and learning (Dale 1994). If a learning climate is to be established then experimentation is encouraged and there is recognition that people learn from experience and from mistakes (Pedler *et al.* 1991). The workshop called 'Making Better Mistakes – Banishing the Blame Culture from the OU' tackled some controversial and difficult issues. The workshops had a broad appeal making it possible for any member of staff regardless of status to meaningfully participate.

The mistakes workshops show the way the programme was prepared to take risky steps to encourage new attitudes and behaviours, and a positive attitude to risk is essential if an organization is to be experimental and innovative (Leonard-Barton 1994).

A people's movement for action and change

In spite of its top down beginnings the programme after time became identified by many of its participants as a people's movement for change. Its prime purpose was seen as working with the staff to bring about changes in the way the university managed itself.

Another strong feature of the programme which emerged from the workshops was its focus on action. As a change process the programme sought to stimulate and encourage staff to think about changes and to introduce these changes themselves. It was an approach which sought at the grass roots level to bridge the traditional strategic divide between planning and action. In an organization where action was frequently slow in coming often because of the long and sometimes ponderous decision-making processes involved, this was almost like a call to arms. It was a challenge to the bureaucratic heart of the institution. Further, it had backing from one of the university's most senior managers the PVC, Strategy. In an article in *Open House* Geoff Peters wrote:

> New Directions is also about action. The activities are designed by staff volunteers and emphasise practical results. The over-used phrase 'think globally act locally' really does fit the New Directions activities. Staff sort out where the University needs to go and then they take action to help get there.
>
> (Geoff Peters, *Open House*, July 1995)

These comments also acknowledge the role of volunteers and their part in New Directions activities. The workshops provided an opportunity for grassroots involvement which had been eagerly taken up by a small number of staff. The original aim of the programme to involve all staff led unexpectedly to a change in the 'hands' of those who guided it and even some aspects of the ownership of the programme. The PVC, Strategy and his office team came to work in partnership with the participants or the 'people' themselves. The programme had become, as one manager described it: 'A dynamic programme of enthusiasts seeking creatively to change the OU for the better.'

Difficulties and opposition

The programme was not enthusiastically supported by all staff and many were antagonistic or highly sceptical. A number of senior managers were openly hostile and wanted to know 'when the university was going to stop wasting money on this nonsense?' Attempts were made to deal with this.

> There was concern that many senior staff saw *New Directions* as a 'people's movement' which was potentially threatening and it was important that everyone was on board and involved. Therefore the PVC (Strategy and Development) personally invited all senior managers to the planned autumn events.
>
> (Parsons and Russell 1995: 2)

One senior manager described how many of his colleagues, particularly those who had not been there, thought the 1994 conference posed a threat. They thought that the Vice-Chancellor and the PVC, Strategy, were taking too much notice of 'the lower groups in the organization'. Some senior staff thought that 'revolution was in the air'.

Tensions were created in some areas where managers did not support the programme and in some instances refused to let their staff attend. Some staff were suspicious of the motives behind the workshops, others thought that it was just a public relations exercise. Others complained that it did not involve enough academics or regional staff to be truly representative. Further, not everyone saw advantages in bringing together a mixed group of staff. One senior member of regional staff wrote:

> I cannot see that getting together a group of staff, most of whom do not sit on decision-making committees and none of whom are in positions of management, can genuinely influence the policy changes that need to come about. I feel it would have been more productive to convene groups of staff who share similar perspectives and concerns.
>
> (McMillan 1999: 261)

It was not an unsurprising response, for as Stacey *et al.* (2000) observe the traditional reaction to perennial problems is to set up a meeting which ensures that the 'right' people are invited to attend. This is the traditional management mindset which fails to question its own behaviours.

A programme that is perceived or described as a people's movement for change or one that involves the 'grass roots' of an organization is unlikely to be welcomed by the traditionalists who view their role as essentially controlling and who have a vested interest in maintaining the status quo. This much could have been predicted.

Impact and flows of change

A significant feature of the programme was the rich flow of ideas which the workshops generated, especially during the early years. These had an influence on strategic discussions and some senior management thinking.

The ideas were so prolific that they have generated papers which have been discussed twice by the Vice-Chancellor's weekly meeting, a summary paper went to SPRC [Strategic Planning and Resources Committee] last month, and at the last meeting of the OU's senior team managers were able to talk through some of the issues and to hear a very interesting report of how Operations and some other units had been bringing their new directions people together to consider change in their area.

(McMillan 1999: 264)

The series of workshops which focused on major strategic themes provided staff with a chance to discuss these themes directly with the senior manager responsible for their development. Thus a bottom-up process was created whereby a small number of staff from across the university were able to directly input to the strategy-forming process.

So for example, when earlier this year we were drafting an international strategy, we held open workshops on the 'OU going global.' The results were then fed straight into the preparation of a first draft and those who attended the workshop were able to comment knowledgeably on the thinking as it developed further.

(McMillan 1999: 264)

Staff who had taken part in the programme thought that their thinking, their feelings and often their behaviours had been influenced. The IES study confirmed that people spoke of an increase in confidence and self-esteem which they attributed to the personal impact of the programme. They also spoke of having obtained a much wider view of the University and their role in it. A significant number thought that their involvement in the programme had directly influenced the way they did their job. Examples given were as follows: improved communications in own areas; managerial style now more personal; more tolerant and analytical of own mistakes; making better provision for their own staff's development; reading more on complexity science and applying some complexity-based ideas.

The programme not only affected those who had actively participated but also influenced many of their working colleagues. This influence varied from being something small and passing to something more significant. Some people spoke of mindsets being affected and even shifted. This they considered was mainly due to the realization that strategic issues were something they could contribute to. However, large numbers of regional staff were hardly affected, especially large numbers of regional secretarial and clerical staff.

To summarize, many staff spoke of how the New Directions process:

- made the staff think about the OU and its situation
- encouraged discussion about strategic issues
- acted as a catalyst for change.

There were dissenters, however, one senior academic observed that the university as an institution valued the democratic process but because of its hierarchical structure and bureaucratic procedures found it impossible to implement its ideals in practice. He stated that the OU 'gives lip service to this kind of thing ... but the structures mitigate against it' (McMillan 1999: 274). There was a view too that the programme had been too small to be really wide ranging in its impact and needed to include more staff.

Because the OU is a large and complex organization with matching procedures it would not be easy to change, as some of the barriers created 'include some of the individuals who helped create the university and are therefore very wedded to the organization they created' (Tamkin and Barber 1998: 18). In spite of this, however, the IES report found 'considerable commonality of response describing an organization that had become more flexible and less hierarchical, more sharing and more open with information' (Tamkin and Barber 1998: 48). This it was observed was congruent with the style of New Directions which sought 'to enhance communications and create a more open organizational culture' (Tamkin and Barber 1998: 48). One interviewee stated:

> I think the University is changing a lot at the moment, some of it is attributable to New Directions, perhaps only a small amount. New Directions had been a good oil making it go more smoothly it was an outlet for individuals at any level to voice difficulties and uncertainties, to vocalise those in a non-threatening way.
>
> Tamkin and Barber (1998: 48)

Tamkin and Barber (1998: 18) refer to the university's management development programme and conclude that together with New Directions one of the outcomes they created: 'was a move away from an organization that was resistant to change to one where there is a growing awareness of the need to change. There is also a perception that it had become more open.'

Over time the programme changed. In 1995/6 external changes led to a financial downturn and budget cuts. This change of climate and the mood change that it engendered had a profound effect on the staff of the university and on the programme. People spoke of heavy workloads, 'gloom' and 'disillusionment'. Much of this was put down to senior managers reverting to old behaviours and of encouraging a period of retrenchment. Thus a change in the university's external environment affected the attitudes of many of the OU's managers and their response was to rely on more traditional ways of thinking and behaving. As Merry (1995) points out most people are unwilling to make deep level or second-order changes as they are afraid of the unknown and the change in external circumstances may have deepened that fear.

Learning, discovery and change

If learning is another word for change (Handy 1990), then there is much evidence to suggest that changes were taking place for those involved in the programme.

Significant numbers of staff believed that they had learnt or discovered something as a result of their participation in New Directions.

One secretary told how the confidence she had gained as a result of running a workshop at the conference had 'acted as a spur to go on and take some management courses' (McMillan 1999: 294). Further, she had arranged a meeting with the Director of Personnel to discuss some of the issues that had arisen from the conference. As Leonard-Barton (1994) makes clear, it is essential that people feel respected and have good self-esteem if they are to learn. One administrator described how he felt encouraged to carry on trying to make changes and believed the conference had created more channels through which to contribute to change.

There is considerable evidence of double-loop (Morgan 1986) and generative learning (Senge 1992, 1994) where the learning was powerful enough to be recognizable at a conscious level and to be deliberately translated into new patterns of thinking and new behaviours. For example, one middle manager who had not been used to participating in such wide-ranging discussions described how he had learnt to talk to people through New Directions and now was able to participate more effectively in all kinds of group situations. Some thought that the conference had broadened their outlook on life at the OU and that they now saw things differently. For example, one manager now realized that, before the conference, his view of the university had been too narrow. His horizons had stretched and he saw new ways he could contribute to his role. As a result he was now involved in National Vocational Qualifications as an assessor and verifier and was involved in writing national standards for the Royal Society of Arts.

One academic described how the conference had made a significant impact upon his thinking. His generative or double-loop learning had led to recognizable action and change. He had been very affected by the discussions on different terms and conditions and recalled how 'the telling example' of a secretary not being allowed to take out an inter-library loan had influenced his thinking, especially in the context of the OU as a learning organization. He had attended Conference workshop given by Rover Cars and had followed up by writing around the OU to see if anyone was carrying out any research on Rover. He went on to make a bid for research funding to set up a learning programme at the university. He also had written a paper on the 'OU and the Learning Society' which explored the OU's contribution to learning in the UK.

The IES study found considerable evidence that both learning and a change in attitude took place as a result of participation in the programme. But it did also find some less than positive responses. One employee thought he had never learned anything useful at the workshops or on any training courses. The study observes that those who did not feel positive about their learning experiences did so because they had had different expectations about the kind of learning that the event offered. Most thought learning was all about the acquisition of knowledge and skills. Thus if the event did not offer knowledge or skills-based outputs then the expectations of the learners were not met. The attitude of these respondents reflects traditional notions of learning whereby once the skill or knowledge was acquired then the process was over. Learning was not viewed as a continuous life-long process, but rather as a series of discrete events.

Other staff identified learning more about the university. One, a senior manager, with over ten years at the university, thought he had learnt more about the values of the university and its sub-cultures. The IES study comments that the OU and the retail company also in their study, were the only two out of the five organizations they studied where interviewees 'spontaneously mentioned that they had learned about their organization' (Tamkin and Barber 1998: 32).

The IES report also noted that in the OU there had been a two-way learning process in which participants had gained a better understanding of how their colleagues perceived them and also a better understanding of how the university worked. This, the report noted, was particularly true of the junior staff who had previously had difficulties understanding the organization. However, there were deeper, more subtle learning and discovery processes taking place which respondents identified and which they believed had affected their behaviours and outlook akin to Merry's (1995) notion of evolutionary learning.

Additionally, the IES report notes that participants in New Directions

> found a greater appreciation of the university's structure, the work of colleagues in different parts of the organization, the workings of the committee system and an appreciation of how others viewed their own department.
>
> (Tamkin and Barber 1998: 28)

The study also notes that, because many of the participants in New Directions were in relatively junior positions they found the opportunity of mixing with people from other areas very valuable and insightful. Some managers changed their style as the result of feedback from subordinates during the workshops and thus became co-learners and reflective practitioners (Dale 1994).

There are implications here for organizations considering a change strategy and any change process should always take into account the complex, dynamics of real life systems and processes. Further if it is to have a good chance of success then a change process should consider taking into account the strategic thinking capabilities of all its staff and their assessment of the needs of the organization at that time. In some individuals and some parts of the university New Directions had a significant impact and second-order change (Dale 1994) and double-loop learning (Morgan 1993) took place. In Stacey's (1992, 1996a) view an organization needs to consider three kinds of change, closed, contained and open-ended, if it is to survive. The New Directions programme provided an opportunity for some employees to explore issues related to closed and contained changes and to take follow up action, and it created an environment in which open-ended changes were encouraged and emerged.

The 1994 conference – rich flows for change

The 1994 one-day conference is worthy of special consideration as it is a microcosm of the whole New Directions programme. It created a change process within a change process and like a fractal reflected the overall pattern of the programme.

But how did it contribute to the New Directions change processes?

The planning team decided that the conference would try to stimulate people to become involved and to take individual action to change the university. There would be speakers from other organizations to introduce new ideas and share their experiences on change, interactive workshops, and opportunities for the staff to come together pool their knowledge and ideas and put their recommendations to top management. The staff of the university responded positively to the call to join in the conference. Employees from all areas, categories and levels of seniority attended. The opportunity to participate was highly appreciated and especially the opportunity to express views directly to top management, and the atmosphere on the day was described as 'buzzing'.

Speakers from other organizations that had undergone major changes included Rover and the Metropolitan Police and the feedback comments on these sessions were exceptionally positive. The OU has many cultures, but exposure to stories of changes in other organizations served to introduce a measure of challenge and diversity into the existing cultural perspectives of some of the conference delegates. The speakers from the external organizations also introduced new information into the organization which is essential if creativity and change are to flourish (Nonaka 1988).

Table 6.1 summarizes the main issues to emerge from the group 'action' sessions which were drawn together and presented in the final plenary session. These indicate how staff from all walks of working life were aware of the challenges the university faced from its external environment. But a major thread running throughout was the importance of also addressing internal issues and especially staffing concerns, if effective change was to be achieved. The emergence of what could be described as a 'democratic strategic action plan' is discussed further in the next sub-section.

The conference as part of New Directions sought to bring about changes in the university. Thus progress on any of the issues raised provides a conventional measure of how effective the conference and New Directions had been in influencing and even changing aspects of the university. It had raised issues that may well have already been under consideration but in doing so it had turned a spotlight on them and raised their profile. Table 6.1 shows that of the seven issues raised significant progress was made on four of them, some progress on one of them and no progress on the remaining two. Details of how these issues were followed up are provided in Appendix 3.

Participation in the conference made a major impression on a number of people. One manager, for example, had been 'really recharged' by the conference and believed it had encouraged her to become more politically active, to approach the General Secretary of the Association of University Teachers at their council meeting shortly after the conference, and to join the National Executive. Other staff were so enthused that they had decided to take action themselves. One secretary in the marketing team had approached the PVC, Curriculum Development, to talk about the need to market things differently.

Table 6.1 Conference issues and outcomes

Issue/theme	Outcome/follow up
Staff policy: equalization of staff terms and conditions; more staff development; need for a Pro-Vice-Chancellor for staff	Significant progress made
Marketing strategy: need to improve; importance of customer research and corporate identity	Significant progress made but more needed
New technology development: fear that university was being left behind; need for multi-media developments	Very significant progress made
Need for improved communications: better bottom-up communications and more effective and appropriate information giving	Significant progress made but more needed
Low staff morale: due to conflicting messages; barriers between staff; working on a treadmill	No progress
Need for leadership and for better people management skills	No progress
Need for a flatter organization structure and better co-operation between departments	Some progress

Because there was widespread representation of staff at the conference so word spread around different levels and in different areas of the organization. This spread of involvement added to the existing response dynamics and further amplified existing feedback loops as well as creating new ones. All this contributed to the energy for change within different areas of the University.

The conference was reported in *Open House* as 'an outstanding success' and Geoff Peters notes that 'already a number of developments have taken place as a result'. The report listed several follow-up activities including:

- the setting up of the team of volunteers from the conference to form the staff survey team
- the production of a user-friendly version of the Staff Policy Committee Action Plan to be circulated to all staff
- an invitation to all staff to input to the next stage of the New Directions programme.

All staff were recommended to read the conference report as it would provide them with 'some valuable insights as regards the information exchanged and ideas shared' (McMillan 1999: 298).

To summarize, the conference had been a New Directions one-day event with 100 delegates which had sought to stimulate visioning of the future and ideas for changing the university. It had made a considerable impression on many of those there and appeared to exert a range of influences on some other staff too. Some of the positive aspects of the conference were as follows:

- it influenced or gave an impetus to a number of significant and recognizable changes
- it boosted the flow of change within the university
- it enabled the grassroots of the university to articulate their views and be heard by senior and top managers
- it encouraged and inspired many staff to take actions of their own
- it provided a fertile learning environment
- it was a successful landmark event that put New Directions on the university map.

Some of the mainly negative aspects were as follows:

- it raised anxiety levels for those staff who felt threatened by changes, especially in new technologies
- it failed to reach most of the regional staff
- it added to the irritation some managers felt about New Directions
- it increased the perceived marginalization of academic staff.

Emergence of a democratic strategic action plan

A significant outcome of the conference was the emergence of a new 'grassroots' strategic action plan. The delegates had taken the university's official strategic action plan ('Plans for Change') absorbed and digested it via the workshops and together with their own ideas and thoughts produced a 'democratic' version. This clearly stated priorities for action if the university was to successfully change itself and meet the challenges of the future. This strategy for action was prepared for, and presented under the aegis of the final plenary session of the conference which had called upon the delegates to make presentations under the heading of 'Strategic Recommendations for the Future'. The delegates at the conference in rising to the challenge of the final session had produced a realistic strategy for future action (see Table 6.2).

Table 6.2 summarizes the seven main themes or issues to emerge from the conference and considers them from four simple aspects: internal/external focus, core or heart of the issue, a SWOT (strengths, weaknesses, opportunities and threats) analysis, and time focus. It shows a predominantly internal focus that puts people- or staff-related themes at the core. As an action plan it sees internal issues as a priority. The importance of organizational structure and the need for a flatter organization is linked to the need for better communications and staff or people management issues. The plan would appear to be saying that the university needs

Table 6.2 Democratic strategic action plan

Issue/theme	Focus	Issue core	SWOT	Time focus
Staff policy: equalization of staff terms and conditions; more staff development; need for a Pro-Vice-Chancellor for staff	Internal	People and equality	Weakness	Present
Marketing strategy: importance of customer research and corporate identity	External and internal	Marketing and income	Opportunity	Present and future
New technology development: fear that university was being left behind	External and internal	Technology and multi-media	Opportunity and threat	Present and future
Need for improved communications	Internal	People/organization management	Weakness	Present
Low staff morale	Internal	People management	Weakness	Present
Need for leadership and for better people management skills	Internal	People management/development	Weakness	Present
Need for a flatter organization structure	Internal	Organization structure	Weakness	Present

to put its internal house in order if it is to succeed in achieving its strategic objectives. Although it has a predominantly internal focus there are important external aspects too which it recognizes as critical for future success. It acknowledges the importance of new technology developments and the competitive threat that these pose if the university falls behind. For an institution that uses distance methods to deliver its products this is a highly critical issue. The focus on marketing recognizes the need to address the university's external profile by creating a strong corporate image. This too is important if the university is to succeed in increasing its student numbers. Further, more effective marketing research is needed to ensure that new markets are reached and existing ones kept satisfied.

A simple SWOT analysis highlights five areas of perceived weakness, two opportunities, one of which could also constitute a threat if not addressed and it views the issue of low staff morale as a crucial weakness. Thus the institution was perceived as having significant weaknesses and limited opportunities. It is not a very healthy profile. Its time focus was fixed chiefly on present needs for action. This democratic approach to strategic change is one that does not rely heavily on the introduction of major financial, structural or procedural changes as part of a planned management exercise. Rather, it is an approach that sees people as the necessary lifeblood of achieving strategic change. As the text from one of the presentation slides puts it: 'The importance of achieving the university's goals lies with the commitment, motivation and enthusiasm of its staff.'

As a democratic plan for strategic action it seeks to involve everyone in an organization and sees strategic thinking and strategic activity as an unfolding symbiotic process. Thus randomly selected groups of staff in an organization who become actively involved in an organization-wide change intervention can make a realistic and valuable contribution to strategic institutional agendas.

Teams in action – energizing changes

The conference planning team and the staff survey team were two very significant features of the New Directions programme. Both enabled small groups of staff to contribute to the New Directions change process by focusing on a particular project and making it happen. The two teams together with the 1995 action group influenced the flow of the programme and energized the dynamics for change.

Why did people volunteer to join these teams? To take on additional roles and responsibilities is not something that people seek to do lightly. People volunteered because they had an interest in strategic issues; they wanted to do something active to support changes in the university; or they had been encouraged by their experience of the programme and even 'inspired by the conference'.

There proved to be many advantages to working in the volunteer teams. People were enthusiastic and keenly interested. They believed in what they were doing and were highly motivated and committed. Most importantly, there were no political or departmental agendas to get in the way. However, there was one significant drawback which relates to the difficulties of having to squeeze time out of the working week to participate. This is perhaps more a comment on the status of volunteer teams in the organization than on the nature of the teams themselves.

There proved to be a number of advantages also in working in a group composed of a mixture of staff drawn from all categories and grades, both in terms of getting the tasks completed and in terms of individual development and shared understandings. Team members found that they learnt more about how other areas of the university operated and about different working roles. Within the teams there was a genuine exchange of viewpoints, a sharing of ideas and considerable listening. For both teams coming into contact with staff they did not normally work with was a refreshing and enjoyable experience.

The success of the teams probably owes much to the way in which they were able to work effectively as coherent and efficient groups. The conference team appears to have been especially spontaneous and creative in its way of working, whereas the survey team was especially focused on its prime purpose, i.e. the survey. This suggests that the nature of the projects affected the way the teams worked. Ideas and creativity were needed to design a conference that would appeal to all OU staff, whereas the design of a survey document required exploration and understanding of both the issues and survey methods.

An important feature of both teams was the sense of equality and the relaxed and democratic way in which they worked. There was the potential in each team for hierarchical patterns to emerge and predominate, encouraged by existing roles in the university. This, however, did not happen. Instead the traditional pecking order was replaced by a network of equals.

The teams broke with tradition in that neither had a formal chair or traditional leader. The traditional model of guidance was replaced by a collective or shared leadership approach which arose out of the open, enabling style of the teams and their strong sense of shared purpose. Initially I had acted as a facilitator or guide in each team, but this role diminished as the teams grew together.

The teams used brainstorming to generate ideas and solve issues, and focused on getting things done and deciding what had to be done and who would do it. Decisions were readily made and often made on the basis of action. In other words, if someone was willing to carry something out then the team would back them. One team member described decisions as being taken creatively and said: 'What seemed to be the best idea always came out on the top of the pile and everybody swung behind it'.

Belbin's (1981, 1993) work on teams is so well-known that it is often used as a guide to ensure that an effective team is put together. But these were teams that were put together at random with no thought for the provision of complementary skills and attributes. On the face of it, the teams were a disparate mix of staff with many hurdles to overcome if they were to work together effectively. But in reality they did have things in common which would help to create the team. They had all responded to the call to support New Directions and they were very motivated and committed to their project's purpose and as Dale (1994) suggests a group of people in an organization who share a common purpose can effectively work together as a group of co-learners.

Given that the two teams were made up without any consideration of the skills, abilities and experience needed to carry out their tasks, what else contributed to their success? Team members supported and encouraged each other and there was considerable discussion and debate. These are also attributes of a group of co-learners (Dale 1994). Further evidence of co-learning is provided by one of the clerical staff who observed that: 'everyone developed the skills needed during the life of the team'. Many of the team members still kept in touch and still formed part of a supportive network of colleagues long after the lifetime of the team.

In summary the teams were quite different to other OU project teams because:

- they were informal
- they included a wide cross-section of staff
- they were much more open
- there was no hierarchy 'not even a relaxed hierarchy'
- there was no person who overruled others in the team
- there was 'no desperation' that arose from people coming along with different agendas
- everyone shared a common aim, and therefore:
  - they were purposeful and directed
  - there was a great deal of energy.

The two teams had many self-organizing aspects which are discussed in detail in Chapter 7 which builds upon facets of the teams explored in this section and compares them with other types of team.

The New Directions legacy

When I arrived at the university in 1986 I found a successful and well-respected organization that had steadily and gradually been developing and expanding its range of activities over a number of years. Change, if there was any needed, was a gradual process. People appeared to be resistant to notions of more transformative change. I could sense complacency, even smugness, in some quarters. There was a feeling in some areas that the quality of the university's teaching was all that mattered and other issues were of much lesser importance. I remember many bitter conversations as people disputed the notion of students as customers. These discussions were often acrimonious as people fought to preserve provider-led teaching approaches.

However, the environmental changes that took place over the following years began to impact on the thinking of many staff. People were beginning to become concerned as the ground started to shift. It was at this time that the New Directions programme commenced. I believe it appealed to those who actively wanted to change things, as they perceived dangers in the air. The programme gave an outlet and a voice to their views and their concerns. Their enthusiasm infected many people who were on the periphery of these strategic issues and brought them in. The programme brought into clearer focus the threats that external changes and internal weaknesses posed and made it more difficult to argue in favour of the status quo and incremental change. I consider that in many ways the programme caught the tide of the times.

I know that participation in the programme awakened my own thinking on strategic matters which had previously lain dormant, and I do not think I was alone in this. Hundreds of staff, especially middle managers and junior employees became aware of the strategic challenges facing the university and consequently the need to make changes to deal with them. Further, they were encouraged to make their own changes and to improve things in their own areas of influence; and I know from my research and from personal observation that many did this.

I interviewed Geoff Peters, PVC, Strategy, mid-way through 1999 and he told me that he had wanted the programme to capture some of the energy and innovation prevalent at the university in its early days. It was a time when anything had seemed possible. From his perspective, New Directions began at a time when people were 'saying no' to things. But since then new ways of working had developed and there were a lot of new initiatives coming on-stream. People were now ready to change things. He cited, by way of example, how at the workshops people had said that it was not possible to take on new students after August to commence their studies the following February. Now they were arguing whether or not to enrol after Christmas. Importantly, they were not saying this could not be done, but rather we can do it, although there might be some risks attached. It was an approach which he thought 'was unthinkable five or six years ago'. He believed the programme had helped people to become more flexible and student-focused and that it had encouraged them to take action. He cited how several faculties now produced courses twice a year instead of only once a year. In his opinion New Directions had achieved 'a process of getting the OU to change'. He heard people still talking positively about the programme, including one of the new Pro-Vice-Chancellors. In his view there had been significant changes in individuals, he referred to several progressive administrators and myself. He spoke of how there had been: 'a breaking down of organizational structure and work ... a general broadening of roles in the OU. People more willing to consider organizational change' (Peters quoted in McMillan 1999: 392).

His perception was that there had been many changes, although many more were still needed. Some of the changes that had happened had worked better because of the influence of the programme because there was 'a readiness to change, to do things that are more flexible' (interview with Geoff Peters, personal notes).

Change is very much a matter of perception and for Geoff Peters and those involved in the IES study, their perception was of an institution that had changed in a number of ways. The staff survey too found lots of evidence of people wanting to change things. It is also my perception that the university has indeed changed in many ways. However, my perception is also that, paradoxically, at the same time it has not changed. The cumbersome bureaucratic structures still remain hindering and slowing up communications and decision-making and sludging up the streams of creative activity. New areas have been set up to promote entrepreneurial activities and better links with business and commerce, but they are linked to the formal structures of the institution and so have to deal with bureaucratic approaches. On the other hand, however, there is general recognition that the OU cannot rest on its laurels and that it must keep moving and responding to the world outside. People no longer debate the need to change the university. The debate has moved on to: how do we change? There is little or no argument about students as customers and the importance of teaching with a student-centred focus. Of the six new directions set out in 1993 (see Appendix 1) there has been perceptible progress, but the structure and its inherent procedures and supportive practices and endemic bureaucratic thinking (strenuously denied everywhere!) still work against the achievement of simplicity, subsidiarity and quality assurance.

Geoff Peters acknowledged that, towards the end of the programme, New Directions had rocked the boat too much for some. The top management team had developed many misgivings and he felt it necessary to try and tone down its activities and gradually withdraw his involvement. It seems to me that the programme was thus effectively disturbing the organization's equilibrium and beginning to make real changes in hearts and minds when people lost their nerve, or ran out of energy or were overtaken by other events.

In early 1999 Geoff Peters organized another series of strategic workshops called 'Shaping the future of the OU'. These used several of the successful approaches developed in the early workshops. So the New Directions legacy continued in a more subtle form and with some aspects absorbed into the formal processes.

New Directions as a strategic change model

The New Directions change process was just one part of a significant institutional long-term change process that the University began during 1993/4. The University sought to introduce changes via the actions required in its strategic action plan, 'Plans for Change', and one of the key ways it did so was via a more rigorous university-wide planning process. This approach was highly 'deliberate' (Mintzberg and Waters 1989) and required detailed plans for action at departmental level which linked to 'Plans for Change' and the budgetary planning requirements. This approach to strategy, with its heavy emphasis on information gathering and analysis, accords with the mechanistic aspects of the university and traditional notions of change as discussed in Chapter 4.

The New Directions process that evolved was a very different change driver. It was essentially a spontaneous, participative process that developed out of a consultation exercise on the university's strategic action plans. It was influenced by several modes of strategic change especially some of the newer interpretations of change and innovative practice, particularly the learning organization. It was also inspired and influenced by ideas drawn from complexity and these are specifically discussed in the next chapter.

New Directions had its origins in the bureaucratic, traditional side of the university as part of a planned and highly formulated approach to strategy. But as the workshops unfolded so the strategy became less imposed, more emergent and an 'unintended order' (Mintzberg and Waters 1989) emerged that echoed notions of order found in self-organizing systems. The role of self-organization in the programme is discussed further in the next chapter.

The programme reflected many of the patterns which Quinn (1989) considered necessary for successful change initiatives. These included the development of informal networks, the testing of ideas, and the spreading of awareness and support for change ideas. But the programme did not pause to solidify and did not approach things in a logical, step-by-step fashion. Thus it did not match Quinn's logical incrementalism.

Mintzberg and Waters (1989) point out that an emergent strategy is a real world approach that enables strategic learning to take place. Further it is possible to develop a learning approach to strategy (Pedler *et al.* 1991) whereby strategic plans are developed and revised as part of a structured learning process. The New Directions programme did not deliberately set out to establish a structured learning process, but rather learning emerged out of a real world laboratory. The use of feedback loops as part of the process also led to continuous evaluation and reshaping of strategic visions in a way akin to Pedler *et al.*'s (1991) model. The use of feedback using multiple methods and the responsive nature of the programme enabled learning to flow from individuals and groups and around parts of the organization in a way that contributed to continuous organizational learning (Garratt 1995). Most importantly there was genuine listening and feedback from the organizers of the programme, the PVC, Strategy, and the New Directions volunteers.

Leonard-Barton (1994) states that a learning environment is based on egalitarianism and the assumption that everyone can contribute to the organization and such beliefs underpinned New Directions activities.

Involving people in strategic action planning and giving them a voice in their own future can create powerful positive emotions. The programme boosted the confidence and self-esteem of those involved such that they were able to make their own changes. This suggests that by creating feelings of excitement and optimism a change intervention can stimulate learning and energize individuals and groups of people to do things differently. This is to act directly and appeal positively to the emotions of people, rather than to ignore how people will react to strategic planning and then deal with the emotional fall-out when it arises. Such an approach recognizes the importance of the emotions as well as the intellect and incorporates them into the change process, so rejecting reliance on the traditional, rational, logical approach.

Pedler *et al.* (1991) recognize that it is people who provide the energy in an organization and they explore the notion of energy in the learning organization or company as a series of flows. They describe how, in a learning culture, the flow of ideas and action between the individual and the collective creates an energy for development, learning and thus change. It is a model which the New Directions programme with its flow of ideas, information, feedback and individual and collective action at all levels maps onto.

The visioning style of strategic management in vogue in the 1980s encouraged many organizations to make changes, although all too often only cosmetic ones (Moncrief and Smallwood 1996). Thus the pattern of activity at the workshops, with their focus on visioning the future, may appear to be drawing on a poor model of strategic change process. Yet as Pedler *et al.* (1991) point out, why should people change unless they have a new vision before them that will not become a reality without changes being made and learning taking place? Further, a picture of a desired future is essential for any learning company (Pedler *et al.* 1991). Also the gap between the vision and reality can lead to creative tension and energy for change (Senge 1992, 1994). This was an important factor in creating some of the enthusiasm for change amongst some of the programme's participants.

First-order change is a feature of the bureaucracy (Dale 1994) but not second-order change. This is because in Morgan's (1986) view bureaucratic organizations tend to operate in a way that actually impedes second-order change or double-loop learning. But the programme was able to provide an environment which overcame many of the factors which hindered the development of deep-level learning. It encouraged participants to think for themselves, to challenge long-accepted norms and facilitated the development of relationships across departmental boundaries. Participants developed a wider vision of the institution and their role within it. The programme demonstrates how an organization such as a bureaucracy can facilitate the development of double-loop learning as Morgan (1986) suggested by:

- encouraging an open approach to the discussion of strategic change
- by facilitating the exploration of issues from many perspectives
- by recognizing that people can make mistakes and can learn from them
- by encouraging a bottom up approach to the strategic planning process.

New Directions demonstrates that one of the advantages of using a responsive, participative and open approach to organizational change is that it facilitates the flow of change through learning. Thus the programme by encouraging, facilitating and enabling learning in all its many forms created a dynamic for change amongst those involved.

The next chapter considers how the programme meshes within a complexity-based framework and how it suggests a number of real-life complexity based approaches to change.

7   Complexity in action

The New Directions programme fits perfectly with the 'chaos' model of organizational development. From the start it set out to encourage us to link up in different
ways, to support and develop 'Plans for Change'. There was no pre-planned list
of activities. Numerous projects developed as we went along, as more people
became actively involved. ... And there's more to come. Although I don't know
exactly what.

> (Carol Russell, New Directions Action Group, *Open House*, July 1995)

In this chapter I continue to offer evidence from my research on the forms and
patterns created by people within the organizational setting of the Open University
as they engaged in a particular set of activities and processes over a four-year
period. The evidence and rich observation from this case study shows how
complexity science may be usefully applied in understanding human organization
and organizations. As the programme evolved so learning arose from developing
theoretical understandings of complexity and also from practical experimentation
and real-life observation. This chapter considers the programme from a complexity
perspective and show how it maps onto complexity theories. It also offers a simple
model for participative strategic change.

Understandings of change and the butterfly effect

Conventional management tends to think of organizational change in a cause
and effect way, as did many of the people interviewed at the university. This
approach to change supports the view that change can be managed in an orderly
fashion and brought about by a series of logical, planned steps devised to achieve
a predictable future. This accords with the mechanistic approach to change and
reflects the traditional face of the university. However, most of the staff who
participated in New Directions had mixed views on change. On the one hand
they considered that the traditional approach was desirable, but at the same time
they also favoured a more individual, free-flowing and creative approach. An
approach which draws on some of the more radical and dynamic views of change
described in Chapter 4. This in many ways reflects the complexity of the university

with its traditional bureaucratic aspects, its mould-breaking, radical past, its espoused values of equality and its innovative and creative teaching approaches.

New Directions and those involved in it, however, recognized the importance of the individual and how small changes by one person could make a major difference over time. They were aware too that creative individuals in particular could make a significant impact on an organization (Wheatley 1994). This notion was taken on board by many of the participants, one of whom stated, that if 'everyone makes a one per cent effort' then it has 'a dramatic effect on the change process'. One of the programme's 'principles' published in its leaflets states: 'We will achieve far more if 100 of us devote one per cent of our time and energy to changing what we do, than if one person devotes 100 per cent'. Although most people thought change was brought about by traditional methods, at the same time they also believed that the individual, given the opportunity, could also make a difference to the future of the organization. Thus they unconsciously subscribed to the notion of the butterfly effect.

When one looks at the New Directions programme then there are examples of sensitive dependence on initial conditions or the butterfly effect at work. The workshops themselves provide evidence of the difference small changes can make over time. The original workshops led to the 'themed' workshops which themselves influenced policy developments, and further workshops, for example, on international developments and new technology (see Figure 7.1).

The 1994 conference, too, was a one-day event that led to a series of unexpected events and influences. As the evidence in Chapter 6 shows, it affected a number of individuals personally and led to new learning and new behaviours. The reactions of the staff to the conference workshops led by external speakers shows how exposure to events in other organizations can lead to unexpected outcomes. All these small changes were amplified by non-linear feedback systems which individuals and groups created as they interacted with colleagues. Thus the perturbations which arose from the conference joined with those that arose from the workshops, from the briefings, from publications, from coverage in *Open House* and from conversations and emails to create a complex new dynamic. This influenced and encouraged new thinking and new policy developments and, as the Institute for Employment Studies (IES) study reported, led over a period of time to discernible changes in the institution (Tamkin and Barber 1998).

Self-organization at work

As described in Chapter 6 the New Directions programme began as a set of consultative workshops for all the staff, but over time it developed into an innovative programme of activities continuing for some four years. In the autumn of 1996 Carol Russell, a key member of the conference team, produced a map showing the origins of New Directions in 1993, how it developed in 1994 and 1995, and the themes that it raised. The map is a personal snapshot of how the programme's history looked at that time through the eyes of a key activist, and it shows in diagrammatic form how she believed the programme evolved. This map has been adapted and is shown as Figure 7.1.

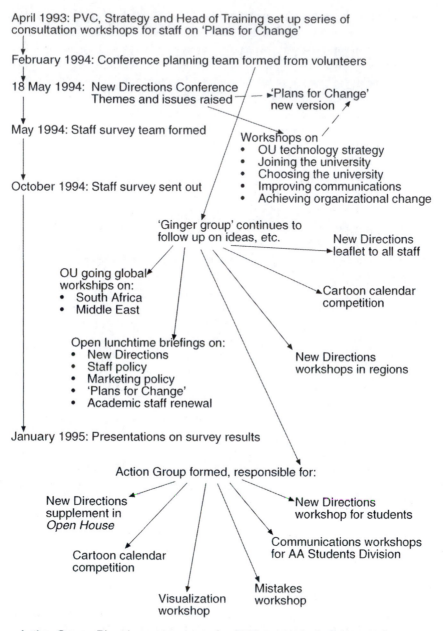

April 1993: PVC, Strategy and Head of Training set up series of consultation workshops for staff on 'Plans for Change'

February 1994: Conference planning team formed from volunteers

18 May 1994: New Directions Conference Themes and issues raised — → 'Plans for Change' new version

May 1994: Staff survey team formed

Workshops on
• OU technology strategy
• Joining the university
• Choosing the university
• Improving communications
• Achieving organizational change

October 1994: Staff survey sent out

'Ginger group' continues to follow up on ideas, etc.

New Directions leaflet to all staff

OU going global workshops on:
• South Africa
• Middle East

Cartoon calendar competition

Open lunchtime briefings on:
• New Directions
• Staff policy
• Marketing policy
• 'Plans for Change'
• Academic staff renewal

New Directions workshops in regions

January 1995: Presentations on survey results

Action Group formed, responsible for:

New Directions supplement in *Open House*

New Directions workshop for students

Communications workshops for AA Students Division

Cartoon calendar competition

Visualization workshop

Mistakes workshop

Action Group: Planning commences for 1996 events including a conference

Figure 7.1 Spread of activities map (adapted from a map drawn by Carol Russell)

The map shows clearly how the success of the first workshops led to further workshops the following year which picked up on the themes emerging from year one and the 1994 conference. The programme was not planned, co-ordinated or controlled in a linear way in accordance with the rational view of management theory. The programme, or rather those who organized it, took an opportunistic approach to change, building on ideas, actions and events in a spontaneous way that is essentially self-organizing (Morgan 1993).

If one looks at the map one sees waves of activities spreading across the university and the emergence of the volunteer groups and the ripples of activity that they then created. None of this was pre-planned. Once the work of the conference team was over the members of the team took it upon themselves to follow up on the conference issues and ideas and to support new activities. Then, after the staff survey work was completed, the 1995 New Directions action group was created by a group of enthusiasts including staff from both of these teams. These groups arose as a natural response to the events around them creating themselves into informal networks. This unplanned response to events whereby individuals formed groups around specific issues and interests and worked to deal with them lies at the heart of self-organization in organizations (Stacey 1996a). The key role played by the New Directions teams in energizing and organizing the process was discussed in Chapter 6. Their self-organizing aspects are discussed in detail later in this chapter.

As discussed in the last chapter, the programme began as essentially a 'deliberate' strategy and became primarily a rather 'emergent' or 'consensus' strategy (Mintzberg and Waters 1989). A 'consensus' strategy is one which is driven not by top management but evolves through the 'results of a host of individual actions' (Mintzberg and Waters 1989: 13). Further, 'an emergent strategy means, not chaos, but in essence unintended order' (Mintzberg and Waters 1989: 17). Thus the highly 'emergent' or 'consensus' strategy with its notions of many individual actions and unintentional order resonates powerfully with notions of self-organizing systems.

There are many parallels between the staff volunteers in the New Directions programme and Morgan's (1993) self-organizing termite colony. For example, they did not follow any predetermined plans but responded to emerging situations and events in a spontaneous way. But although they may not have worked to any predetermined plan they had a strong sense of what they were trying to achieve. They wanted to change the way the OU did things, and this purpose informed and guided their actions.

Spontaneity is one of the key attributes of self-organizing systems and was a key feature of the New Directions change process. It had picked up on ideas/ events/issues as they arose from the workshops or from the staff and had responded spontaneously. For example, one of the action group wrote:

> At several New Directions events last year, staff had suggested we should also be asking students what kind of OU they'd like to see in the future. So in the usual New Directions fashion, we decided to get some students together and ask them.

> (McMillan 1999: 344)

This spontaneous, opportunistic, 'let's have a go' response is a hallmark of the volunteers and the programme and it accords well with Morgan's (1993) description of a self-organizing termite colony approach.

The programme had both planned and spontaneous features, in that the content was put together spontaneously but the structure evolved over time in support of the activities and the ethos of the programme. It had what one senior manager described as 'structured spontaneity'. He added that it became 'more freewheeling' as it went on, yet there was still 'a structure within it' like 'a self-imposed hierarchy' (McMillan 1999: 344). In other words, order emerged from within the self-organized systems, without the need for strong controlling mechanisms. This is an example of Kauffman's (1996) 'order for free' whereby self-organizing systems create their own internal patterns of order.

The New Directions programme had begun with a sense of purpose which was to change the institution by involving its staff. Thus the overall programme had a clear sense of direction and an understanding of the desired outcomes to be derived from this. This is essential for a self-organizing approach to managing change (Morgan 1993). Once the programme began to unfold, so fresh objectives emerged but still within the framework created by the programme's overall purpose. Again these objectives were not pre-planned but were a spontaneous response to events. As Morgan (1993) points out, a self-organizing termite looks for opportunities to create 'mounds' of activity, or projects to undertake which are consistent with the overall direction in which they wish to move forward. Further, just as New Directions encouraged staff to take action themselves to change the university, so self-organizing termites encourage others to take their own actions in support of the overall project.

> Termites attract termites. The 'mounds' of activity that you initiate or support will often energize, focus, and mobilise others of similar mind. They will help yet others create new perspective and leverage on their situations, thus adding to the momentum.
>
> (Morgan 1993: 61)

There is evidence which was discussed in Chapter 6 to show that the behaviour of the volunteers and those who attended events did indeed attract others to participate in the programme. The people who came forward to create the staff survey team spoke of being inspired and excited at the conference and wanting to become a part of the programme. The activities of the volunteers created an energy and a momentum which enabled the programme to roll forward for some four years and to evolve in a free form way as Figure 7.1 illustrates.

Fractals

During 1993 and 1994 a rich and complex programme of activity developed out of the initial programme of workshops as Figure 7.2 shows. Each small circle represents a different category of staff. Only one workshop is shown but it is

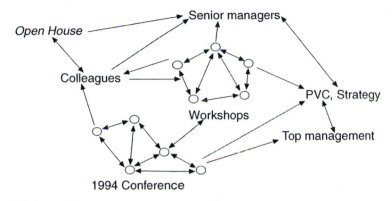

Figure 7.2 Interactions

representative of the many workshops that took place. All these events followed a similar pattern. There was always a mix of staff from all categories, grades and locations and the process involved visioning, creative presentations, free-flowing discussions and feedback. The content or the theme at each workshop may have been different, but the processes always followed a recognizable pattern as did the style and behaviours of the organizers and facilitators. Ideas and suggestions were fed back to the university's top management from whence they cascaded out to senior and middle managers. The 1994 conference was in many ways a scaled-up version of the workshops. Even without showing all the events that took place and the number of attendees at each it is possible by looking at the diagram to grasp the richness of the interactions and the possibilities for feedback and amplification of key themes.

The programme with its patterning and self-similarity which was repeated on a number of levels, sometimes on different scales, throughout the organization has many of the aspects of an organizational fractal as described by Wheatley (1994). These are also, in her view, to be observed in self-organizing systems. The New Directions programme had visions of an OU of the future, strongly valued all the people in the university and believed in openness and equality. These and other features of the programme, such as its spontaneous and free-flowing nature, all suggest that it was essentially self-organizing and fractal in nature.

Shadow systems

As Stacey (1996a) points out there are often many shadow systems in bureaucratic organizations where they offer a way of coping with the mechanistic face of the organization. Shadow systems are network of contacts that are informal, self-organizing and operate outside the formal structures (Stacey 1996a). The university, like any other traditional organization, has many shadow systems formed by staff who network and work together often to circumvent the more cumbersome organizational procedures. The New Directions programme encouraged the formation of informal networks and created a network of shadow systems under its aegis. The workshops and other events brought together staff from all over the university. Many gained important insights into how other staff contributed to the work of the OU and how they could perhaps work together in the future. New informal networks of social contacts were created which had the potential of becoming new shadow systems, which many of them did over time.

The New Directions groups were made up of New Directions enthusiasts who responded to the programme and its approach and in so doing created networks of like-minded people. People spoke of forming new relationships which still endure. They created and supported a shadow system that existed outside the formal system. The PVC, Strategy, had an important role, for his support created the 'space' for the New Directions shadow systems to flourish.

The 1995 action group provides a good example of a shadow system or network that accords with many features of Stacey's (1996a) description of a self-organizing shadow system. It was not set up by prior intention or design, but arose as an unplanned response to the 'situation' at the time. It existed outside the formal university structures although it reported informally to the PVC, Strategy. The group came together to address a number of issues and, although it lasted for only two years, people within the group continued to keep in touch afterwards. It sought in a number of ways to introduce innovations and changes and challenged the status quo of the OU. Further, its existence added to the tension already existing between the formal systems and other New Directions inspired shadow systems. It was a tension which made many senior managers uneasy and even hostile.

Stacey (1996b: 20) describes how the 'creative play' of a self-organizing shadow system is subversive and will ultimately replace parts of the existing formal system. This happens because members of the shadow system act in highly creative and innovative ways while operating in this system, yet at the same time they are carrying out their normal role in the legitimate system. When any learning that takes place in the shadow system is transferred to the 'everyday' role then part of the formal system is changed. As was discussed in Chapter 6 considerable learning took place within the shadow system created by New Directions and many staff spoke of changes in the way they carried out their jobs as a result. Thus the self-organizing shadow system worked through learning to introduce changes into the formal system.

In 1996 the external environment changed and senior managers became fearful and fell back on traditional controlling behaviours. Thus the orderly, formal system was strengthened. At the same time New Directions was partly absorbed into the formal system as some of its ideas were adopted. For example, the lunchtime briefings were taken up by the Public Relations department and became 'On the Record'. Further, many of those previously active described how they felt over-whelmed by the new challenges and extra workloads and how energy drained away from the programme. Thus the New Directions self-organizing shadow system was weakened and much of the creativity that challenged the status quo was lost.

A complex adaptive system in action

In many ways the New Directions programme was something of a chameleon adapting itself to suit different circumstances. As one senior manager observed

New Directions was changeable in that sometimes it was a ginger group, at other times almost allied to the structure, and at other times it was a counter organization group and almost subversive. This corresponds to Stacey's (1996a) 'fluid, shifting aspect' of a shadow system. Those involved were responding to events and learning how best to adapt and respond themselves to changing times and changing agendas for action. As discussed in Chapter 6 there is considerable evidence that complex or double-loop learning and adaption took place amongst those who were involved in the programme. Thus the programme could be described not only as a self-organizing shadow system but also as a complex, adaptive system. It could be described as a complex, adaptive system because:

- its survival depended on learning, adaption and innovation (McMaster 1996)
- The agents or individuals in the system interacted in a way that constituted learning (Stacey 1996a)
- it was both self-organizing and learning (Battram 1996)
- it interacted in a non linear, responsive way with other agents or individuals (Stacey 1996a)
- it acquired information about itself and its environment using feedback and used feedback to construct its own models (Stacey 1996a)
- it observed the reactions it provoked and the consequences of these to revise the way it responded and behaved, in other words it used feedback to adapt and learn (Stacey 1996a)
- patterns of behaviour emerged that could not have been predicted and could not be ascribed to one individual, thus it had emergent properties (Lewin 1993; Merry 1995; Waldrop 1994).

Emergence

Emergence is a key feature of a complex, adaptive system (Coveney and Highfield 1995; Lewin 1993; Merry 1995; Waldrop 1994) and there is evidence of emergence and other self-organizing principles in the patterns of behaviour which became identifiable as the New Directions way of doing things. In the same way that a flock of birds self-organizes and a number of key principles emerge to ensure an effective and spontaneous response to circumstances that the whole flock follows (Waldrop 1994), so too did unwritten and unintentional principles emerge which the New Directions groups followed. Various levels of learning were experienced by those who were involved in the programme and there is evidence of complex or double-loop learning that changed the way a number of individuals viewed the world and the way they behaved. Their thinking and behaviour changed influenced by their belonging to a larger entity, an entity which they had helped to create. This in Lewin's (1993) view is another example of the phenomenon of emergence.

No-one could have foretold the way the New Directions programme would evolve. But a series of workshops, briefings, and publications coalesced into a greater whole that was described by staff as a 'movement' for change and as the 'people's programme'. In other words, out of all the workshops and other activities unexpectedly emerged a greater whole. It became an unexpected collective expression of individual energies, beliefs and aspirations.

Self-organizing teams at work

The conference planning team and the staff survey team both fit Stacey's (1996a) description of self-organizing groups as ones that arise spontaneously around specific issues, communicate and co-operate about the issues, reach a consensus and give a committed response to the issues.

When I compared the teams with Stacey's (1996a) definitions of self-organized and self-managed teams, the evidence showed that both teams could be described as self-organizing, although the survey team also had significant attributes of a self-managed or empowered team. This would appear to reflect the nature of the team's project and its link with the formal organization of the university (i.e. it was carrying out a project on behalf of the Staff Policy Committee). The teams were also compared with ten other characteristics which were theoretically informed by my reading of the literature including Capra (1996), Kauffman (1996), Merry (1995), Morgan (1993), Wheatley (1994) and my own thinking. These were that a self-organizing team in an organization setting:

- knows what it has to do
- has meetings that are loosely structured
- the team's purpose influences the structure of the meetings
- its decision-making is mainly spontaneous
- there is freedom in its meetings to explore lots of ideas
- there are lots of ideas which emerge spontaneously
- there is a lot of energy and enthusiasm.

Overall, the conference planning team closely matched these definitions but the survey team less so. Table 7.1 shows how closely the two teams matched both Stacey's and my own definitions (see Figure 7.3).

My research also provided additional data on team working which added to and built on Stacey's definitions of self-managed and self-organized teams. This makes it possible to show these differing approaches to team working set against the organizational contexts of four simple models of organizations (see Figure 7.3).

In this figure the first eight statements that describe self-managed and self-organizing teams are based on Stacey's (1996a) definitions. The final six descriptions shown in italics are derived from my own research. The definitions that describe a traditional team or committee are based on my own observations and research and in relation to the definitions for self-managed and self-organizing teams.

The top of the diagram shows a line representing the changing flow of team working from the very formal committee system on the left to the very informal self-organizing team on the right. At the bottom of the diagram two other lines represent the flow of organizations and time from the bureaucracy on the left to

Committee / Traditional team	Self-managed or empowered team	Self-organizing team
Part of formal structure	Part of formal structure	Not part of formal structure
Formal and permanent	Formal, temporary or permanent	Informal and temporary
Not spontaneously formed	Not spontaneously formed	Spontaneously formed
Controlled by senior management	Indirectly controlled or steered by senior management	Boundaries influenced by senior management
Managers decide 'who' and 'what'	Managers decide 'who' and 'what'	Team members decide 'who' and 'what'
Represent and reinforce the hierarchy	Replace the hierarchy	Often in conflict with or constrained by the hierarchy
Represent senior management	Empowered by senior management	Empowered by team's members
Strongly shared culture	Strongly shared culture	Cultural difference provoke and constrain
Little or no sense of shared purpose	*Some sense of shared purpose*	*Strong sense of shared purpose*
Order via controlling, formal processes	*Order achieved via recognized processes*	*Inherent order emerges*
Behaviours governed by procedures and roles	*Behaviours influenced by procedures and roles*	*Behaviours predominantly spontaneous*
Strong sense of role commitment	*Strong sense of team commitment*	*Strong sense of personal and team commitment*
Low levels of energy and enthusiasm	*Variable amounts of energy and enthusiasm*	*High levels of energy and enthusiasm*
Little or no learning possibilities	*Possibility of some learning*	*Co-learning community*
Bureaucracy Traditional organization	Modern / traditional	Complexity organization
20th century		21st century

Figure 7.3 Team-working in organizations – a fluid spectrum of process (adapted from McMillan 2000: 191)

Table 7.1 Self-organizing teams

Team	Stacey's (1996a) definitions – match	My definitions – match	Overall match
Conference planning team	70%	80%	75%
Staff survey team	46%	63%	54.5%

Source: Adapted from McMillan 2000: 186.

the emerging twenty-first century or complexity management organization on the right. This model thus represents a flow of time as well as process from the bureaucratic and classical models of organizations at the beginning of the last century, through the adaptive, experimental models of the 1980s and 1990s, to the latest emerging concepts. The organization of the 1980s and 1990s are referred to as 'modern/traditional' because although many adapted their structures and updated working practices most still thought in a traditional way about people and processes.

A model is necessarily a simplified and interpretative representation of reality and the reality is that in most organizations and most teams there are facets of more than one model. But it shows how self-organizing principles used in a team context are an extension, or further development, of today's self-managed or empowered teams and a move towards a complexity orientated view of team working.

The 1995 New Directions action group

The New Directions action group was a ginger group which formed spontaneously in early 1995 in response to the issues that had been thrown up by the conference and the staff survey. It defined its role as a group dedicated to motivate and enable change in the university by encouraging local action and creativity. It would listen to all the staff, keep them informed and empower them to take action. It fits well with Stacey's (1996a) description of a shadow system or network, as discussed earlier, and his description of self-organizing team as 'a fluid network process in which informal, temporary teams form spontaneously around issues' (Stacey 1996a: 333).

When it first met in January 1995 the group used brainstorming and discussion to forge its new identity and an electronic whiteboard to facilitate and record the process and outcomes. The group agreed what everyone considered New Directions stood for and proceeded to develop a shared vision of the OU of the future. It then moved on to its priorities for action and set up project groups for 1995 with names attached to each project. Seven projects were listed and four were achieved during the year. The action group at its first meeting had used the meetings' style and processes developed by the earlier teams. It had quickly explored the issues, made decisions via consensus and agreed actions and responsibilities. A shared commitment had encouraged self-organization and experience had enabled it to self-organize to deliver.

A key feature of self-organization is that people empower themselves (Stacey 1996a) and the new group did just that, for example, when it devised and ran a programme of activities and 'experimental' workshops designed to challenge the 'blame culture'.

Moving towards the edge of chaos

By the late 1980s the Open University existed in a stable state not far from Kauffman's (1996: 26) 'frozen, ordered regime' and the kind of rigid organization that is in danger of ossifying and dying (Merry 1995). But at its height the New Directions programme moved involved individuals and those areas of the university influenced by its activities away from a stable position and closer to the edge of chaos. The New Directions movement created a dynamic that actively challenged the status quo in some areas. It created a self-organizing shadow system and also spawned several small shadow systems as delegates from the conference and the workshops formed new networks. Thus over a four-year period there was a surge of new networks and a nest of fresh shadow systems was created. As a result, information and energy flowed in new patterns across all these new webs and connections and in Battram's (1996) view, extra information flows between living cells moves them closer to the edge of chaos. It created a rich learning environment that involved individuals and groups who changed their views and behaviours and thus their bit of the organization. It actively experimented and took risks in the cause of innovation and creativity, key attributes of existing on the edge of chaos (Merry 1995).

If the New Directions programme was operating close to the edge of chaos how much of the university did so too? Given that some 23 per cent of the staff, chiefly from its central headquarters at Walton Hall, were involved in the programme, then it is clear that as an institutional whole it would not have been operating at the edge of chaos. However, there were pockets of activity, particularly in the administrative areas where activists and others tried to emulate the principles and approaches of New Directions and, for a time, moved their own bit of the university nearer to the edge of chaos.

Complexity ideas and key players

As I wrote earlier in this book, I came across ideas of chaos theory in 1993 as the programme began. During that year and those that followed I continued to read further on complexity and to attend presentations on complexity and allied topics including seminars led by Ralph Stacey, Frijof Capra, Brian Goodwin and Gareth Morgan in order to further my learning and understanding.

As a pragmatist and an experimenter, I deliberately introduced complexity principles into the programme and sought to influence key people and those who worked with me, particularly the facilitators on the workshops. I worked very closely with Carol Russell who became a lead volunteer in the programme and who herself started to study complexity. We wrote a number of papers together and she is now studying for her doctorate and using complexity as a defining feature. At meetings of the 1995 action group Carol and I would use complexity-derived notions to inform discussion and practical applications. People were encouraged to let go and see what happened if they did not too tightly prescribe things.

Geoff Peters had wanted to overcome the hierarchical barriers that blocked or slowed action for change and deliberately sought to bypass many of the management structures, believing that individuals needed to take action if things were to change. In my view, his commitment to empowering the individual and his preparedness to let go and support the volunteers enabled self-organizing processes to flourish for a time.

Mapping onto complexity

The New Directions programme shows that it is possible to use ideas derived from complexity to create an effective and innovative change process in a traditional, hierarchical organization in the bureaucratic mould. The programme created a spontaneous process for change that drew on self-organizing principles and used self-organizing teams. It created a 'backcloth' (Johnson 1996) which offered non-academic as well as academic staff the opportunity to self-organize. It did this by offering all categories of staff a chance to become involved and by the open, responsive way it did it, created the conditions for several self-organizing systems to emerge.

The self-organizing systems created by the programme responded and adapted to events and ideas as individuals engaged in double-loop learning. Their learning and consequent revision of outlook and attitudes led to new actions and fresh interpretations of the organization and their role in it. Complex adaptive systems are all about learning and changing (Merry 1995). This was the experience of the activists in the programme and their double loop learning ensured that their self-organizing systems developed into complex adaptive ones (Stacey 1996a).

Complex learning and adaption push a system to the edge of chaos (Merry 1995; Waldrop 1994). This is where complex adaptive systems flourish and where an organization is at its most creative and innovative (Stacey 1996a). As the New Directions programme showed, the creation of a new shadow system in an organization, typically a bureaucracy, where people are familiar with shadow systems, can have a profound effect on parts of the organization if the shadow system creates a tension with the formal systems that pulls towards the edge of chaos. New Directions by creating several self-organizing shadow systems, which also were complex adaptive systems, pushed some individuals and some groups away from an equilibrium state (Michaels 1990) and closer to the edge of chaos. This is an excellent place to be, but it requires balancing between a rigid, ossifying order and a deeply chaotic state where things begin to disintegrate (Kauffman 1996; Merry 1995). The university with its very orderly systems and controlling mechanisms provided a counterweight to the more radical tendencies of New

Directions and so, paradoxically, helped maintain the programme and the pockets of New Directions-inspired activity at the edge of chaos. Although a traditional bureaucratic organization does not readily provide the right kind of environment for a self-organizing change intervention to flourish, this suggests that should such an intervention take root it is unlikely to tip the organization over into the chaotic realm where it would disintegrate. Thus I would suggest that an effective way to change a bureaucracy is not to rely on restructuring by cutting out layers of management and procedures, but rather to provide the right environment for a number of self-organizing change processes to flourish alongside a restructuring process. Change the way people think and work and then they will through their thinking and behaviours introduce new ways of doing things that will further change structures and accompanying procedures as part of an ongoing process.

As discussed in Chapter 5, Stacey (1996a) has developed a complexity-based theory of organization which is based on nine propositions. How well does the Open University and the New Directions programme map onto this? Evidence from the programme supports seven of the nine propositions. This is summarized as follows:

- The nature of the programme, its emerging dynamics, the spread of its influences, the range of interactions and responses all support the notion of an organization as a web of non-linear feedback loops connecting people and other environments.
- As a non linear feedback system the university operated predominantly in conditions of stability, but changes in its environment produced instabilities which it responded to with its strategic planning moves. These were designed to help it cope with these instabilities and to adapt to them. The New Directions programme helped to pull parts of the university and certain individuals and groups away from stability and towards the edge of chaos.
- The paradoxical nature of organizations is reflected on many levels by the university and the programme. Some individuals were excited by the prospect of change and changes, even radical ones, and others were hostile and afraid.

  Some of the university's strategic activities, such as the new unit planning process sought to control and predetermine activities and outcomes. While others like the New Directions programme sought to let go and react spontaneously to events.
- An organization that is pulled too far into stability will ossify and find real difficulties in responding to events. The university had evolved since its radical inception into a traditional, hierarchical bureaucracy and it had failed in many ways to change sufficiently to meet the new challenges emanating from its external environment. As the conference showed, staff were seriously concerned that the institution was under threat from other providers, and was being left behind in terms of multi-media development and the use of effective marketing strategies. Agreement to have a staff survey to find out how people felt about working at the university had been talked about for some 18 months before it was picked up. In the meantime staff morale had fallen. There were

pockets of instability in some areas that produced new ideas for teaching and student services and these provided a small pull away from equilibrium. 'Plans for Change' and the New Directions programme sought to add to this pull. The university was not pulled far enough towards non-equilibrium to test whether or not it would disintegrate in such a position.

- Traditional analytical long-term planning methods and controls can only be successfully applied to the short term and not the long term. The use of the 'Investors in People' initiative in a highly formalized and preplanned way linked to the new unit planning processes, was given very significant funding and staffing resource, yet failed to deliver across the whole university over a three-year period. The development of the New Directions programme from a short, planned exercise in consultation to a spontaneous and free-flowing programme of activities that unexpectedly unfolded over a four-year period could not have been predicted. Both these interventions demonstrate how it is not possible to predict nor control the medium-term future and thus not the long-term future.

- The programme supports the notion of long-term planning as a spontaneous self-organizing process out of which new strategic directions may arise. The emergence of the democratic action plan from the conference supports this possibility. Spontaneous self-organization arose from the activities of different groups of staff as they grappled with strategic issues and experienced the learning that these interactions stimulated.

- The New Directions programme showed how it was possible for people in an organization, and therefore, managers, to create realistic visions of the future and thus discover the possible longer-term future of their organization.

Stacey (1996a) described the successful organization as one which has irregular cycles and unconnected trends and because of its own dynamics cannot know what the specifics of its future will be. The New Directions programme existed for some four years and thus the study of this programme is not long enough, in my view, to determine whether or not the university maps onto this aspect of the model of the successful organization.

Nonaka (1988) describes some of the ways an organization can create chaos or fluctuations in order to transform itself. How well did the New Directions process map onto his conclusions drawn from research on Japanese companies? The programme mirrored several of his ideas as follows:

- Via its early workshops in particular, it offered strategic visions which were open to interpretation and debate. This did lead to creativity.
- New information entered the organization or the system via the use of external speakers at the two conferences.
- It promoted creative discussions between groups of staff and encouraged experimentation.
- It stimulated dynamic co-operation and encouraged employees to change their points of view.

- It set up self-organizing teams which were protected by senior management (the PVC, Strategy).

But it did not seek to seek to create a crisis and provoke extreme reactions from people. This is an extremely risky strategy, which Nonaka admits can put people under extreme pressures and even cause the organization to disappear. Indeed, when a crisis did arise in late 1995/6 and the funding situation became critical it did not lead the university into creative new ways, instead many managers fell back upon the old way of doing things.

Nonaka's (1988) observations of renewal in Japanese firms convinced him that an organization needs a strategic vision which is open to interpretation if it is to create renewing chaos. Further, it needs processes which encourage 'creative dialogues' between groups of staff regardless of status, and opportunities for experimentation and debate. These factors create fluctuations in ideas and points of view which if amplified by a series of feedback loops and fed back into the organization stimulate waves of change. The university's strategic action plan provided the strategic vision around which the workshops created a flow of dialogue and debate which was amplified via a variety of feedback systems and over time set up waves of change across those areas of the institution involved in the programme. Thus the case study evidence supports Nonaka's ideas and shows that it is possible to effectively transfer some of them from a Japanese context into an English one. However, his notion that people need pushing to the edge by using extreme pressure is one that I do not believe would transfer well and was not one that was used in the New Directions process.

Complexity teaches us to look for flows and patterns in organizations rather than static structures. Wheatley (1994) emphasizes the importance of recognizing the energy flows in an organization. Evidence from the programme supports Wheatley's contention that energy comes through relationships and is encouraged by participative management and the formation of self-organizing teams. It also confirms Capra's (1996) definition of a self-organizing system as one that has a constant flow of energy and matter (information) and non-linear interconnectedness. Thus the case study evidence supports the notion of the importance of energy as a resource and a stimulus for change. This suggests that organizations should not only pay considerable attention to the 'hard' resources available for organizational change processes but also the 'soft' energy available, which is less readily identified.

The workshops stimulated and encouraged the free flow and creation of information within the programme which Nonaka (1988) considers one condition necessary for the deliberate generation of chaos. Wheatley (1994) describes how a mixture of people working together can self-organize, weave potent visions of the future and create a rich fractal dynamic that energizes the organization. This notion is supported by evidence from the case study. The programme brought together a significant number of staff from all categories, grades and locations and gave them the opportunity to exchange ideas, to challenge each other and the status quo and to engage in interactive learning experiences. This created two things: energy and excitement for many of those associated with the programme; and information which flowed in a variety of feedback loops between individuals in the workshops, between colleagues and groups. This matches Wheatley's descriptions and supports her notion that using the right kind of workshops can stimulate and create a series of local change dynamics.

Thus, if one considers the New Directions programme in the light of complexity science, then there is significant evidence to show how insights and principles derived from complexity can work to influence and introduce processes for change in a complex and traditional organization like the OU.

A model for participative strategic change

In a New Directions style change process there are many employees at all levels involved in considering the future of the organization. Thus the total cumulative knowledge, experience and ingenuity involved in dealing with the unpredictable is considerably greater than that available when using more traditional and less participative interventions.

In Figure 7.4 I have used icebergs as a metaphor to model how a traditional, hierarchical organization may change while it is undergoing a New Directions style change process.

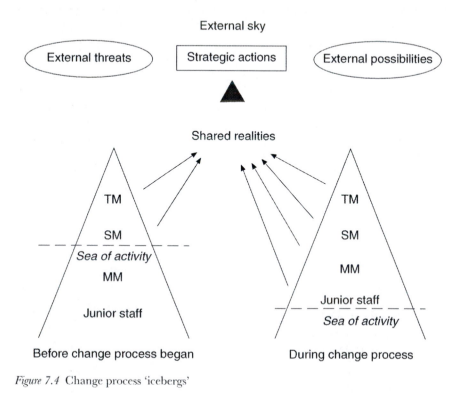

Figure 7.4 Change process 'icebergs'

The iceberg represents the staff layers in the organization. TM equals top management, SM, senior management and MM, middle management. As the iceberg on the left shows most of the time most of the people in an organization are submerged under a sea of everyday activity. In other words, they are doing their jobs and making things happen. They are not in a position to focus on and to study the external sky around the organization. Some may get glimpses of what is happening, but for most it is not their prime concern. It is left to the top managers and some of the senior managers to watch the external sky and to consider how best to react and respond to its ever-changing nature. They are often well aware that most of the staff do not share their concerns nor appreciate the sometimes difficult nature of their position.

But, as the iceberg on the right shows, while an organization undergoes a widespread New Directions style change process then the sea of activity recedes from time-to-time and all levels of staff have an opportunity to consider the external sky and how best to respond to it. More staff are able to understand better the challenges faced by the managers on the top of the iceberg. Some of these realities become shared and with this better understanding. This is particularly important in times of change. There is some sharing of response as the layers of staff in the iceberg share possibilities, explore future visions and consider appropriate actions. Some sense of shared purpose emerges. This is enhanced as people learn together. A whole new source of ideas, insights, energies and collective wisdom is now deciding how best to work with the 'weather' of the external environment to ensure the survival of the organization.

As the evidence from the case study shows, the New Directions programme was a complex change process in which groups of active enthusiasts became heavily involved and played a key role in creating pockets and flows of change. Aspects of the programme mapped clearly onto some accepted models of change and learning, notably the learning organization. It is possible to view the programme as representative of an approach that seeks to include what it perceives as the most useful innovative thinking, along with accepted models of strategic change and an infusion of ideas from complexity. All this was taking place within a complex, complicated, organization dominated by a hierarchical structure and a bureaucratic tradition, albeit with pockets of innovation and self-organization.

8 Future possibilities, future choices

The intuitive mind is a sacred gift and the rational mind is a faithful servant. We have created a society that honours the servant and has forgotten the gift.

Albert Einstein

For managers interested in working with concepts from complexity science the challenge is: how do I move towards a complexity-based organization? How do I begin this journey when I live and work in an environment that is largely unaware of these ideas, especially with reference to their application in management and business. How do I begin when I am surrounded by traditional management concepts many of which are antithetical to such proposals? How do I begin this task of transition? This chapter offers a 'twelve principles' model designed to facilitate a complexity-based change process and also a 'transition strategy' model. Both models are based on real-life research and offer managers a way to move their organizations towards a complexity-based model of organization.

What other possibilities does complexity science offer that could help managers and organizations to adapt and survive in the turbulent conditions of the twenty-first century? Understanding of complexity offers managers and researchers alike fresh perspectives on organization theory and practice, and these and possibilities for the future are explored in this chapter, particularly via the 'fractal web' model. This offers a speculative way of considering organization structure and design principles that takes into account the interconnectedness of all facets of organizational life and enables them to flourish in a dynamic interplay.

Twelve principles for encouraging a complexity-based change process

If a New Directions style approach to organizational change is taken, then resources are required to set up workshops and project teams and to encourage fresh flows of information with infusions from outside the organization. But once the systems start to self-organize then the dynamics they create tend to engender their own energies. As the teams demonstrated, the staff involved were able to carry out their project work in addition to their normal roles. Some people may become highly energized and motivated, as did the staff who spontaneously created the 1995 action group. It is likely that energy will also be demanded of those managers with controlling tendencies who will need to refrain from interfering. A participative approach to envisioning the future and a self-organizing response may prove more effective and less demanding on both people and resources than a traditional one with all the preplanning, analysis and resources that it involves.

The New Directions teams and the 1995 action group showed that people can organize and get on with things without waiting for someone to tell them what to do. They experiment and learn from each other, new behaviours are developed and new patterns and principles for being emerge. This is true emergence where it is not possible to predict what eventually happens nor to reduce the patterns of activity to any one individual's action. It is a very effective way of delivering discrete change events in project form. Knowing that small perturbations can over time lead to major changes, i.e. the butterfly effect, suggests that organizations need not rely on major change initiatives to make a difference. Additionally, small changes are often more palatable than large ones and can have the added advantage of being unopposed.

If an organization wishes to encourage a complexity-based change process then the following twelve interdependent principles provide a model based on the real life experience of the New Directions programme. Further, the model offers a change process using complexity principles which resonates well with some of the newer approaches to organizational change based on involvement and learning.

1   Stimulate changes at the micro level, primarily by focusing on people as individuals, encouraging them to think and to behave differently. Workshops and a range of creative activities and events can help to do this. Small changes constantly happening at this level can affect the larger systems and, over time, real changes can occur. Bring in information from other organizations that will highlight differences, stimulate discussion and encourage individuals to consider new ways of doing things. These together with more traditional changes at the macro level will move the organization away from equilibrium and towards the edge of chaos.

2   Facilitate this micro level process by setting up a series of workshops about the future plans of the organization which bring together mixed groups of staff from all areas, categories and levels to share ideas and experiences. This approach will:
    *   awaken many staff to the opportunities and threats the organization faces and encourage strategic thinking at the operational level
    *   provide those staff who actively want to become involved with an opportunity to contribute to future strategy development
    *   further encourage individuals to bring about changes themselves and so help to start small individual waves of change
    *   create fresh flows of information across the organization
    *   enable individuals to develop new perspectives on their roles; learn more about their organization; engage in active learning experiences

- involve a wide range of people in the change process which will help create multiple change dynamics at an individual and group level which have the potential to bring about significant changes over time
- provide the right conditions for the development of self-organizing networks which will challenge the formal systems.

3   Ensure that a senior manager with strategic responsibilities is at every 'strategic' workshop to brief people on the organization's current strategic plans, to give advice, to listen actively to ideas and recommendations for action from the staff, and to feed back to senior management.

4   Use 'strategic' workshops to create energy for change. It can often be difficult for people to discuss visions of the future because of their awareness of the gap between reality and the vision, but this gap produces creative tension which Senge (1992, 1994) identifies as an energy source. Use workshops explicitly to explore the 'gap'. An organization needs to take positive action to make the vision a reality and so reduce the gap. If this is a slow process then frustration and emotional tension arise. But for some individuals the gap will produce energy for change.

5   Invite people to form self-organizing teams. These will encourage a self-organizing process for a range of change activities to emerge within an organization. The teams may also stimulate more changes by moving ahead on specific change projects. Further, each group has the potential to create a range of learning experiences and thus opportunities for individual and group learning. They may organize further activities that stimulate local changes.

6   Provide the right environment for a self-organizing change process to emerge. This includes providing safe organizational 'space' for experimentation and learning and recognition of the role that humour can play in developing and maintaining equality of participation. Most importantly consider the ethos, values and type of activities associated with the process, as shown in Table 8.1.

7   A complexity-derived change process is essentially free-flowing and unplanned but it could use a more traditional and 'deliberate' approach to strategy as its starting point. Such an approach blends the 'old' with the 'new' and by so doing avoids excessive shifts of approach that both individuals and organizations often find hard to handle. This makes it a useful 'transition' model of

Table 8.1 Environment, ethos, values and activities

Environment	Ethos and values	Activities
Safe	Egalitarian	Fun
Stimulating	Open	Experimental
Responsive	Democratic	Challenging
Supportive	Reflect those of the	Use mixed staff groups
Non-political	organization if possible	Offer a variety of learning opportunities

Source: Adapted from McMillan 2000: 188.

strategy. Further, such a change process integrates spontaneous and intuitive approaches with planned and rational ones and merges the 'old' and 'new' scientific paradigms in a healthy balance (Capra 1996). The 'transition' model is discussed in the next sub-section.

8 Use experienced, skilled and trusted facilitators to ensure equality of involvement and to help with the dismantling of cultural and hierarchical barriers which could block the free-flowing nature of the process and impede equality of participation. Further, they should be used when setting up self-organizing groups to encourage the development of collective experience and the emergence of group adaption. The facilitators should understand the thinking and the principles that underpin self-organizing groups and will need to develop a high level of credibility with the groups themselves.

9 The change process should aim to work with those who want to be involved. One way to do this is by the creation of an involving process that uses self-selection or volunteering. Such a participative process creates an opportunity for people who need outlets for their energies and ideas.

10 Create the conditions for the use of self-organization and other principles derived from complexity to emerge by not only providing the right context but also the kinds of beliefs and behaviours, both espoused and actual that underpin the process. Table 8.2 suggests some of the beliefs and behaviours that help.

11 Ensure that there are several key people involved in the process who understand some of the core concepts of complexity, such as self-organization, the butterfly effect, emergence, concepts of order and disorder, and the 'edge of chaos'. They will encourage participants to let go and see what happens and to feel comfortable not trying to predict events or control outcomes.

Table 8.2 Beliefs and behaviours

Beliefs	Behaviours
One cannot predict the future	Relaxed
Expect the unexpected	Responsive
People networks and interactions create change	Listening
dynamics	Feeding back
Humour and fun can encourage changes	Communicating
Individuals can make small changes which may	Letting go
be very valuable and should be encouraged	Trusting
Experimentation goes hand in hand with innovation	Supportive
Energy and enthusiasm in people are a real resource	Sharing
Change is both seen and unseen	. Adaptive
Change cannot be easily measured	'Walking the talk'
Real change will probably feel very uncomfortable for	Restraining controlling
a time but it is part of an ongoing learning and	tendencies
adaption process	Resolute
	Encouraging others to let go

Source: Adapted from McMillan 2000: 188.

12 In most organizations perceived radical approaches to change have many critics and detractors and a complexity-based change process will need powerful support and supporters if it is to get off the ground and survive long enough to have significant and recognizable effects. In this respect the process is like any traditional change intervention, in need of powerful support.

A democratic or grass roots strategic action plan may emerge from a complexity-based change process as it did from the New Directions programme. A 'democratic' strategy is not strategy in the traditional sense but rather if fully realized is about all the people in the organization enacting the strategy which unfolds as they act. This accords with Stacey's (1996a) nine-point theory of organization whereby new strategic directions spontaneously emerge as a result of a self-organizing process created via political interaction and group learning.

When introducing a complexity-derived change process then it is very helpful if everyone in an organization views change and the change process in a fresh light. Organizations are entering an era of unprecedented change (Handy 1990) and the unpredictable nature of the real world means that long-term planning is not an effective tool for delivering the future (Morgan 1993). Notions of change as a predictive, orderly, cause and effect phenomenon are no longer useful. The world is much more complex and unpredictable, and newer approaches to change are needed (Morgan 1993; Durcan *et al.* 1993). Looking at real-life models, such as living systems with their self-organizing attributes and their complex learning and emergent properties can suggest new, realistic models to use within an organizational context.

The transition strategy model

There are powerful resonances between the work of modern writers like Handy and Morgan, their innovative views on organizations, and notions of the learning organization with concepts from complexity science. Morgan (1993) considers that if managers are to learn how to cope with the flow of unpredictable events that shapes their working lives then they will need to become skilled in handling disorder and in helping their organizations to self-organize and evolve. In his view, consideration of the behaviours of a self-organizing termite colony can teach managers a great deal about how to deal with a turbulent world. There is a direct link here between some of the more innovative approaches to change and complexity science.

Handy (1990) points out that organizations will need to think and act very differently if they are to survive. He suggests that one way of doing this is to reframe the way we see the world. As discussed in earlier chapters, ideas from complexity challenge the existing paradigm and enable one to reframe one's world view. Learning is key to the development of complex adaptive systems and thus by espousing ideas from complexity one is able to link together Handy's notions of reframing and learning in another meaningful way.

Notions of double-loop learning (Morgan 1993) and second-order change (Dale 1994) features of learning organization theory accord well with aspects of the complex adaptive systems of complexity science. Real learning and real change have a symbiotic relationship that is recognized both by theorists from complexity and the learning organization. Here is a bridge between organization/management theory and scientific theory.

Writers on the learning organization consider that change and learning are key to survival (Pedler *et al.* 1991). Complex learning is viewed as a prerequisite for real change. A learning organization encourages people at every level to learn afresh and to reframe their world (Handy 1990). Complexity considers group learning and adaption skills as vital for the survival of a species. Thus these two approaches both support a symbiotic notion of change and learning. Individuals in groups learn from each other and from the complex series of interactions that is always taking place in their group. Socially-organized insects, birds and mammals all engage in complex, adaptive learning activities in order to survive. Organizations can use this model to improve the learning, adaption and therefore the survival chances of their own species, the organization. By creating richly diverse groups they provide a complex range of new interactions and experiences that stimulate learning. By using mixed groups an organization can help to raise the levels of complex learning for individuals and groups and thus the level of adaptive skills within those parts of the organization where they have significant influence.

Morgan (1986) points out the difficulties of fostering double-loop or complex learning in bureaucracies. The case study evidence reinforces Morgan's proposals on how to overcome this by creating a learning/change intervention which values openness and reflection, encourages challenge and debate on important issues, and creates a participative or grass roots involvement in planning. Further, it supports his belief (1993) in the importance of the role of shared understandings and personal empowerment in the creation of more effective organizations and, most importantly, the value of using self-organization as a way to bring about constructive change.

Thus by considering learning organization concepts and complexity concepts and the role they played in the New Directions change process it is possible to construct a 'transition strategy' model for organizational change (see Figure 8.1). The model is a hybrid strategy because it draws on many influences and existing strategic approaches and it has some roots in traditional ideas. But it offers a strategic approach which creates a bridge between old and new and serves to integrate traditional theories of organizational change with more innovative and radical models, while moving into the complexity science domain.

The 'flow of explicate changes' refers to Bohm's (Morgan 1986) theory of implicate and explicate order. This acknowledges newer notions of change discussed in Chapter 4. The 'old world view' reflects classical science and its influence on organizations, discussed in Chapter 3. The 'new world view' is that which is emerging from the challenges of complexity science, reviewed in early chapters. 'Traditional' approaches to strategy have been discussed in relation to the New Directions case study and include Mintzberg and Waters (1989), Eccles (1993)

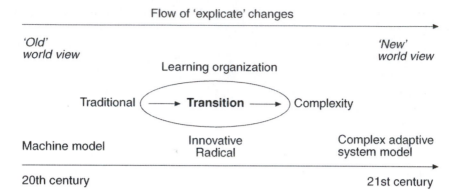

Figure 8.1 Transition strategy model

and Quinn (1989). The influence of ideas drawn from the learning organization is indicated and the work of writers like Morgan and Handy is indicated by the reference to 'innovative' and 'radical'.

A transition strategy is not a fixed approach but a process that draws on a rich flow of theories and ideas. Its core purpose is to flow in the direction of a complexity-dominated approach that resonates with the emerging new world view (Toffler in Prigogine and Stengers 1984). Thus, as it moves forward, so it makes a break with the past in the sense that it diminishes its influence and looks forward. It is an approach that is integrative and not divisive as it seeks to provide an inclusive bridge of the 'old' and established with the 'new' and the challenging. It is not as radical as some of the proposals from Stacey and Nonaka, but it may prove more digestible in more traditional organizations where ideas on change still draw strongly on the classical scientific framework and where notions of revolutionary change would be resisted. It offers a realistic way to move from the 'machine model' perception of the organization to the notion of an organization as a complex adaptive system. Thus moving over time away from the predominant model of the twentieth century to an emerging twenty-first century model.

To move towards a complexity-style model of organization the transition strategy approach would suggest using the twelve principles put forward earlier in order to introduce complexity ideas and practice. This should encourage a participative style strategic change process as discussed in Chapter 7. It should be possible to do this in a traditional organization and with reference to some traditional strategic change models, as New Directions demonstrated. Using a participative approach and the twelve principles puts the involvement of the people in an organization at the core of an organization's strategic thinking and so taps into a wealth of ideas and experiences. In some cases this may lie just below the surface, in others, where there has been little or no democracy and plenty of control, then it may be buried under a thick layer of suspicion and cynicism. Using a transition strategy involves adopting a participative, learning process that is infused with self-organizing principles and which involves people, both intellectually and emotionally, and seeks to energize them and so create a change dynamic within their own spheres of influence. One of the possible outcomes of using a transition strategy may be the emergence of a 'grassroots' or 'democratic' strategy for action as discussed in Chapter 6.

Once a transition-type change process is underway, then a number of related change dynamics should emerge. There should be a communications dynamic as information and ideas arise and create new patterns of response. There should be a responsiveness dynamic and, most importantly, there should be a learning dynamic that becomes more and more powerful and complex as participants' experiences increase and intensify.

A 'transition' approach to change is a real-world change strategy that enables an organization to blend the strategic with the operational. It is a systemic approach whereby both the thinking and planning parts of the organization and the operational or producing processes are involved in the change intervention. This replaces what Senge (1992) describes as the dichotomy between those who think and those who do. It offers an integrated, real-world approach where thinking and activity happen simultaneously. Also it helps to negate and balance out a long tradition where in the Anglo-Saxon world there is a tendency to reward people for the grand plan or the impressive strategy, and to see the implementation of these as separate and lesser things (Dawson 1996).

The fractal web

Western culture and the Newtonian–Cartesian paradigm has encouraged linear thinking such that we have a tendency to think in a linear fashion and consequently to see the world linearly (Senge 1992). And as Senge points out this creates real difficulties for managers as they tend to try to deal with complex, dynamic problems with a language designed for simple, static, problems. Further, this linear use of language encourages and facilitates traditional, linear thinking. Complexity reminds us, however, that we do not live in a linear world and that theories of change do not fit neat linear models. The natural world is full of surprises whereas linear models have very little potential for providing surprise (Stevenson and Harmeling 1990).

Human activity is essentially non-linear, yet traditionally organizations are designed from a linear perspective. This is reflected in the horizontal linearity of the typical structural hierarchy of management and the vertical linearity of formal communications and accountability systems. Linear models when used as the underpinning structure for management systems offer very little flexibility and very limited systems for communication flows. Information may flow up and down an organization and even across the different levels and functional boundaries but its flow is restricted. Compare this design with the pattern of a spider's web. Here is a star burst design where a message in the form of vibration travels at speed across the whole structure and where every thread has access to the same unfiltered and undiluted information. A linear organization is not an organization of equals. It is founded on notions of authority, albeit implicit authority in some companies.

Complexity suggests that organizations move away from linear thinking and the linear models that this encourages and instead seek new patterns of thinking and behaving that are more in tune with the realities of both the natural world and the uncertainties of the twenty-first century.

Many writers have pointed out the importance of an organization's form and how this affects its strategy, technology, environment and culture (Miller 1989; Mintzberg and Waters 1989). Handy (1990, 1993) has written on the importance of the relationship between culture and organizational design and the need for new organizational forms. Pascale *et al.* (2000: 197) consider 'design is the invisible hand that brings organizations to life and life to organizations'. If an organization is to achieve maximum performance then its structure must fit with or match the rate of change in its environments (Burns and Stalker 1961). Structure has a key role in the human dimension of an organization affecting as it does many aspects of human resource management (Mabey *et al.* 2001).

Management's role in the design of organizational structures is often a neglected responsibility (Senge 1994) and the importance of organization structure is frequently overlooked. The management literature tends to focus on the content of corporate or business strategies, but rarely in relation to structure (Miller 1989). Organizational design is not well understood and conventional management education does not include the development of any understanding of the principles of corporate design (McMaster 1996).

I would describe an organization's structure as the architecture that is both visible and invisible which connects and integrates all aspects of an organization's activities so that it operates as a complete dynamic entity. Thus an organization's structure is vital. If its structure and its underlying design principles are not in tune with its core purposes and its many environments, then it is unlikely to successfully survive. For as Senge (1994) points out, what use is the captain of the ship asking his crew to turn to starboard sixty degrees, if the rudder will only turn to port, or the ship takes six hours to respond to the command? Morgan's (1993) termites self-organize to create a free form of architecture that mirrors their way of working and satisfies their core purpose. They create a physical structure that is perfect for the rearing of the next generation and the colony's overall survival. Thus the physical form they create and their working practices and principles are in harmony. Evolution ensured that. But what of today's human organizational forms both metaphorical and physical?

As discussed earlier in this book the modern organizational form is based on design principles which are predominantly derived from the classical scientific (Newtonian–Cartesian) paradigm. This is reflected in practices and invisible structures as well as physical form. Table 8.3 shows some stereotypical classical science design principles and compares them with principles derived from a complexity approach. McMillan's (2002) table showed seven attributes but I have built on this and added 'closed' and 'open'.

The linearity of the traditional approach to organization design is reflected in organization charts, lines of communication, chains of responsibility and accountability and even in physical structures. Such an approach supports hierarchical notions and controlling aspirations. Reductionism is evident in

Table 8.3 Organization form and design principles: a comparison

Classical science principles	*Complexity science principles*
Linear	Non-linear
Hierarchical	Non-hierarchical
Reductionist	Holistic
Controlling	Self-organizing
Inflexible	Flexible
Uniform	Diverse
Centralized	Networked
Closed	Open

Source: Adapted from McMillan, 2002: 130.

compartmentalized approaches whereby corporate tasks are broken down into specialized functions and functioning. The need for detail and close examination of activity pervades every aspect of organizational life from business planning to job descriptions. A holistic overarching approach to people's roles and to organizational activity is rarely taken in this kind of organization. Uniformity and a lack of flexibility go hand in hand. When carried to extremes everyone in the company is expected to subscribe to the organization cultural doctrine and wear the corporate 'uniform' whether Gucci shoes or the ubiquitous dark business suit. If one company takes over another one then blending in is usually required. Areas of activity and information are bounded or closed off (only possible in a compartmentalized organization) and only accessible to certain staff. This is usually related to hierarchy and the need for control. All these design principles work together to support and reinforce each other and the paramount organizational ethic. Thus when a traditional organization tries to slim down or radically restructure it is exceptionally difficult to change things. Removing layers still leaves intact other linear attitudes. For example, at the end of the last century almost every organization experimented with changes in structure (Ashkenas *et al.* 1995). Companies sought to become leaner and fitter by making large structural adjustments. Many failed, however, to capitalize on this and introduce new systems of working (Mabey *et al.* 2001) and there were losses in terms of skills and experience too. In spite of all the experiments at the time most organizations were still essentially bureaucratic (Mabey *et al.* 2001; Morgan 1986). Structures were changed but there was a lack of understanding about the importance of the relationship between structure and internal and external processes and human interactions.

Some changes were taking place, however. Ashkenas *et al.* (1995) describe how there was a shift in notions of design criteria. Organizations no longer valued size, specialization, role clarity and control but sought instead speed, flexibility, innovation and integration. This shift resonates well with many of the principles that arise from a complexity approach to organization design. Senge (1994) describes one innovative approach to organizational form that has emerged. Johnson & Johnson, the US baby care company, is an organization with a structure built upon a foundation composed of purpose and core values. This is an approach that resonates well with complexity science principles, especially self-organization. In 1982 their clear sense of purpose enabled them to effectively handle a major crisis that threatened its survival. Another example is St Lukes, the award winning advertising and communications company, which was referred to in an earlier chapter. This built itself on 'invisible' structures: values and moral principles (Lewin and Regine 1999). Although the company now finds itself in some difficulties it was for a number of years hugely successful. Another example of an organization using complexity principles to underpin its structure is the US company SENCORP referred to in Chapter 5.

How might an organization structure look which is based on design principles derived from complexity science as shown in Table 8.3? How might it work? In order to begin to answer these questions I decided to focus on four key features of complexity: self-organizing principles; complex adaptivity; fractals; and notions of patterning, rhythms and flow. A model was then devised by thinking about biological forms and the human heart and circulatory system in particular (see Figure 8.2). This shows the 'fractal web' which is a speculative model of organization structure based on the design principles described. It is designed so that it embraces environmental intelligence gathering and distribution, distributed leadership principles and the possibility for rich flows of communications.

> The model has non-linear interconnectedness; is designed to allow a constant flow of energy and matter (information) throughout its whole; and via its 'arteries' is open to its environments, all characteristics of a self-organising system as described by Capra (1996). The structure allows for employees to

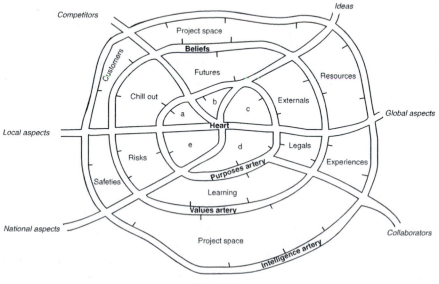

Figure 8.2 The fractal web (adapted from McMillan 2002: 133)

respond spontaneously to events guided by an overall sense of direction and purpose – key attributes of self-organization … .

(McMillan 2002: 131)

People are able to form into self-organizing project teams as they respond and react to information and ideas flowing through the organization and the right kind of supportive environment is created by the organization's ethos and set of values. Thus the importance of the five inner 'chambers' of the web and the beliefs and values artery and the purpose/s artery. These nourish the heart of the web which in turn feeds the whole organization ensuring that everyone shapes, shares and understands the key principles of the organization.

The structure is designed so that it is able to develop all the key attributes of a complex adaptive system 'by recognising learning and experimentation needs and the key role they play in facilitating dynamic adaptability and spontaneous responsiveness to change' (McMillan 2002: 132). The organization is able to unfold as it learns and to grow new bits of structure as a result of its own activities and responses to the external environment (McMaster 1996). Most importantly, the structure has space for individuals to experiment, change and adapt co-operatively which will enhance organizational sustainability (Allen 2001).

Fractal patterning is the key design principle which influenced the shape of this organizational structure. The simple web pattern is created by the circularity of the arteries which are replicated on different scales. Every level is imbued with the beliefs and values of the organization. 'However you slice the structure it is a fractal one' (McMillan 2002: 132).

The fractal web is a very flexible organizational form with all the necessary arteries and spaces or chambers needed to function effectively, but if it needs to expand then it adds more arteries or extends existing ones and so creates more spaces – whatever is needed. If it needs to contract then it narrows its arteries or reduces their length. It adjusts its size by a kind of organic expansion or contraction that still maintains the integrity of the overall structure. It is essentially a project or 'theme' based organization with flexible 'spaces' for the lifetime of each project. The size of the space or the number of spaces allocated to a particular 'theme' indicates the number of resources involved and the amount of activity. These are able to expand or contract in response to the individual, group or organization's needs, as may the number of different types of space. Thus each space is dynamic and not fixed. The overall structure 'is flexible and responsive to the needs of the organization with changeability built into the design. In other words, its shape is able to ebb and flow as it renews itself' (McMillan 2002: 133).

The arteries running from west to east collect intelligence from the external environment. Examples of external sources of information are shown in italics. These sources will vary for individual organizations, as will the number and size of the project or theme spaces at any given time. Some features are considered essential in order to comply with external obligations and requirements. For example, there are legal, financial and safety responsibilities and obligations which have to be met. Any organization needs a range of resources in order to function.

These include people, and other soft and hard resources. These are shown in their respective spaces in the web as legals, resources and safeties. Thus some three spaces cover a wide range of conventional functional areas.

Information, knowledge and energy from inside and outside the organization are pumped around the structure by the arteries and the capillary system. This is essential for learning to take place and for the development and enrichment of knowledge. The capillaries help carry rich and diverse information around the organization ensuring that this flows from the spaces into and out of the large arteries.

> Feedback becomes 'feedaround'. The larger the space the more small vessels are connected to it to ensure that organizational flow continues. If two small vessels join then a new small artery is formed. It is a very co-operative system with considerable positive feedback and high synergy and this will support organizational sustainability (Allen 2001). The structure enables the organization to operate like a complex adaptive system by supporting learning and adaption and by enabling itself to constantly revise its shape in response to learning from events and intelligence gathered.
>
> (McMillan 2002: 133)

The heart or confluence area of the organization is where the east–west arteries meet, mix and flow into each other. Here they are encircled by the purposes artery. 'This creates a rich mixture which circulates through all the system influencing and guiding in symbiosis with other cells of information or intelligence as they feed in' (McMillan 2002: 134). The inner chambers marked a, b, c, d and e represent the essential principles of the organization. In the Open University, for example, these would be the guiding principles of openness: openness to people, to places, to methods, to environments and to ideas. These contribute to and enrich the confluence of flows and flow around the organization energizing activities, giving clarity to direction and decision-making. This will add to its capacity to generate an ongoing flow of new knowledge that will ensure its survival (Allen 2001).

Everyone participates in learning; speculates on the future; take risks and experiments; works on projects; observes external aspects; shares experiences and knowledge; exchanges information; draws on resources; observes safety and legal requirements; embraces customers; and relaxes from time to time in the chill out space. This is achieved by moving people around the organization and ensuring that they spend time in different spaces, and several spaces at one time too, even if they are specialists. A legal expert, for example, will always spend a percentage of his or her time in the legals space, but they will also be active in other spaces too. In this way they contribute their knowledge around the organization and it is not held captive in one specialist area. Employees will also spend time as 'intelligence' specialists. This means that they have a major responsibility for ensuring that 'nutrition' flows around the arterial system. Thus making sure that intelligence is exchanged and fed around the whole organization. Further, people will also spend time gathering intelligence from external sources such as competitors or shareholders, or seeking opportunities or information on different perspectives. Such specialist roles will not be permanent but the taking on of different roles will facilitate connectivity, encourage learning and a deep understanding of how the whole organization works.

The chill-out space acknowledges the ebb and flow of human energy as it responds to a range of real life situations. Human rhythms can fluctuate, sometimes people need to slow down, or pull out, and reflect on events. It recognizes too that people have an existence outside the organization and that activities in other social contexts can affect their life within the organization and vice versa. As noted earlier it is possible to push people towards a far-from-equilibrium existence which can lead to personal disintegration. The chill-out space is all about recognition of an individual's emotional needs and the importance of this to the organization's effective functioning.

> The design principles also include the notion of continuous flow as essential to nourish the organization. Information and ideas flow throughout in waves of changing depth and speed as they respond rhythmically to the external landscapes and internal responses. If, for example, the global perspectives artery and the opportunities artery both feed in important and exciting information that the futures space responds to enthusiastically then a powerful flow would unfold throughout the structure.
>
> (McMillan 2002: 133)

The rate of flow in the organization and the degree of interconnectedness between individuals, plus the diversity of the population will determine how well the organization will survive and do well over time (Slocum and Frondorf 2000). In the fractal web model communications and interconnectedness are the structure. They are inherent attributes of the organizational form, they are non-linear in nature and free-flowing.

Where is leadership in this model of organization? It is intended that leadership would be distributed throughout the organization on a day-to-day basis. Employees should be well-informed and knowledgeable enough to make most operational and non-strategic decisions without reference to the whole organization. Strategic-level decisions would be shared collectively unless it is agreed to hand them over to a specific group. Guidance and policy should be provided by the shared core principles (which are constantly revisited) and the organization's beliefs and values. Like socially-organized insects, employees would be guided by a collectively derived and supported sense of purpose. Further, because they move around the organization and spend time considering and working on a range of organizational projects and support systems so they should have wide knowledge of the whole organization and its needs. However, individual leaders or groups of leaders may emerge frequently in response to specific issues or organizational needs. So, for example, if there is a major cash flow crisis then a group of informed and interested people (including financial specialists) would take the lead in searching for a solution, and would continue to lead until the crisis is resolved. Once the particular issue is resolved then the leadership role would diminish and disappear. Thus no one person would lead the organization on a permanent basis. Although a number of people may emerge over time who because of experience and or ability frequently act in a leadership capacity.

The fractal web is a product of the imagination, but it was an imaginative process that drew on knowledge from hard science, real-life research, long-time observations and experience of organizational life. It is a speculation, and I would argue that researchers and writers should not be afraid to play with their ideas and their intuitions in a way that is unconstrained by current notions of what constitutes validity. To do so is to join distinguished company, for Albert Einstein is renowned for his observation that: 'Imagination is more important than knowledge. Knowledge is limited. Imagination encircles the world.'

The model is a first prototype and as Allen (2001) points out it is impossible to predict the success of a particular design and wide explorations are necessary as part of the design and innovation process. However, I am confident that experimenting with the use of design principles derived from the complexity paradigm will offer managers radically new ways of restructuring as part of an ongoing change process.

> Further, I would suggest that the use of design principles derived from a thorough understanding of the complexity paradigm offer a way forward that will break effectively with past approaches that are no longer relevant, and in some cases positively damaging to organizations and individuals. The use of these principles will facilitate the development of new structural forms that are more resonant with the times and therefore designed to respond to conditions of rapid change and uncertainty.
>
> (McMillan 2002: 135)

New perspectives, new possibilities

Morgan (1986) points out that many writers on managing change fail to explain the underlying dynamics. I would contend that one of the difficulties is that managers in looking for evidence of change tend to look for discrete entities or specific bursts of activities. They try to measure quantitatively in order to produce impressive statistical analyses. Change is observable, but not always and not always over short or prescribed time scales. Observable change may be realized at an individual level through self-observation and self-realization, or through shared realization in groups when individuals observe and share their observations on the differences that have taken place within themselves over time. The dynamics of change are created by human activity and the amplification of feedback loops of process and learning. Deep-level, second-order change is not always readily detected by traditional methods and is more likely to be discovered by looking for flows of learning and adaption, flows of fresh information, flows of innovative ideas and flows of new behaviours.

A complexity-based change intervention is applicable and useful because people are essentially self-organizing, and unimpeded and unrestrained human systems are essentially self-organizing systems. Yet paradoxically the longing for order in an apparently disorderly world has encouraged the belief that synthetic, manmade systems can deliver order. This has led to the development of the complex and complicated controlling systems used to impose order that underpin many modern organizations. But the control and order they seek to create, however, is constantly disturbed and threatened by human needs and behaviours. There is an inherent disharmony in this arrangement. A complexity-style approach to organizations takes into account this human factor and shows how new notions of order via self-organization can work successfully in a 'manmade' environment and harmonize intrinsic human needs with those of the organization that their collective activities have created.

Complexity is a new science and as the history of science shows all new collections of theories and insights take time to gain universal acceptance and establish themselves in the mainstream. Complexity science is no exception. After some thirty or so years its validity and contribution to the advancement of science is now recognized by the scientific community. However, the debate still continues on how useful, how appropriate and how valid is its application in other non-scientific domains. I would argue that if we consider humans and their collective activities as living systems – and this is generally accepted – then it is entirely appropriate to use known science to further our understanding of these. I do not see the problem that others have with this application and I suspect too much reductionism and protectionist thinking may have influenced such attitudes. People are socially-organized creatures and thus to study the creature is to study the way they organize and the forms and patterns their organizing activities take.

I believe that we have just begun the process of discovering and creating new organizational forms for the twent-first century and that we need to let go of the old ways of thinking and our entrenched ideas on what is effective and what is not. McMaster (1996) believes that it is emergence rather than design that is responsible for most companies. He states that he has yet to speak to a founder of an organization who does not privately admit that their organization came about by chance. Further, many are happy to accept that their organizations emerged as a result of the interaction between chance events and their own efforts. While acknowledging that organizations are complex adaptive systems it was the notion of an organization as an emergent phenomenon that led McMaster to state that this suggests a new theory of organization. A theory that suggests that an organization has its own characteristics, its own intelligence, its own ability to learn, and its own culture.

> This theory implies that these qualities exist independently of the founder, management, and people currently in that corporation. Even though some of the specifics that were intended and planned by individuals can be traced to individual personalities or to the results of specific historical accidents, what now exists has a life of its own.
>
> (McMaster 1996: 9)

To McMaster this means the end of out-of-date machine theories of organization and recognition that the universe is a dynamic self-organizing system, a system in which organizations and ecologies continuously interact with each other. Managers therefore need to adopt a new approach to organizations, one that radically affects the ways they view their responsibilities. This, in my view, is to restore the primacy of the senses and intuition and to reinstate the vital role they play along with intellect and rationality in guiding us in understanding our world. McMaster (1996: 7) suggests that managers become more like horticulturists in a rain forest with responsibility for the 'health and survival of a particular plant species in that forest'. If they do their job well the species will flourish, if they fail the species will weaken and its place in the forest will be taken by other species. This calls for a revolutionary new way of looking at organizations and considering how best to behave within them.

Writers like Gareth Morgan and Margaret Wheatley, too, consider it is time to see the world with fresh eyes and to try and envisage new ways of doing things and new ways of seeing things unaffected by mechanistic models. I believe that using insights from complexity can greatly assist in developing such new ways of interpreting the world and in devising real life approaches that may work in transforming organizations.

It is possible to think of the learning organization approach as a conscious attempt to develop a new way of thinking about organizational life. It is in many ways an evolved transitional approach which resonates strongly with both old and new attitudes to change. I would suggest that today many organizations and their managers are ready for a transitional approach to change that is more radical and dynamic than that of the learning organization and the use of ideas and theories from complexity make this a possibility.

Organizations in their many guises play a dominant role in the life of individuals. How they act is crucially important for our survival and well being. It has almost always been so. Early organizations like village councils, craft guilds, religious bodies and state institutions played a key role in daily lives and had a powerful local influence. Today that influence is more potent and widespread as there are more organizations locally, nationally and internationally that affect our lives. This impact significantly affects the way we live and work and the quality of that life. Unfortunately, too many organizations and state institutions are conceived and perceived to act and exist in ways that are often unrealistic and out of touch with the real world. I would posit that much of this is due to the mechanistic influence of Newtonian–Cartesian thinking which has distanced intuition, holism and sensitivity from organizational thinking, decision-making and accountability. There is, as Capra (1996) pointed out, an imbalance in the predominant mode of thinking that is at least unhelpful and at worst severely damaging. I believe that the mainstreaming of ideas and insights from complexity can address that imbalance. Further, complexity offers alternative solutions and a fresh range of possibilities that should help address the raft of issues that organizations and individuals face at all levels. Issues which need to be resolved if organizations are to flourish and working life is to be enriched.

There are many facets to the flow of change and a range of aspects which themselves mutate and differ over time. Change and changing is experienced in many ways and quite differently between one individual and another, and between one organization and another. Each person will have their own unique experience of life and life events, and how they interpret these will change from moment to moment and from one point in time to another. To neatly define such perceptions and to capture them in tidy timelines is to diminish and reduce the complexity of their reality. In our endeavours to understand and describe these things we have a long way to go and much to discover and learn.

Appendix 1

Plans for change

New Directions 1993–7

1   From long to short response times
2   From complexity to simplicity
3   From provider-led to customer-centred provision
4   From an expenditure to an income culture
5   From centralism to subsidiarity
6   From quality control to quality assurance

Appendix 2

Diary of events

1993

April	New Directions Workshop – 'How to Achieve Quality Growth for the OU of the Future' × 3
May	New Directions Workshop × 2
July	New Directions Workshop × 1
November	New Directions Workshop × 1
December	New Directions Workshop × 1

1994

January	Electronic Strand Workshop × 2
February	Joining the University Workshop × 1
March	Choosing the Open University × 1
	Conference planning team formed
April	Improving Internal Communications Workshop × 2
May	NEW DIRECTIONS CONFERENCE
	Staff survey team formed
June	Achieving Change Workshop × 1
August	New Directions cartoon competition announced
October	Lunchtime briefing – Geoff Peters, PVC, Strategy. New Directions and 'Plans for Change'
November	The Regional Centre of 2001 – Birmingham Region
	Lunchtime briefing, Philip Marsh, Director of Personnel
	The OU Going Global Workshop – Office for International Collaboration
December	The Regional Centre of 2001 – London Regional Office
	Lunchtime briefing, Ted Atkinson, Director of Marketing
	Calendar cartoon competition prize winners receive prizes from Geoff Peters, PVC, Strategy

1995

January	*New Directions Action group first meeting*
	The Regional Centre of 2001 – Newcastle Regional Office
February	OU Going Global Workshop – Office for International Collaboration
	The OU in the 21st Century Workshop
May	Lunchtime briefing, Geoff Peters, PVC, Strategy. The new 'Plans for Change'
June	Workshop for OU students in R04 – Birmingham
	Making Better Mistakes Workshop
	Lunchtime Briefing, Geoff Peters, PVC, Strategy. The new 'Plans for Change'
July	Communications Workshops for AA (Students) × 2
	New Directions 1996 Cartoon calendar competition announced
September	Lunchtime briefing, Tim O'Shea, PVC, Quality Assurance and Research, and Academic Staff Renewal Visualization Workshop
October	Communications Workshops for AA (Students)
November	Making Better Mistakes Workshop
December	New Directions 1996 cartoon calendar competition winners receive prizes from Geoff Peters, PVC, Strategy

1996

February	Communications Workshop for AA (Students)
May	Communications Workshop for Centre for Modern Languages
July	Communications Workshop, for Cambridge Office
September	New Directions Conference and Fair (80 participants)
November	Making Better Mistakes Workshop

1997

January	*New Directions Action Group disbands*

Appendix 3

Conference issues

1. Staffing issues

Within two months of the conference, *Open House* reported that talks were taking place on addressing 'unjustified' differences in terms and conditions which had been a major issue raised at the conference. A schedule of differences had been drawn up by personnel division and sent to the trades unions and further discussions were due to take place in the autumn. The decision to go ahead with a staff survey was seen as a response to the staffing issues raised by the conference. A Pro-Vice-Chancellor with responsibilities for staff matters in the strategic context was appointed four years after the conference.

2. Marketing

This issue has been progressed with a reorganization and the setting up of OU World Wide with the posts of development manager and marketing manager as key roles. There had been a lunchtime briefing session on marketing. However, it was felt that more work was needed on market research and on what was described as an amateurish approach.

3. New technology development

Significant progress has been made on the development of new technologies and a great deal has changed. There was general agreement that these actions may have already been under consideration but that the conference had given them a major impetus.

4. Improved communications

Several activities were seen as directly attributable to the conference and New Directions including the provision of lunchtime briefings for all staff on strategic issues. These were mainstreamed as 'Off the Record' lunchtime briefings by the public relations department. A series of communications workshops had also been organised by the New Directions action group in response to the conference plea for better communications.

5.   Low staff morale

It was felt that no progress had been made on the issue of low staff morale, and that the downturn in the University's financial situation during 1996–8 had further lowered staff morale.

6.   Need for leadership and for managers with better people skills

Leadership was not an issue identified by those who were active in the programme. They had felt empowered by the conference and by the programme to take action themselves. However, some of the non-activists were expecting changes to be made for them. Their view of management drew on traditional notions of leadership where senior managers were meant to plan for the future and to direct their staff towards it. This they did not think their managers were doing and thus they articulated the need for leadership.

7.   Need for flatter organization and better co-operation between departments

It was felt that there had been some progress as there were now more ad-hoc groups in the University and more recognition of the need to cut across formal structures. Inter-unit contracting had also changed attitudes between departments. Apart from the ad-hoc groups the conference and New Directions were not seen as directly contributing to these developments.

Bibliography

Allen, P.M. (2001) 'A complex systems approach to learning in adaptive networks', *International Journal of Innovation Management*, 5(2): 149–80.

Anderson, C. and Bartholdi, J.J. (2000) 'Centralized versus decentralized control in manufacturing: lessons from social insects', in McCarthy, I.P. and Rakotobe-Joel, T. (eds) *Complexity and Complex Systems in Industry: A Conference Proceeding*, Warwick University, Warwick, September.

Ashkenas, R., Ulrich, D., Jick, T. and Kerr, S. (1995) *The Boundaryless Organization Breaking the Chains of Organizational Structure*, San Francisco: Jossey-Bass.

Battram, A. (1996) *The Complexicon: A Lexicon of Complexity*, London: Local Government Management Board.

Belbin, R.M. (1981) *Management Teams: Why they Succeed or Fail*, London: Heinemann.

Belbin, R.M. (1993) *Team Roles at Work*, New York: Butterworth Heinemann.

Berreby, D. (1996) 'Between chaos and order: what complexity theory can teach business', *Strategy and Business*, Spring 1996.

Bohm, D. (1980) *Wholeness and the Implicate Order*, London: Routledge and Kegan Paul.

Brewer, E.C. (1978) *The Dictionary of Phrase and Fable*, New York: Avenel Books.

Briggs, J. and Peat, F.D. (1989) *Turbulent Mirror*, New York: Harper and Row.

Burns, T. (1990) 'Mechanistic and organismic structures', in D.S. Pugh (ed.) *Organisation Theory* (3rd edn), London: Penguin Books.

Burns, T. and Stalker, G.M. (1961) *The Management of Innovation*, London: Tavistock.

Capra, F. (1983) *The Turning Point*, New York: Bantam Books.

Capra, F. (1996) *The Web of Life*, London: HarperCollins.

Carlisle, Y. and McMillan E. (2002) 'Thinking differently about strategy: comparing paradigms', Proceedings on CD-ROM of Australian and New Zealand Academy of Management Conference, La Trobe University, Beechworth, VIC, December.

Cooksey, R.W. and Gates, R.G. (1995) 'HRM: a management science in need of discipline', *Asia Pacific Journal of Human Resources*, 33(3): 15–38.

Costello, N. (1992) 'Strategic change and the learning organisation', unpublished thesis, Judge Institute of Management Studies, University of Cambridge.

Coulson-Thomas, C. and Coe, T. (1991) *The Flat Organisation: Philosophy and Practice*, Corby: British Institute of Management.

Coveney, P. and Highfield, R. (1995) *Frontiers of Complexity*, New York: Fawcett Columbine.

Dale, M. (1994) 'Learning organizations', in Mabey, C. and Iles, P. (eds) *Managing Learning*, London: Routledge in association with the Open University.

Dawson, S. (1996) 'Judged on merit', *People Management,* Institute of Personnel and Development, 8th August: 25–6.

Durcan, J., Kirkbride, P. and Obeng, E. (1993) 'The revolutionary reality of change', *Directions – The Ashridge Journal,* September: 4–9.

Eccles, T. (1993) 'Implementing strategy: two revisionist perspectives', in Hendry J., Johnson, G. and Newton, J. (eds) *Strategic Thinking: Leadership and the Management of Change,* Chichester: John Wiley.

Foss, N.J. (2000) 'Internal disaggregation in Oticon: interpreting and learning from the rise and decline of the spaghetti organization', 5th revision, *LINK,* Department of Industrial Economics and Strategy, Copenhagen Business School. Available online http://www.cbs.dk/departments/ivs/staff/njf.shtml (accessed 4 February 2003).

Fowler, A. (1997) 'Let's shed a tier', *Personnel Management,* Institute of Personnel and Development, March: 21.

Fuller, T. and Moran, P. (2000) 'Moving beyond metaphor', *Emergence,* 2(1). Lawrence Erlbaum Associates. Online. Available HTTP: <http//ehostvgw18.epnet.com> (accessed 4 February 2003).

Garavan, T. (1997) 'The learning organization: a review and evaluation', *The Learning Organization,* 4(1): 18–29.

Garratt, B. (1995) 'An idea that has come of age.' *Personnel Management,* Institute of Personnel and Development, September 1995.

Gleick, J. (1993) *Chaos,* London: Abacus.

Goodwin, B. (1997a) *How the Leopard Changed its Spots,* London: Phoenix, Orion Books.

Goodwin, B. (1997b) 'Life living at the edge of chaos', Valedictory Lecture, Open University, 16 July.

Gribbin, J. (1999) *The Little Book of Science,* London: Penguin Books.

Hampshire, S. (1956) *The Age of Reason,* New York: Mentor Books, The New American Library.

Handy, C. (1990) *The Age of Unreason,* London: Arrow.

Handy, C. (1993) *Understanding Organizations* (4th edn), London: Penguin Books.

Handy, C. (1994) *The Empty Raincoat,* London: Hutchinson.

Johnson, J. (1996) 'Design and control of self-organising complexes', *Proceedings of the 1996 International Workshop on Control Mechanisms for Complex Systems,* Las Cruces, New Mexico, 8–12 December.

Jones, A. (1994) 'A learning in organizations model', in Bradshaw, D.C.A. (ed.) *Bringing Learning to Life: The Learning Revolution, the Economy and the Individual,* London: Falmer Press.

Kakabadse, A., Ludlow, R. and Vinnicombe, S. (1988) *Working in Organizations,* London: Penguin Books.

Kanter, R.M. (1990) *When Giants Learn to Dance,* New York: Touchstone, Simon and Schuster.

Kauffman, S. (1996) *At Home in the Universe: The Search for Laws of Self-Organization and Complexity,* London: Penguin Books.

Koontz, H. and O'Donnell, C. (1955) *Principles of Management: An Analysis of Managerial Functions,* New York: McGraw-Hill.

Koontz, H. and Weihrich, H. (1988) *Management,* Singapore: McGraw-Hill.

Kotter, J.P. (1995) 'Leading change: why transformation efforts fail', *Harvard Business Review,* March–April: 59–68.

Larsen, H.H. (2002) 'Career management in non-hierarchically structured organizations', paper presented at the 2nd International Human Resource Management in Europe

Conference, Athens, October 2002. Available online: http://www.mbc.aueb.gr/hrconference (accessed 3 February 2003).

Law, A. (1999) *Open Minds*, London: Orion Business.

Leonard-Barton, D. (1994) 'The factory as a learning laboratory', in Mabey, C. and Iles, P. (eds) *Managing Learning*, London: Routledge in association with the Open University.

Lewin, K. (1951) *Field Theory in Social Sciences*, New York: Harper and Row.

Lewin, R. (1993) *Complexity: Life on the Edge of Chaos*, London: Phoenix.

Lewin, R. and Regine, B. (1999) *The Soul at Work*, London: Orion Business.

Lorenz, E. (1979) 'Predicatability: does the flap of a butterfly's wings in Brazil set off a tornado in Texas? Paper presented at the Meeting of the American Association for the Advancement of Science, Washington, 29 December.

Lovelock, J. (1989) *The Ages of Gaia*, Oxford: Oxford University Press.

Mabey, C., Salaman, G. and Storey, J. (2001) 'Organizational structuring and restructuring', in Salaman, G. (ed.) *Understanding Business Organisations*, London: Routledge.

Macintosh, R. and Maclean, D. (1999) 'Conditioned emergence: a dissipative structures approach to transformation', *Strategic Management Journal*, 20: 297–316.

Massarik, F. (1990) 'Chaos and change: examining the aesthetics of organization development', *Advances in Organization Development*, vol. 1.

McMaster, M.D. (1996) *The Intelligence Advantage: Organizing for Complexity*, Newton, MA: Butterworth-Heinemann.

McMillan, E. (1999) *The New Sciences of Chaos and Complexity and Organisational Change: A Case Study of the Open University*. Unpublished thesis, Open University.

McMillan, E. (2000) 'Using self organising principles to create effective project teams as part of an organisational change intervention: a case study of the Open University', in McCarthy, I. and Rakotobe-Joel, T. (eds) *Complexity and Complex Systems in Industry: A Conference Proceedings*, Warwick University, Warwick, September.

McMillan, E. (2002) 'Considering organisation structure and design from a complexity paradigm perspective', in Frizzelle, G. and Richards, H. (eds) *Tackling Industrial Complexity: The Ideas That Make A Difference*, Cambridge: Institute of Manufacturing, University of Cambridge.

Merry, U. (1995) *Coping with Uncertainty: Insights from the New Sciences of Chaos, Self-Organization and Complexity*, Westport, CT: Praeger.

Michaels, M. (1990) 'The complex dynamics of change', *The Chaos Network*, 2(2): 1–3.

Miller, D. (1989) 'Configurations of strategy and structure: towards a synthesis', in Asch, D. and Bowman, C. (eds) *Readings in Strategic Management*, London: Macmillan Education.

Mintzberg, H. and Waters, J.A. (1989) 'Of strategies, deliberate and emergent', in Asch, D. and Bowman, C. (eds) *Readings in Strategic Management*, London: Macmillan Education.

Moncrief, J. and Smallwood, J. (1996) 'Ideas for the new millennium', *Financial Times*, 19 July: 10.

Montuori, A. (1993) 'Evolutionary learning', *World Futures*, 36: 189–97.

Morgan, G. (1986) *Images of Organization*, Newbury Park: Sage.

Morgan, G. (1993) *Imaginization*, Newbury Park: Sage.

Mumford, E. and Hendricks, R. (1996) 'Business process re-engineering RIP', *Personnel Management*, Institute of Personnel and Development, May: 22–9.

Nonaka, I. (1988) 'Creating organizational order out of chaos: self renewal in Japanese firms', *California Management Review*, Spring: 57–73.

Parsons, E. and Russell, C. (1995) 'A programme for organisational change: new directions at the Open University. a case study', Briefing Paper 14, Universities and Colleges Staff Development Agency, Sheffield.

Pascale, R.T. (1990) *Managing on the Edge: How Successful Companies Use Conflict to Stay Ahead*, London: Viking Penguin.

Pascale, R.T., Millemann, M. and Gioja, L. (2000) *Surfing the Edge of Chaos*, London: TEXERE Publishing.

Pedler, M., Burgoyne, J. and Boydell, T. (1991) *The Learning Company*, London: McGraw-Hill.

Perry, W. (1976) *Open University*, Milton Keynes: Open University Press.

Peters, T. (1987) *Thriving on Chaos*, New York: Harper and Row.

Pettigrew, A.M. and Whipp, R. (1991) *Managing Change for Competitive Success*, Oxford: Blackwell.

Pickard, J. (1996) 'A fertile grounding', *Personnel Management*, Institute of Personnel and Development, October: 28–37.

Prahalad, C.K. and Hamel, G. (1990) 'The core competence of the corporation', *Harvard Business Review*, May–June: 79–91.

Priesmeyer, H.R. (1992) *Organizations and Chaos: Defining the Methods of Non Linear Management*, Westport, CT: Quorum Books.

Prigogine, I. and Stengers, I. (1984) *Order Out of Chaos*, London: Heinemann.

Pugh, D.S. (1990) *Organization Theory* (3rd edn), London: Penguin Books.

Pugh, D.S. and Hickson, D.J. (1996) *Writers on Organizations* (5th edn), London: Penguin Books.

Quinn, J.B. (1989) 'Managing strategic change', in Asch, D. and Bowman, C. (eds) *Readings in Strategic Management*, London: Macmillan Education.

Roberts, P. (1998) 'John Deere runs on chaos', *Fast Company*, 19: 164.

Rose, S. (1998) *Lifelines*, London: Penguin Books.

Rosenhead, J. (1998) 'Complexity theory and management practice', Working Paper Series LSEOR 98.25, London: London School of Economics.

Ruelle, D. and Takens, F. (1971) 'On the nature of turbulence', *Communications in Mathematical Physics*, 20: 167–92.

Rumelt, R. (1995) *Inertia and Transformation*, Corporate Renewal Initiative Reprint Series, Paris: INSEAD.

Salaman, G. (2001) 'The emergence of new work forms', in Salaman, G. (ed.) *Understanding Business Organisations*, London: Routledge.

Semler, R. (1989) 'Managing without managers', *Harvard Business Review*, September–October: 76–84.

Semler, R. (1994) *Maverick*, London: Arrow Books Limited.

Senge, P.M. (1992) *The Fifth Discipline*, New York: Doubleday.

Senge, P.M. (1994) 'The leader's new work: building learning organizations', in Mabey, C. and Iles, P. (eds) *Managing Learning*, London: Routledge in association with the Open University.

Shakespeare, W. (1980) 'The Tempest', in Alexander, P. (ed.) *William Shakespeare. The Complete Works*, London: Collins.

Slocum, K.R. and Frondorf, S.D. (2000) 'Business management using a fractally-scaled structure', *Complexity and Complex Systems in Industry: A Conference Proceeding*, Warwick University, Warwick, September.

Slocum, K.R. and Frondorf, S.D. (2003) 'A fractal management model', available online: http://www.nextscale.com (accessed 12 February 2003).

Stacey, R.D. (1992) *Managing the Unknowable*, San Francisco: Jossey-Bass.

Stacey, R.D. (1993) 'Strategy as order emerging from chaos', *Long Range Planning*, 26(1): 10–17.

Stacey, R.D. (1996a) *Strategic Management and Organisational Dynamics*, London: Pitman Publishing.

Stacey, R.D. (1996b) *Excitement And Tension At The Edge Of Chaos*, Complexity and Management Papers No. 6. Complexity and Management Centre, University of Hertfordshire, Hertford.

Stacey, R.D., Griffin, D. and Shaw, P. (2000) *Complexity and Management: Fad Or Radical Challenge To Systems Thinking?*, London: Routledge.

Stevenson, H. and Harmeling, S. (1990) 'Entrepreneurial management's need for a more "chaotic" theory', *Journal of Business Venturing*, 5: 1–14.

Stewart, G., MacLean, D. and MacIntosh, R. (2000) 'Applying complexity theory in organisations (comparing experiences)', in McCarthy, I. and Rakotobe-Joel, T. (eds) *Complexity and Complex Systems in Industry: A Conference Proceedings*, Warwick University, Warwick, September.

Stewart, I. (1997) *Nature's Numbers*, London: Phoenix, Orion Books.

Swift, J. (1733) *On Poetry*, quoted in Coveney and Highfield 1995: 172.

Sykes, J.B. (1976) *The Concise Oxford Dictionary of Current English*, Oxford: Oxford University Press.

Tamkin, P. and Barber, L. (1998) 'Learning to Manage', Draft Report, Institute for Employment Studies, University of Sussex, Brighton.

Taylor, R., Micolich, A. and Jonas, D. (1999) 'Fractal expressionism', *Physics World*, October: 25–8.

'The Tempest' (1960: 7) in Alexander, P. (ed.) *William Shakespeare. The Complete Works*, London: Collins.

Tetenbaum, T.J. (1998) 'Shifting paradigms: from Newton to chaos', *Organizational Dynamics*, 26(A): 21–32

Toffler, A. (1984) 'Preface/Introduction', in Prigogine, I. and Stengers, I. (eds) *Order out of Chaos*, London: Heinemann.

Turner, I. (1996) 'Working with chaos', *Financial Times*, London, 4 October: 14.

Waldrop, M.M. (1994) *Complexity*, New York: Penguin Books.

Waldrop, M.M. (1996), 'The trillion-dollar vision of Dee Hock', *Fast Company*, 5 (October): 75.

Walsham, G. (1993) 'Management science and organizational change: a framework for analysis', in Mabey, C. and Mayon-White, B. (eds) *Managing Change*, London: Paul Chapman.

Weick, K.E. (1987) 'Substitute for corporate strategy', in Preece, D.J. (ed.) *The Competitive Challenge: Strategies for Industrial Innovation and Renewal*, Cambridge, MA: Ballinger Publishing.

Wheatley, M. (1994) *Leadership and the New Science*, San Francisco: Berrett-Koehler.

Wickens, P. (1995) 'Getting the most out of your people', *Personnel Management*, Institute of Personnel and Development, March: 28–30.

Wille, E. and Hodgson, P. (1991) *Making Change Work*, London: Mercury Books.

Willis, R. (2001) 'A complexity and Darwinian approach to management with failure avoidance as the key tool', Open University Complexity Science Research Centre, Technology Faculty. Online. Available: http://technology.open.ac.uk/ccc/csrc/index.htm (accessed 7 March 2003).

Winograd, T. and Flores, F. (1991) *Understanding Computers and Cognition*, Reading, MA: Addison-Wesley.

Index

165
95
70

Printed in the United Kingdom
by Lightning Source UK Ltd.
110735UKS00003B/112-135